Thomas Reid on Religion

Edited by James J.S. Foster

with an introduction
by Nicholas Wolterstorff

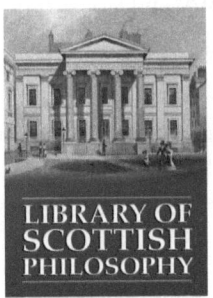

IMPRINT ACADEMIC

Copyright © James J.S. Foster, 2017

The moral rights of the author have been asserted.
No part of this publication may be reproduced in any form
without permission, except for the quotation of brief passages
in criticism and discussion.

Published in the UK by Imprint Academic
PO Box 200, Exeter EX5 5YX, UK

Distributed in the USA by
Ingram Book Company,
One Ingram Blvd., La Vergne, TN 37086, USA

ISBN 9781845409289

A CIP catalogue record for this book is available from the
British Library and US Library of Congress

Full series details:

www.imprint-academic.com/losp

Contents

Series Editor Note	v
Editor's Introduction	1
Introduction to Reid's 'Lectures on Natural Theology' by Nicholas Wolterstorff	20
Lectures on Natural Theology	29
Lecture 73rd	29
Lecture 74th	39
Lecture 75th	45
Lecture 76th	51
Lecture 77th	59
Lecture 78th	67
Lecture 79th	73
Lecture 80th	81
Lecture 81st	89
Lecture 82nd	97
Lecture 83rd	106
Lecture 84th	112
Lecture 85th	119
Lecture 86th	124
Lecture 87th	134
Appendix I — Published Material	141
Appendix II — Lecture Notes	179
Appendix III — Personal Papers	214
Bibliography	220
Index of Names	227

Series Editor's Note

The principal purpose of volumes in the *Library of Scottish Philosophy* is not to provide scholars with accurate editions, but to make the writings of Scottish philosophers accessible to a new generation of modern readers in an attractively produced and competitively priced format. In accordance with this purpose, certain changes have been made to the original texts:

- Spelling and punctuation have been modernized.
- In some cases the selections have been given new titles.
- Some original footnotes and references have not been included.
- Some extracts have been shortened from their original length.
- Quotations from Greek have been transliterated, and passages in languages other than English translated, or omitted altogether.

This volume of Thomas Reid's thoughts on religion is rather different to others in the series, including the selection from Reid's major philosophical works. Much of it is hitherto unpublished material, most especially the student notes of lectures Reid gave over many years on natural religion. Previously, only a rather poor quality version of one set of notes had been published. Now, thanks principally to a year working in Scottish archives on a Fulbright Scholarship, James Foster has provided students and scholars with a definitive version based on a comparison of all the surviving students' lecture notes. By placing them in the context of other relevant selections from Reid's writings on religion, both published and unpublished, the volume allows readers for the first time to consider Reid's thoughts on religion in the round.

The importance of this volume in the *Library of Scottish Philosophy* is further marked by the inclusion of a specially commissioned introduction in which the distinguished philosopher of religion and Reid scholar Nicholas Wolterstorff reflects on the contents of the lectures.

Gordon Graham,
Princeton, April 2017

James J.S. Foster

Editor's Introduction

Thomas Reid (1710–1796) was one of the greatest thinkers of the Scottish Enlightenment. In his own time he was seen as an able opponent of the scepticism of David Hume and a stalwart proponent of 'Common Sense' philosophy. His ideas were influential both in his native Scotland and abroad, notably on the French philosopher Victor Cousin (1792–1867), and the American father of Pragmatism, Charles Sanders Pierce (1839–1914). Although his star dimmed considerably both in Europe and the United States during the ascendency of Kantian and post-Kantian idealism in the nineteenth and twentieth centuries, he has experienced something of a renaissance in the last forty years.[1] Today he is known chiefly for his epistemology and his defence of 'first principles' — propositions that are necessary for reasoning, but are themselves based not on reason, but on intuitive judgements of evidence. This narrow lens, however, does not reflect the interests of the man, who was widely read and intensely interested in a diverse range of topics including chemistry, optics, astronomy, mathematics, ethics, politics, economics, and farming.

The genesis of this volume may be traced to a Fulbright post-graduate scholarship which I was awarded in 2012 to study at the Research Institute for Irish and Scottish Studies

---

[1] See Kroeker's 'Thomas Reid Today', *JSP* 13(2), for an excellent review of Reid scholarship since the twentieth century.

(RIISS) at the University of Aberdeen. At the time, I was completing a doctoral dissertation on Thomas Reid's moral philosophy, and found myself frustrated with Reid's frequent but oblique references to theological concerns. Piety and religion were clearly important to his ethics, as evidenced by such passages as:

> Every man... who believes in God, while he is careful to do his duty, may safely leave the care of his happiness to Him who made him... This shows the strong connection between morality and the principles of natural religion; as the last only can secure a man from the possibility of an apprehension, that he may play the fool by doing his duty.[2]

What 'religion' means for Reid, though, is not immediately clear. I proposed, therefore, to study the extensive set of Reid's autograph manuscripts, housed in the University of Aberdeen Library, and the five sets of student notes from Reid's lectures held by libraries in Aberdeen, Edinburgh, and Glasgow. These student notes were particularly interesting because none of Reid's own notes from his lectures on natural theology, given at Glasgow University, have survived. My hope was twofold: first, to make an accurate transcription of all of the notes from Reid's lectures on natural theology; and second, to get a clear picture of Reid's religious views. This volume is the result of those labours.

The longest and most complete set of notes from Reid's lectures on natural theology at Glasgow was taken by George Baird in the academic year 1779-1780. Absent a few exceptions—noted below and in the text itself—there is little of interest in the other four sets of student notes on these lectures that is not found in Baird's notes. With the permission of the Mitchell Library, these appear below. As Nicholas Wolterstorff has generously provided an introduction to the Baird notes, I will not comment on them here. It may be helpful, though, to establish the context of these lectures by spending a few pages on Reid's religious views in general. Unfortunately, unless further discoveries are made, it appears that no sermons, doctrinal statements, confessions,

---

[2] *Active Powers*, 194.

or treatises on revealed religion by Reid still survive. Our picture of Reid's religion must therefore remain incomplete. We may, however, gain some insight into Reid's beliefs from his biography and from his allusions to and discussions of religious topics in his voluminous writings.

Reid's Life and Faith

Early Life and Education

Thomas Reid was born in 1710 in the town of Strachan in Kincardineshire, Scotland, to Margaret and Rev Lewis Reid, a Church of Scotland minister. We know little of Reid's early years, but it is certain that his life was a time of foment among Christian factions in Scotland. In 1715 and 1745, members of the Roman Catholic Stuart dynasty tried to wrest back the thrones of England and Scotland from the Protestant Hanoverians. Although neither attempt was successful, they exacerbated durable tensions between Scottish Presbyterians, who largely resisted the risings, and Scottish Catholics and Episcopalians, many of whom were sympathetic to the Stuarts. Reid not only lived through these uprisings, but felt their effects in his family which, though largely Presbyterian, contained staunch Episcopalians on his mother's side.[3] There was also significant friction within the Presbyterian Church of Scotland itself. In Reid's time, the conflict existed largely between two parties: the Evangelicals, who emphasized the strict Calvinism of the Westminster Confession and a populist church polity; and the Moderates, who, though still orthodox Christians in the broad sense, were not strict Calvinists and supported the role of patronage in church governance.[4]

At the age of twelve, Reid entered Marischal College in Aberdeen, graduating four years later in the spring of 1726. In October of that same year, he returned to Marishcal to study for the ministry. In 1731, having completed his courses

---

[3] See *Correspondence*, 189.
[4] For more on the debates between the Evangelicals and Moderates, see especially Sher's *Church and University in the Scottish Enlightenment*, and Ahnert's *The Moral Culture of the Scottish Enlightenment*.

in divinity, Reid was licensed to preach in the Church of Scotland by his home presbytery of Kincardine O'Neil. He then served as a supply preacher and as clerk of the presbytery, until, in 1733, he was appointed librarian at Marischal. After three years of service, Reid travelled to Cambridge, London, and Oxford with his friend John Stewart, where they met with several distinguished scholars and visited his uncle, Dr George Reid. Upon his return in 1737, Reid became the parish minister of New Machar, in Aberdeenshire, by the appointment of King's College, Aberdeen.[5]

Minister at New Machar and Regent at King's College

The internecine conflict of the Church of Scotland became viscerally real to Reid upon his arrival in New Machar. Accounts differ as to the details, but Reid's early biographers agree that he initially experienced staunch opposition and even physical violence from Evangelical parishioners, who demanded the people of the parish be allowed to call their own minister. In time, however, this initial animosity turned to amity. Reid was neither a charismatic, nor particularly original preacher. The most charitable account of his pulpit oratory describes his style as 'clear, plain, mathematical... little indebted to voice or action'.[6] Further, as was common in Reid's time, he frequently read the sermons of celebrated pulpit orators, including the Anglican Archbishop John Tillotson, the Anglican clergyman and philosopher Samuel Clarke, and the non-conformist Welsh preacher Christmas Evans. Despite this deficiency, however, Reid soon won the affection of his parishioners through diligent care and charity.[7] In this undertaking he was aided by his wife, Elizabeth, his cousin and the daughter his uncle George, whom he married in 1740. Over the course of their fifty-two year marriage, Reid and Elizabeth would have nine children,

---

[5] In 1860 King's College and Marischal College joined to form the University of Aberdeen.

[6] Ramsay, *Scotland and Scotsmen in the Eighteenth Century*, 472. Cf. AUL MS 2814/1/45 for a remarkably uncharitable account.

[7] See Fraser, *Thomas Reid*, 33–34.

only one of whom, his third daughter Martha, would survive him.

It is also during this time that Reid wrote the most personal attestation of his faith of which we have record. According to Alexander Campbell Fraser, in March 1746 Elizabeth took ill and, fearing her death, Reid composed a prayer in which he vowed 'to turn from... backslidings, to express my thankfulness by a vigorous discharge of my duty as a Christian, a minister and master of a family, and by alms of ten pounds sterling to the poor in meat and money' if his wife should live.[8] The original manuscript of this prayer is now lost, but a catalogue of Reid's papers dated 1864 shows that such a prayer did exist, and that Reid thought it important enough to keep for the rest of his life.[9] In total, Reid served as minister of New Machar for fifteen years, during which time he not only fulfilled his ministerial duties, but undertook philosophical and scientific pursuits, including participation in a scientific observation of a solar eclipse and the publication of his first scholarly article, 'An Essay on Quantity', both in 1748.

In 1750, on the strength of his academic reputation, Reid was appointed to the position of regent at King's College, Aberdeen. As a regent, Reid was responsible not for a single subject, or a rotating schedule of courses, but the general education of an entire class over their four year career. This, it seems, was a position that well suited him and his wide-ranging interests in natural science, mathematics, politics, and philosophy. While at King's, Reid played a major part in retaining and reforming the regent system, became a founding member of the Aberdeen Philosophical Society, and worked on the material which would ultimately become his first book: *An Inquiry into the Human Mind on the Principles of Common Sense*. This work, a detailed investigation into the five external senses and reply to the 'ideal' system typified by Hume's epistemology, was published in 1764.

---

[8] Ibid., 35. See also Appendix III.
[9] AUL MS 2814/1/80.

Teaching at Glasgow

Later that same year Reid became the successor to Adam Smith in the Chair of Moral Philosophy at the University of Glasgow. This position required him to lecture on a less comprehensive but still broad range of topics, including pneumatology, theoretical and practical ethics, and politics. It is from this period on that most of the existing autograph material and all five sets of student notes originate. It is therefore the period of Reid's life in which we begin to find his most explicit statements regarding religion.

In both his own time and ours, Reid's philosophy has been seen as primarily concerned with questions of epistemology. But according to Reid himself, his concern with epistemological questions is secondary and due to the deleterious effects that the 'ideal system', and the scepticism it leads to, has on his first pedagogical priority, the cultivation of virtue.[10] For Reid, this latter and more important issue is not only a matter of personal virtue or civic prosperity, but of religious devotion. As he writes in a lecture on humanity's duties to God:

> Virtue that disdains any aid of Religion stands upon a very slippery foundation & will hardly be able to endure any severe trial. For how can we conceive a man to believe himself under an obligation to reverence his parents and at the same time to owe no Reverence or filial Affection to his Maker and father in heaven… I conceive that those who profess to be friends to Virtue while they hold in contempt Piety toward God, must either be hypocrites or very grossly deluded.[11]

We will return to the relation between religious belief and virtue below, but, taken together, these observations show that, to Reid, the teaching of true religion was critical to his vocation as a professor.

---

[10] See, for example, *Inquiry*, 202; *Politics and Society*, 145.
[11] *Practical Ethics*, 23–24. See also Appendix II.

The Intellectual Powers and the Active Powers

Reid retained his chair at Glasgow University until his death, but retired from teaching duties in 1780 in order to work on his two largest works. These volumes—*The Essays on the Intellectual Powers of Man* (1785) and *The Essays of the Active Powers of Man* (1788)—were based on his lecture notes during his tenure at Glasgow, and may profitably be read as one work, containing the most mature statement of Reid's anti-speculative philosophy. In these we also find evidence for Reid's beliefs on four matters related to religion: divine causality, free will, the permission of evil, and the relationship between virtue acquisition and salvation.

Regarding the first, Reid is adamant that there can be no effect without a cause, and that no true cause can be anything but an agent 'endowed with will and intelligence'.[12] For Reid, this means that the forces of nature described by natural laws are not strictly causes of anything. Properly, they are the regular effects of divine will. 'Whether it be the Supreme Cause alone, or a subordinate cause or causes', all natural causality is ultimately derived from divine agency.[13] According to Reid, from this it follows that the beauty of the natural world ought to be ascribed not to the intrinsic merit of the creation but to the excellency of its creator.[14] Although he rarely mentions the related topic of miracles, Reid's defence of their existence follows directly from this understanding of divine agency.[15] It is the continuously-active will of God that produces all the derivative causes and effects in the natural world. They do not run on their own, because they are not themselves agents. Thus, a choice to act in a way contrary to the regular order of nature, i.e. perform a miracle, is completely within the power and prerogative of God.

According to Reid, divine agency is also the foundation of human agency, which 'in its extent, and in its exertions, is entirely dependent upon God, and upon the laws of nature

---

[12] *Active Powers*, 33.
[13] Ibid., 39.
[14] *Intellectual Powers*, 595.
[15] See *Active Powers*, 257; and Appendix I.

which he has established'.[16] Human beings, in other words, have both intelligence and free will, and so are real agents, but their agency is contingent on God granting it to them. We ought, therefore, to be humbly thankful for the agency granted to us by God.

We can also ascertain Reid's beliefs with considerable specificity on the relationship between human agency and divine foreknowledge. In a long section of the *Active Powers*, Reid defends the compatibility of perfect divine foreknowledge and human freedom. As the relevant texts are reproduced in Appendix I, I will not rehearse Reid's arguments in detail here. It is worth noting, however, that these arguments are closely related to Reid's response to the problem of evil. In short, Reid believes that God permits evil partly to provide the necessary opportunities for human beings to grow in virtue by choosing well in the midst of difficulty. Reid is careful to say that this theodicy is not sufficient to account for all the evil in the world, nor its distribution. The full account is, for now, a divine mystery. However, Reid is adamant in affirming that human beings have free will, and that God can in no way be blamed for any morally imperfect action.

Finally, to return at last to the relationship between piety and virtue, as the development of moral character was Reid's chief pedagogical concern, it is not surprising that he returns to it at the close of the *Active Powers*. Here we find a powerful, if somewhat vague, statement on the relationship between virtue acquisition and religion:

> We may therefore conclude, That what we know in part, and see in part, of right and wrong [God] sees perfectly; that the moral excellence which we see and admire in some of our fellow-creatures, is a faint but true copy of that moral excellence, which is essential to his nature; and that to tread the path of virtue, is the true dignity of our nature, an imitation of God, and the way to obtain his favour.[17]

---

[16] *Active Powers*, 45.
[17] *Active Powers*, 362–63.

Although perhaps unremarkable to a modern reader, in context, this stress on moral formation is telling. According to the strict Calvinism of the Evangelicals, God's favour is granted to the elect before any reformation of character, only by the grace of God, and never on account of the merit of the receiver. From this perspective, an emphasis on the meritoriousness of a virtuous person smacks of heresy; of claiming credit for what can only be God's work. According to the Moderates, on the other hand, virtue acquisition and righteousness before God go hand in hand. They cannot be easily separated into two moments of justification (being declared righteous before God) and sanctification (actually becoming righteous before God). The Evangelicals of Reid's time would doubtless consider the above statement — as they did their Moderate opponents — heretically Pelagian. Without more textual evidence, however, we should hesitate to accept the Evangelical circumscription of orthodoxy. Although it is beyond the scope of this introduction to examine, the relationship between justification and sanctification has been a vexed question in Christian theology since at least the time of Augustine (354–430). And Reid's statements touching this subject are by no means beyond the scope of broad orthodoxy.

Unpublished Papers

Beyond the published works from this time we also find valuable clues as to Reid's religious beliefs among his unpublished papers. One of the challenges that a modern reader faces when seeking Reid's religious views is his vocabulary. When speaking of God, Reid frequently uses phrases such as 'The Author of Nature', 'Supreme Being', 'Deity', and 'First Cause'. Much less frequently does he refer to Jesus, and even then often as a passing example. Certainly, Reid repeatedly insists that reason and revelation — which in Christian theology primarily means the life and teaching of Jesus Christ — are fully complimentary.[18] Yet his circumlocution and vagueness may still give the impression that Reid

---

[18] See e.g. *Practical Ethics*, 9; *Active Powers*, 374; and the 'Lectures on Natural Theology' below.

held to some version of Socinianism or deism, instead of Trinitarian Christian theism. One line in a long and biting criticism of materialism, written in retirement, however, gives us good reason to reject this interpretation.

In early 1774, the English dissenting clergyman and proponent of materialism, Joseph Priestly, published a fiercely critical book on Reid entitled *An Examination of Dr. Reid's Inquiry into the Human Mind*. Reid had previously been aware and critical of Priestley's materialism, but following this publication Reid wrote extensive engagements of Priestley's philosophy.[19] Among this material is a paper entitled 'Some Observations On the Modern System of Materialism', probably prepared for a lecture before the Glasgow Literary Society. In this paper Reid attacks Priestley for doubting the Christian doctrine of the Trinity—the belief that there is one God in three persons: Father, Son, and Holy Spirit.[20] Reid's reticence on Christology ought to give us pause in assuming too much about his views on divinity.[21] But, unless we read Reid as opportunistically hypocritical here, it seems that Reid was an orthodox Trinitarian.

In the same discourse, we also find hints of Reid's view of the Eucharist. Reid, it seems, was no admirer of the Roman Catholic and Lutheran doctrines of trans- and consubstantiation. Mocking Priestley's views on the permeability of matter, Reid remarks that 'those who think themselves obliged to maintain these mysterious doctrines, will be thankful for a discovery, which affords them an aid that was much wanted'.[22] Although we cannot infer too much from his brief comments, this negative attitude was consonant with Presbyterian doctrine, which viewed the belief that the Christ's body and blood becomes materially present with the bread and wine at communion as superstition. It is also consistent with Reid's frequent warnings against 'superstition' and 'enthusiasm', against anti-rational religion of all kinds,

---

[19] See Paul Wood's 'Introduction' in *Animate Creation*, 31–56, for the complex history of these papers.
[20] *Animate Creation*, 194.
[21] Although, cf. Fraser, *Thomas Reid*, 34.
[22] *Animate Creation*, 195.

in his published and unpublished papers. Interestingly, however, another document, written a few years later, in 1791, points to an openness toward Christians of other churches. In a sympathetic letter to an unidentified Roman Catholic prelate, Reid cheers the prospect of an eventual reunion between their respective churches with the memorable words 'let the pure wine of Rome and Geneva mix, leaving the dregs behind!'[23]

Conclusion

Reid died in 1796, after a short illness. His ashes were initially interred with those of his wife in the university church's burial ground. In 1872, however, the University of Glasgow moved three miles west to its present location, and the Reids' remains were transferred to the Professor's Monument in the necropolis behind St. Mungo's Cathedral. A month after his death, an anonymous epistolary obituary was published in the Glasgow Courier, along with a selection from a late lecture regarding Sir Thomas More's *Utopia*. According to the obituary:

> [Reid] venerated Religion; not the noisy contentious systems which lead men to hate and persecute each other, but the sublime principle which regulates the conduct by controuling the selfish, and animating the benevolent affections. When vilified by intemperate Philosophers, he made no reply being satisfied with having stated what he thought the truth; and when outraged by zealots who most falsely call themselves Christians, he bore the outrage meekly, using no terms either of complaint or reproach. He was, to the last moment, free from that morose, querulous temper, which had been deemed inseparable from age... Every scheme which promised to improve human nature or to alleviate human misery, found in him the most ardent support. He was uncommonly active in establishing the Infirmary at Aberdeen and was an early, vigorous uniform promoter of that in Glasgow. Besides a very liberal subscription, he

---

[23] *Correspondence*, 223. See also Appendix III.

seldom visited the Infirmary without leaving a new mark of his good will.[24]

As with all early accounts of Reid's life, we must be wary of hagiography. Yet, if somewhat burnished, this picture of Reid's religious attitudes well-accords with the one found in his papers. Reid was not immune to party politics, nor innocently ignorant of the role that patronage played in church and university. But though, as a minister and professor, he regularly attended the General Assembly of the Church of Scotland, and was friendly with many of the leading lights among the Moderates, we do not find him among the cut-and-trust of debates against the Evangelicals. Similarly, in letters written near the end of his life, he expresses gratitude for his life, good humour toward the infirmities of age, and confidence in an afterlife.[25] Nor is the extent of Reid's charitable deeds in dispute. In addition to his donations to hospitals in Glasgow and Aberdeen, and other charitable endeavours, Reid helped to found the Glasgow Society of the Sons and Daughters of Ministers of the Church of Scotland, which still assists impoverished children of deceased ministers.

All told, Reid's emphasis on moral formation, the agreement of reason and revelation, and temperate religious practice, point to moderate Presbyterian belief, in both senses of the word. Yet even here we must be careful not to assume too much. According to Thomas Ahnert, the eighteenth-century Moderates were largely sceptical of the use of natural theology, while the Evangelicals embraced it as necessary to show that sin was inexcusable, since God's existence and good nature ought to be obvious to every rational soul.[26] If we may take Reid's lectures on natural theology, as recorded by George Baird below, as indicative of his attitudes toward it, then it seems that, though we have

---

[24] Robert Cleghorn, *Sketch*, 5–6.
[25] See especially *Correspondence*, 230.
[26] Ahnert, *The Moral Culture of the Scottish Enlightenment*, 49 and 131–32. Note, however, that Ahnert's use of the terms 'orthodox' and 'heterodox' may be misleading as follows the Evangelical circumscription of orthodoxy to Calvinism.

good reason to number him among the moderate *literati* of the Scottish Enlightenment, in theology, as in philosophy, Reid remained his own man.

Editorial Principles

In accordance with the aims of the *Library of Scottish Philosophy*, the primary texts in this volume have been modernized. As Baird's and Reid's styles—especially in autograph—are quite different from current convention, this has required many changes in spelling, punctuation, capitalization, and spacing.

The great majority of these changes are small, such as inserting a missing period, changing a capital letter to lowercase, or changing an underlined passage to italics, and have therefore been made silently. For more significant changes, I have adopted the following notation. Where I have translated a short Latin or Greek phrase, I have put the translation in square brackets—[like so]—after the transliteration. Where I have provided a long translation, I have reproduced the original Latin or Greek, but have noted the translation in the footnotes. All translations are from the Loeb Classical Library, except where otherwise noted. Where I have inserted or changed a word, I have put those words in curly brackets—{like so}. In addition, when I have changed, instead of merely added, a word, I have also noted the change in a footnote. On occasion, I have broken up long sections of texts into paragraphs. In such instances, I have indicated the change with a ¶.

For the 'Lectures on Natural Theology' only, I have additionally indicated page breaks and page numbers from the original manuscripts. Page breaks are indicated by a slash—/—with page numbers appearing in subscript following. The 'Lectures on Natural Theology' appear in volumes five and six of the eight-volume set of George Baird's notes. The numbers are therefore formatted as 'volume number. page number': '5.80', thus meaning 'volume five, page eighty'.

In addition to these textual changes, I have also added a number of explanatory footnotes. None of these are original to their texts. Although these notes clutter the page somewhat, I hope they bring additional clarity to Reid's frequent but usually un-cited allusions to Scripture, history, and contemporaneous and classical writers, without negatively affecting readability.

As Gordon Graham states in the 'Series Editor's Note', the 'principle aim of this series' is to 'make the writings of Scottish philosophers accessible to a new generation of modern readers'. For readers of this volume who are inspired to further study of Reid, I highly recommend the volumes of the *Edinburgh Edition of Thomas Reid*, which contain critical texts of and extensive commentary on all of the material found in the appendices, save for the three prayers in Appendix III. Unless otherwise noted, all page references to Reid's work in the footnotes are to the Edinburgh Editions. There is, unfortunately, as yet no critical text of George Baird's notes from Reid's lectures at Glasgow.

About These Texts

'Lectures on Natural Theology'

The 'Lectures on Natural Theology' are selected from George Baird's extensive set of student notes, taken in Reid's last public lecture class, which ran from September 1779 to April 1780. Baird records notes for one hundred and nineteen lectures, addressing the following general topics: intellectual powers (lectures 1–54), active powers (55–70), the soul (71–76), natural theology (77–87), theoretical ethics (88–104a), practical ethics (104b–108), and politics (109–118).[27] Today, these notes, which have been bound into eight volumes, are held in the Mitchell Library in Glasgow.

Baird's notes are one of the five sets of student notes we have from Reid's lectures.[28] As they are almost certainly not

---

[27] Baird mis-numbers the lectures, giving two the number '114'.
[28] The others are:
Anonymous (1766) 'Reid's Essays', Aberdeen University Library, MS 2131/8/VII.
Anonymous (1768) 'Dr. Reid's Lectures', New College Library, Edinburgh, MS Box 32.3.
Archibald Graham (1769) 'Notes of Thomas Reid's Lectures on Pneumatology', Glasgow University Library, MS Gen 760.

in-class notes, but rather an attempt to carefully preserve Reid's last lectures, they are also the most extensive and detailed. Since we have no notes for the 'Lectures on Natural Theology' in Reid's own hand, they are therefore the best source for our knowledge of Reid's views on the topic.

This is not to say that Baird's notes are completely accurate, or even consistently legible. In several places, Baird clearly mis-hears or mis-records what Reid said. And, though he often begins his transcriptions of Reid's lectures in a clear and careful hand, there are many instances of nigh-unreadable handwriting. Thus, although we may consider Baird a conscientious reporter of Reid's lectures on natural theology, we ought to remember that these notes are not Reid's. As every student and lecturer knows, even the most well-intentioned and assiduous note-taking does not guarantee reliability on all points.

My initial transcriptions of Baird's notes were made from high-quality photographs, generously supplied by the Mitchell Library. I initially made 'photo' transcriptions, attempting to render the manuscript pages as faithfully as possible in text. The text was then proofread several times in this format before it was modernized and annotated in accordance with the editorial principles of the *LSP*.

Appendix I – Published Material

Selecting relevant sections from Reid's published materials for a volume on religion is difficult; though not for lack of choice. Reid frequently mentions God in his published works, and often in contexts that parallel passages from the 'Lectures on Natural Theology'.[29] The selections in this volume were therefore included on the basis of two narrow criteria: first, that they included material which significantly expanded upon that found in the 'Lectures on Natural

---

Robert Jack (1775) 'Dr. Reid's Lectures', Glasgow University Library, MS Gen 117.

[29] See Wolterstorff's 'Introduction to Reid's "Lectures on Natural Theology"', below. See also Dale Tuggy's 'Reid's Philosophy of Religion' in *The Cambridge Companion to Thomas Reid*.

Theology'; and, second, that they were long enough to present a sustained argument. The four selections in this section are all excerpted from 'Essay IV. Of the Liberty of Moral Agents' in the *Essays on the Active Powers of Man*: chapters V, IX, X, and XI. Although these chapters are not all contiguous, they may be usefully read as a single sustained reflection on the relationship between divine and human volition. Given the context in which Reid was writing — with the Church of Scotland divided between the Calvinist Evangelical and the non-Calvinist Moderate parties — it is especially worth notice that Reid appeals to no less an authority than Augustine to support his Moderate views. The text of these essays, though modernized here, is based on the first edition of the *Active Powers*, published in 1788.

Appendix II – Reid's Lecture Notes

The three texts in this section are transcripts of Reid's own lecture notes, preserved in manuscript form in Birkwood Collection, housed in the Aberdeen University Library. In each case, my initial transcriptions of these lectures were made in the Wolfson Reading Room of the Aberdeen University Library from the original texts themselves. As with the Baird notes, these transcriptions were originally formatted as 'photo' transcripts, and then reformatted to match the modern conventions of the *LSP*. Unlike Baird's notes, however, these manuscripts sometimes required the additional step of reconstruction. They are, quite obviously, working documents, and Reid commonly wrote sections out of order or as marginal notes, indicating the proper placement of material with notations which — though no doubt clear to him — are often ambiguous.

The first, entitled 'Eloquence of the Pulpit', is an example of this ambiguity. The notes for this lecture, which was part of Reid's larger discussion of rhetoric in his advanced class on the 'culture of the mind' at Glasgow,[30] is fully contained in AUL MS 2131 8/I/6. But the placement of several sections is unclear. The ordering in this volume is my best attempt to

---

[30] See Alexander Broadie's introduction in *Logic, Rhetoric, and Fine Arts*, xiii–l.

restore the order intended by Reid. For a different ordering, however, see Alexander Broadie's critical edition.[31] The second set of notes regards the immortality of the soul. According to George Baird's notes, this topic immediately preceded his public lectures on natural theology.[32] The pages of these notes are split among three manuscripts in the Aberdeen University Library: AUL MS 2131 6/I/26, 6/I/27, and 4/II/19. Despite this complication, the order of this lecture is straightforward, and so the one presented in this volume matches that of Knud Haakonssen and Derek R. Brookes in the Edinburgh Edition.[33] These manuscripts, and the Edinburgh Edition, also contain notes from Reid's lectures addressing two other questions regarding the soul—its immateriality and place.[34] As these notes are in outline form only, however, they have not been reproduced here.

The last set of lecture notes in this section regards our duties to God. Like the notes on the immortality of the soul above, these notes appear to be for lectures given in Reid's public class. According to textual evidence and order of lectures recorded by George Baird, 'Duties to God' was also the first topic addressed in Reid's lectures on practical ethics. Although this lecture is entirely contained in AUL MS 2131 8/IV/2, the placing of one paragraph is uncertain and is therefore noted it in the text.[35] Another placement of this paragraph may be found in Knud Haakonssen's critical text in the Edinburgh Edition.[36] Interested readers are also encouraged to view images of the original manuscripts themselves on the University of Aberdeen's excellent website 'The Papers of Thomas Reid', which provides access to the entire Birkwood Collection and the Thomas Reid Papers of MS 3061.[37] Also available at 'The Papers of Thomas Reid'

---

[31] *Logic, Rhetoric, and Fine Arts*, 240–50.
[32] See also *Practical Ethics*, 3–16.
[33] *Intellectual Powers*, 620–31.
[34] Ibid., 617–19.
[35] See note 28 in Appendix II, below.
[36] *Practical Ethics*, 17–25.
[37] https://www.abdn.ac.uk/diss/historic/Thomas_Reid

website is Giovanni Grandi's detailed and searchable list of Reid's manuscripts held in the Aberdeen University Library.

Appendix III – Personal Papers

This section contains four personal papers relating to Reid's religious beliefs and practice. Of the four, the first is the most uncertain. The text reproduced in this volume comes from Alexander Campbell Fraser's 1898 biography of Reid.[38] According to Fraser, 'The following expression of religious feeling during an illness of his young wife appears among his manuscripts, dated March 30, 1746'.[39] As the manuscript of Reid's prayer is now lost, we have no way of checking the accuracy of Fraser's transcript. The previous existence of the manuscript itself, however, can be independently verified. There is another manuscript in the Aberdeen University Library which lists 'Letters and Papers sent by Mr J. Edmond to Rev Dr McCosh'. Among the papers indicated is 'Dr. Thomas Reid's prayer and confession, 30th March 1746'.[40]

The second and third texts are occasional prayers prepared by Reid. Both of these are copied from manuscripts in the Aberdeen University Library's Birkwood Collection — MS 2131 4/II/9 and MS 7/VII/16, respectively. The former and longer of the two is part of Reid's inaugural lecture, given at Glasgow University after receiving the Chair of Moral Philosophy 1764. The latter is also clearly a public prayer, although its occasion is unknown.

The last of these papers is the draft of a short letter by Reid to an unidentified Catholic correspondent in 1791. It too is part of the Birkwood collection — MS 2131 3/III/8 — and has been included here because it contains the clearest statement of Reid's view of the Christian unity: 'Let the pure wine of Rome and Geneva mix, leaving the dregs behind!'

While the first of these four texts is merely a modernized reproduction of Fraser's account, the last three, like the lectures in Appendix II, were faithfully transcribed from

---

[38] Fraser, *Thomas Reid*, 34–35.
[39] Ibid., 34.
[40] AUL MS 2814/1/80.

their originals held in the Aberdeen University Library, and then modernized for this series.

Acknowledgements

Permission to publish the manuscripts transcribed in this volume has been generously provided by the Mitchell Library, Glasgow, and Special Collections, University of Aberdeen Library. In particular I would like to thank Archie Fischer from the Mitchell Library and Jan Smith and Michelle Gait from Aberdeen. This project could not have been completed without their help. The primary research for this volume took place during a post-graduate Fulbright Research Scholarship, and I am deeply indebted to the US-UK Fulbright Commission and the Research Institute of Irish and Scottish Studies—especially Cairns Craig, Michael Brown, and Adam Hanna—for their help and support during that year. Finally, I would also like to thank Rocki Wentzel for help with translating difficult Latin passages, Lisa Stahl for proofreading the text, Paul Wood for unfailingly responding to my emailed queries, even when the answers turned out to be obvious, Nicholas Wolterstorff, for writing an introduction to the 'Lectures on Natural Theology', and Gordon Graham for his encouragement at every stage of this volume's production. The mistakes herein are, as ever, my own.

Nicholas Wolterstorff

Introduction to Reid's 'Lectures on Natural Theology'

In his published work Thomas Reid refers often to God, doing so with a wide variety of terms: 'God', 'First Cause', 'Supreme Cause', 'Supreme Being', 'Creator', and so forth. However, nowhere in his published work does he explain why he feels entitled to assume that God exists and has the nature that he ascribes to God. Happily, we are not at a complete loss in this matter, because in Glasgow, every year from his appointment to his retirement (1764–1780), he delivered a series of lectures on the topic of natural theology.

Reid devoted his retirement to working up for publication his lectures on the 'powers' of the mind, publishing *Essays on the Intellectual Powers* in 1785 and *Essays on the Active Powers* in 1788. He did not work up his lectures on natural theology for publication, but we know a lot about their content from extensive notes taken by students. The most extensive of these are the notes of George Baird. Baird's notes have previously been published, but the present volume marks a significant advance in our knowledge. James Foster is the first to have worked carefully not only through Baird's notes, but to have compared them to notes taken by Archibald Graham, Robert Jack, and two other anonymous students. By filling in missing words, completing sentences, correcting the grammar, translating non-English quotations, and so forth, Foster has brought to light, in a much more satisfactory form than hitherto, this essential component of Reid's thought.

What drew Reid's attention in his published work was the workings of the human mind. In his early *Inquiry into the Human Mind* and in his late *Essays on the Intellectual Powers*, his questions, more specifically, were mainly two: What accounts for the fact that we get entities in mind in such a manner as to be able to form beliefs about them, in particular, entities other than the present states of our own minds? And what accounts for the fact that often we do not merely entertain thoughts about the entities we have in mind but form beliefs about them: perceptual beliefs, memory beliefs, beliefs in other minds, beliefs in the truth of testimony, and so forth?

To the latter set of questions Reid's answer, in each case, was that we are endowed with innate dispositions — he called them 'powers' — such that, upon having an experience of a certain sort, a belief of a certain sort is produced. In the course of articulating this view Reid spent a good deal of time arguing against alternative explanations current in his day, including Hume's claim that beliefs in other minds and testimonial beliefs are formed by inductive inference.

In recent years this Reidian approach to explaining the formation of some of our most fundamental beliefs has been employed by philosophers and psychologists of religion to explain the formation of basic beliefs about God. The topic of Book One of John Calvin's *Institutes* is our knowledge of God. In Chapter 3 of Book One, Calvin develops the idea that 'There is within the human mind, and indeed by natural instinct, an awareness of divinity' (I.iii.1).[1] Alvin Plantinga interprets — correctly, in my view — what Calvin goes on to say in this and other passages as affirming that there is in human beings a 'Reidian' disposition to believe in the existence of God upon having experiences of a certain sort. Calvin called it the *sensus divinitatis*. Plantinga finds passages in Aquinas in which the same idea is expressed.[2] He then goes on to develop his own 'Reidian' account of the formation of

---

[1] Calvin, *Institutes*, 44.
[2] See Plantinga, *Warranted Christian Belief*, 170–75.

basic beliefs about God, explicitly setting his account within the context of Reid's thought about the workings of the mind.[3]

In cognitive psychology there has been a flurry of discussion in recent years concerning the formation of basic beliefs about God, with something of a consensus emerging about the psychological dynamics at play. The 'Reidian' character of the accounts being offered is explored in an essay titled 'Reidian Religious Epistemology and the Cognitive Science of Religion',[4] authored jointly by the philosopher, Kelly James Clark, and the cognitive psychologist, Justin L. Barrett.

Those familiar with these recent developments in philosophy and psychology of religion will wonder, when they take up Reid's 'Lectures on Natural Theology', whether Reid's approach to natural religion is likewise 'Reidian' in character. Those not familiar with these recent developments but familiar with Reid's published work may also have that question in mind.

Reid's approach to natural theology is not 'Reidian' in that way. He never so much as considers the possibility that there is, in human beings, an innate theistic disposition (or set of dispositions) comparable to our disposition to form perceptual beliefs, our disposition to form memory beliefs, and so forth. The *Lectures* are devoted to giving arguments for the existence and nature of God. Nowhere does Reid appeal to anything like Calvin's *sensus divinitatis*. Though he was an ordained Presbyterian clergyman, there is no evidence in the 'Lectures on Natural Theology' or in his published works that he had ever read Calvin.

Reid employs two arguments for God's existence: the first cause argument and the argument from design. In his way of employing these arguments, and in his interpretation of the epistemological status of certain of their premises, there are,

---

[3] Evans, in *Natural Signs and Knowledge of God*, develops a somewhat different 'Reidian' account of theistic belief than Plantinga's by picking up on Reid's idea of bodily expressions and movements being natural signs of our states of mind.

[4] *JAAR* 79(3).

Introduction to Reid's 'Lectures on Natural Theology'

as we shall see, some distinctively Reidian touches. But the arguments themselves are thoroughly traditional.

Reid dispatches the first cause argument in a few pages. Evidently it did not much interest him, this in spite of the fact that it plays a crucial role in conclusions at which he arrives concerning the nature of God. He opens his statement of the argument by declaring his agreement with the view of 'some authors' that *everything beginning to exist must have a cause*. This principle, he says, is a necessary truth, not a contingent truth at which one arrives by inductive inference. He adds a Reidian touch by noting that it is among those that he calls, in his published work, *first principles*, a first principle being 'a principle to which all who are come to years of understanding assent, and without which we could not act with common prudence for a single hour in life' (11).

Given this principle, that everything beginning to exist must have a cause, we are

> necessarily led to a first cause of all or to an infinite succession of being, one producing another without a cause. The last of these is evidently absurd; for an infinity of beings without a first cause cannot possibly be, because it would be a chain every link of which would be an effect which stood in need of a cause and what is true of a part is equally true of the whole. Thus we are unavoidably led to admit the existence of some external [sic] being, uncaused, necessarily existing and by his power producing everything we see. (11)

Reid's statement of the argument is notably inarticulate at a crucial point. In an infinite sequence of causes and effects there is a cause for everything that begins to exist. The principle is satisfied, or so it appears. So why can there not be an infinite sequence of causes? What's the problem? Reid alludes to what is arguably the problem with his cryptic remark, 'what is true of a part is equally true of the whole'. A traditional objection to there being nothing but an infinite sequence of causes and effects is that, though every event within the sequence has a cause, we are left without a cause for the sequence as a whole. I judge it to be a serious defect in Reid's presentation of the first cause argument that he does nothing more than cryptically allude to this point.[5]

When Aquinas presented the first cause argument in his *Summa Theologica*, the attribute of the First Cause that he highlighted was its aseity: the First Cause is in no way dependent on anything not identical with itself. Aquinas drew from this a long line of additional attributes, beginning with simplicity. A distinctive feature of Reid's employment of the first cause argument is that he nowhere mentions God's aseity, and rejects divine simplicity with the dismissive and rather obtuse remark, 'There have been others who, through a love of simplicity and to reduce the divine attributes to what they think consistent with the unity {of the} divine nature, have included all under divine rectitude and divine wisdom. But it does not appear that by reducing them all under one word, we make the notion of them any clearer' (94).

The attribute of the First Cause that Reid highlights is necessary existence. He says,

> Another attribute of deity is his necessary existence, that is, it is impossible that he could not be. Every being that exists is either contingent or necessary... We call that *contingent* which either might or might not be and that *necessary* which must be. Whatever either might or might not be depends on the will of some agent with power to bring it to pass or not... That we do exist is most certain — but that existence is contingent, the supreme being gave it and he can take it away when he pleases — it depends on his will. But are we to suppose that the supreme being himself exists in the same manner? This evidently would be absurd, he derives his

---

[5] He also disposes quickly with the possibility of a causal circle: 'If we suppose there were two beings, let us call the one A and the other B, then if A created B, surely A could not be created by its own creature...; and the reasoning is the same if to these we add a third being or if we add three thousand or three thousand millions; still the same conclusion will hold. For there is no principle more evident than this that two things cannot mutually be the cause of each other' (11–12).

power and his existence from no other being. Therefore he is not contingent but necessary. (61)

It is mainly from the necessary existence of the First Cause that Reid attempts to derive other attributes of God. He argues, 'The immensity, eternity, and unlimited perfection of the supreme being are necessarily connected with his necessary existence' (100). Some of his arguments concerning the implications of God's necessary existence strike this reader as seriously underdeveloped, if not fallacious. I have in mind, for example, his argument for God's existing at all times and in all places — he calls it God's 'immensity'.

> There is an absurdity in supposing limits to a being, either in time or place, who exists *necessarily*. For this necessity is the same at all times and at all places, and therefore we cannot suppose a being necessarily existing in one place which is not necessarily existing in another place. Though our notion of this kind of existence, as I observed before, is imperfect and inadequate, yet we can have a clearer conception of it by attending to the distinction of truths into *necessary* and *contingent*, and this is an evident property of truths which are necessary, that they are true in all places and at all times, and could not possibly be otherwise... What exists necessarily then exists everywhere and at all times. (67)

Just how does noting that a necessary truth is true in all places and at all times make clear that a being that exists necessarily 'is the same' in all places and at all times?

Whereas Reid's treatment of the first cause argument is cursory, his development of the argument from design is expansive.[6] The argument, if 'reduced to the form of a syllogism [has] two premises', he says. '1) That an intelligent cause may be inferred from marks of wisdom in the effects. 2) There are clear marks of wisdom and design in the works of nature' (51).

About the first premise he says little more than that it is another of those necessary truths that is what he calls a *first*

---

[6] After remarking that the argument 'has commonly been called the argument from *final causes*', he says that he will use the term 'without enquiring into the propriety of it' (51).

principle. 'Thus it appears then that, from marks of design and wisdom, to infer intelligence in the cause is a first principle learned neither by reasoning nor by experience; it is self evident and assented to by all men' (50). He offers an acute argument against Hume's claim that one can arrive at the principle by inductive inference (47ff.). Inductive inferences do not yield necessary truths; and only in one's own case does one observe a connection between design and its cause. As Reid sees it, the only alternative to 'marks of wisdom and design in the works of nature' being the product of an intelligent cause is that they are the result of chance; and that supposition, he insists, is absurd.

> The learned Archbishop Tillotson hath well observed, as, by throwing carelessly in a heap an infinite number of types it is not to be expected that a fine polished poem would be made or even a tolerably sensible discourse in prose, how much less can we suppose that this beautiful system of nature could be the work of blind chance acting by no fixed rules. (20)

Reid dwells at length over the course of several lectures on the second premise of the argument, highlighting 'clear marks of wisdom and design' in the movements of the planets and the stars, in the functioning of plants and animals, in the functioning of the human body, and in the working of the human mind. His discussion breathes a spirit of awe, wonder, and amazement. He says, 'when we attend to the marks of wisdom and intelligence that appears all around, every discovery proves a new hymn of praise to him who is the creator and governor of the world' (51). There is no hint of the possibility that evolution might be the cause of at least some of what he identifies as design.

A theme that Reid sounds over and over in his published works is that of the limits on our attempt to explain things. We explain one law by reference to another, that law by a reference to a third, and so forth. But there comes a point where our explanations run out and all we can do is say, 'This is how it is'. The same theme is sounded repeatedly in the 'Lectures on Natural Theology', this too giving a Reidian touch to a traditional line of argument.

> Our muscles have been shown by anatomists to be admirably fitted for giving motion to the body. How they are contrived is beyond our comprehension, but when a muscle acts we know that it swells in breadth and contracts in length and thus the motion is produced. We know that this power is communicated to them by the nerves, but of the manner of its operation we are entirely ignorant—so far is the wisdom of God beyond the wisdom of man. (37)

My aim in this introduction has been to give the reader some sense of the overall structure of Reid's line of thought concerning natural theology and to call attention to those points where he adds a distinctive 'Reidian touch' to an otherwise traditional argument. Thus, I have taken no notice of the many interesting points of detail in Reid's discussion, nor, apart from raising a question at a couple of points concerning the cogency of Reid's argument, have I critically engaged Reid's arguments for the existence and nature of God.

Let me close by taking note of what he says at the beginning of his first lecture about the relation between natural theology and revelation and the relevance of natural theology. He writes that anything that can be learned from natural theology can also be learned from revelation: 'it is no doubt true that revelation exhibits all the truths of natural religion' (1). And that God has in fact 'enlightened' human beings by revelation is 'evident from a comparison of the doctrines of Scripture with the systems of the most refined heathens' (1).

> It appears a strange phenomenon, that the Jews, who were not more polished and civilized than others, but rather a barbarous people, should have such ideas of deity, his attributes, and government as perfectly agreeable to what our reason dictates. They were not polytheists. They believed in one God the maker of the world, who was eternal, omnipresent, omniscient, who had regard to virtue and a dislike at vice. Now, such refined notions of deity in a nation so rude as the Jews is hardly to be expected, unless by a divine revelation. (115)

But though everything that can be learned about God from natural theology can also be learned from revelation, it does not follow that revelation renders reasoning about God irrelevant. To the contrary.

> It is by reason that we must judge whether that revelation be really so; it is by reason that we must judge of the meaning of what is revealed; and it is by reason that we must guard against any impious, inconsistent or absurd interpretation of that revelation... That man is best prepared for the study and practice of the revealed religion who has previously acquired just sentiments of the natural. (1-2)

It's a very Lockean picture of the relation between reason and revelation![7]

---

[7] See my *John Locke and the Ethics of Belief*, 118-33.

Lectures on Natural Theology

/5.17

Natural Theology
Lecture 73rd, February 11th, 1780

Of all the animals which God has made, it is the prerogative of man alone to know his maker. There is no kind of knowledge that lends so much to elevate the mind as the knowledge of God. Duty to God forms an important part of our duty, and it is the support of every virtue; it gives us magnanimity, fortitude, and tranquillity. It inspires with hope in the most adverse circumstances; and there can be no rational piety without just notions of the perfections and providence of God. It is no doubt true that revelation exhibits all the truths of natural religion, but it is no less true that reason must be employed to judge of that revelation; whether it comes from God. Both are great lights given to us by the father of light[1] and we ought not to put out the one in order to use the other. Revelation is of use to enlighten us with regard to the use of natural religion; as one man may enlighten another in things /5.18 that it was impossible could be discovered by him. It is easy thus to conceive that God could enlighten man. And that he has done so is evident from a comparison of the doctrines of Scripture with the systems of the most refined heathens. We acknowledge then

---

[1] James 1:17.

that men are indebted to revelation in the matters of natural religion, but this is no reason why we should not also use reason here. Revelation was given {to} us not to hinder the exercise of our reasoning powers, but to aid and assist them. It is by reason that we must judge whether that revelation be really so; it is by reason that we must judge of the meaning of what is revealed; and it is by reason that we must guard against any impious, inconsistent, or absurd interpretations of that revelation. As the best things may be abused so when we lay aside the exercise of reason, revelation becomes the tool of low superstition or of wild fanaticism, and that man is best prepared for the study and practice of the revealed religion who has previously acquired just sentiments of the natural. The best notions of the divine nature which we can form are imperfect and inadequate, and are all drawn from what we know of our own mind. We cannot form an idea of /5.19 any attribute, intellectual or moral, as belonging to the deity, of which there is not some faint resemblance or image in ourselves. As we cannot form the least conception of material objects but {they} must somehow or other resemble those we perceive by our sense, so our knowledge of deity is grounded on our knowledge of the human mind. And for this reason I thought it best to give you a view of it before we entered upon this subject.[2] In treating of natural religion, I shall adopt the plan which has been followed by Mr Hutchinson in a tract which he has published and which I shall take this opportunity of recommending to your attention and careful perusal.[3] The first branch is to treat of the existence of God; the second, of his nature and attributes; the third, of his works.

---

[2] These lectures are preceded by lectures on the human mind. For more on the structure of Reid's lectures at Glasgow see esp. 'Introductory Lecture' in *Practical Ethics*, 3–16.

[3] Despite Baird's spelling, Reid refers to the third part Francis Hutcheson's 1742 work, *Synopsis Metaphysicae, Ontologiam et Pneumatologiam Complectens*, 'De Deo' [*Synopsis of Metaphysics, including Ontology and Pneumatology*, 'On God']. As Reid indicates, the tripartite structure of these lectures is borrowed from Hutcheson. But as Haakonssen notes, Reid does not adopt Hutcheson's content. See *Practical Ethics*, xxxiii.

1) The existence of the supreme being is so loudly proclaimed by everything in heaven and earth, by the structure of our own bodies and the no less curious structure of our minds, and indeed by everything about us, that it may perhaps appear unnecessary to confirm a truth so evident. But when we consider its importance and that there have not been wanting persons who have exercised their wit to weaken its evidence, it will appear proper to consider the grounds on which it is suspected and to enquire into the force of the sophistical arguments /5.20 that have been urged against it. I shall therefore point out some observations that appear to have the greatest strength in confirming the important truth. I shall first, however, offer a few remarks on the causes of speculative atheism and consider if it can justly be drawn from this system that there is no God.

I conceive then that there are chiefly two causes that may be assigned for the speculative atheism that has appeared in the world. There were a few among the ancients that professed atheism as Diagoras, Theodorus, and Protagoras, and in later times we are told that Julius Caesar Vaninus suffered death for atheism in the dark ages.[4] What seems to have led them to embrace their opinion may, as I said, be ascribed to two causes.

1) To false systems of philosophy by which they thought to account for the formation of the world and what happens in it without once bringing in a wise and intelligent maker. They conceived that by a mixture of moisture and draughts, the mighty machine of the universe was produced without any intelligence to begin, regulate, or finish its operations. The philosophers of the Ionic School were generally thought to lean to atheism, because that philosophy was chiefly employed in accounting for the formation of the world by chance. /5.21 Everything arose from chaos by a mixture of the elements, and we find that Anaxagoras was the first who

---

[4] Diagoras of Melos, Theodorus of Cyrene, and Protagoras of Abdera, are all fifth-century BC philosophers, and described by Cicero (106–43 BC) as doubting the existence of divine beings. See *De Natura Deorum* [*On the Nature of the Gods*] I.i, I.xxiii, and I.xlii. Lucilio (Giulio Cesare) Vanni was an anti-scholastic Italian priest, executed in Paris in 1619 for the charge of atheism.

thought it necessary to introduce mind into his system and who thought intelligence necessary to put all things in order.[5] All other atheists who differ from Anaxagoras must either hold that the world existed from all eternity without a cause, or was produced without an intelligent cause and author. The ignorance of true philosophy, which leads men to discern marks of wisdom and design in the formation and government of things, may be considered, then, as one cause of speculative atheism. But,

2) It was intended by some to free men's minds from the fear of punishment for their crimes in an after state, to free them from all reflections on the future or remorse for the past. Epicurus, who does not deny the existence of God, but thinks he does not interest himself in the affairs of the world, glories in this as a great benefit done to mankind, that he had freed them from the fears of religion and all the evils which a dread of the gods never fail to create.[6] Lucretius celebrates his praises on this account, and by all his followers he was also reckoned a kind of deity, who had nobly delivered them from the bugbears of religion.[7] He seems to have taken it /5.22 for granted that there was no supreme being, that therefore there was no future life, nothing after death, neither rewards for virtue nor punishment for vice, and of consequence they might pursue their pleasures without any restraint. This was the conclusion, supposing the premise true, which they then drew, but I conceive that these men have reasoned ill even on their principles of atheism, and before I enter on the arguments in proof of the existence of deity, let us consider the conclusions that follow from this system of atheism and whether their conclusions justly can be drawn from it, on account of which it seems to have been adopted by some. It is indeed difficult to reason on a hypothesis so absurd, but let

---

[5] Anaxagoras of Clazomenae (c. 500–c. 428 BC). Although mentioned by Aristotle and Plato, among others, no complete work of this Pre-Socratic philosopher survives. For his cosmogony see fragments B1–17 in, *Anaxagoras of Clazomenae: Fragments and Testimonia*.

[6] Epicurus (341–270 BC). See Diogenes Laertius, *Lives of Eminent Philosophers*, X.123–127.

[7] Titus Lucretius Carus (c. 99–c. 55 BC). See Lucretius, *De Rerum Natura* [*On the Nature of Things*], especially books III, V, and VI.

us for a moment suppose that heaven and earth are either from all eternity without any cause, or were produced by chance without the interposition of any intelligent power. Suppose then that this is the case. Will it follow from thence, 1) that men must perish at death and there is no future existence, 2) that if there is a future life that it will have no relation to the present, and that our happiness and misery in it will not depend on our conduct here, {and} 3) whether it would tend to make us happier in the present life if there was no God, no future state, and all things governed by unalterable laws, than under the persuasion of a universal ruler who governed /5.23 all things wisely and well? These it may be proper to consider a little and see whither they may justly be deduced from the principles of atheism or not.

1) There is no supreme being, therefore there is no future state and men must perish at death. Now to me there does not appear the least shadow of connection between the two propositions. If our present existence is consistent with his nonexistence, why not also a future? That the thinking principle is distinct from the body which we see and feel has already been proved by convincing arguments.[8] Now whatever this principle is—let us suppose it produced by necessity or fate, or any other unmeaning manner you please to give it—why may not that chance which at first united them again disunite them? We see other unions broken which appear equally strict, as that between the mother and the child, the egg and the bird. Thus it appears that, even on the principles of atheism, there is not the shadow of evidence for the position; we may grant the premise, yet the conclusion will not follow. But further, we may observe that in the whole course of nature we have no proof of the annihilation of any other substance that exists. All the operations of nature consist either of the composition or decomposition of /5.24 what already exists without either creation or annihilation. But the soul is a subtle simple principle, and therefore can perish only by annihilation, of which we have no

---

[8] Reid is referring to his preceding lectures on Pneumatology. See especially Reid's third lecture 'On the Nature and Duration of the Soul', Appendix II.

evidence in all nature, and it cannot reasonably then be supposed in this instance. This argument is equally strong even on the supposition of atheism, because it is drawn only from what we observe of the course of nature. We may observe too that it is agreeable to the analogy of nature that we should pass through different states, as different from one another as the present from the future. Neither is this grounded on the supposition of a deity, but retains its full force even allowing the principles of atheism to be true. We see then that the atheist cannot solace himself in this conclusion; that because there is no God therefore there is no future state: he reasons ill even from the principles of atheism.

2) The next conclusion I mentioned was, if there is a future state, will it have no relation to the present, and will our happiness or misery there not depend on our conduct here? And here again I maintain that this will not follow. We have already seen that, granting the principles of atheism to be true, yet we cannot conclude from them that the soul /5.25 will not exist after death. We have seen that there are no good arguments against a future state, nay that there are some arguments in proof of it which retain their force even on the supposition of atheism being just. Let us now then suppose a future state without any supreme intelligent ruler. Then on this supposition let us enquire whither it is certain that wicked men will not be miserable there, or if we will not find our good behaviour here redound to our happiness hereafter? I answer that it is neither certain nor probable that it will not be so. Nor does any system of atheism furnish us with any satisfying evidence that we will not reap the fruit of our doings. Nay, it is probable, on the contrary, that we shall, for 1) where animals pass though different states, the future always has a connection with that which went before. Thus if a chicken in the egg receives any blemish it always retains it — if it loses a foot or a wing it never after recovers it. In like manner, a child in the womb if it brings any defect or disease along with it, it continues through life and often renders its days few and evil. It is analogous then that we should carry our good or bad habits along with us to a future world. That vice is a disorder of the mind is {as} evident as that lameness is of the body. Now, /5.26 we have no evidence that it shall not be continued in a future as it is in the present life. The

excellence and superiority of temperance, prudence, and fortitude above their contrary vices is intrinsic and results from the nature of virtue and vice, and we may as well suppose that twice three will not make six as that there will be no distinction between them hereafter. If, therefore, we reason from analogy, we see that there is a probability of a good man's carrying along with him the fruit of his virtuous improvement of his rational and moral powers. These are his most valuable acquisitions, and if death doth not put a period to his existence we have no reason to think that it will put a period to them. The vicious man has the same probability of feeling the consequences of his bad habits. But, has the Epicurean any probability of finding those objects to gratify his sensual pleasures? Has the votary of ambition any probability to hope that his power will go along with him, or that then he may raise himself to influence and gratify his lust of dominion? Or has the covetous man reason to think that he will carry his idol along with him or that he will draw bills of exchange of this world?

¶ So it appears, then, on the supposition of a future /5.27 state, even without a supreme and intelligent ruler, that every probability promises happiness to the good and misery to the wicked. We see that it is so in the course of things here, and we can only judge of the future by the past. Were we to reason farther on this subject, it would not be difficult to show that whether we suppose the future world to be a social or solitary state, and if social, whether mixed of the good and the bad, or if we suppose the good and the bad separated, that in all of these cases, still the chance is on the side of the good. We have no reason, then, but to think that virtue and vice will always retain their nature and produce their consequences. Let a man habituated to sloth and rapacity and injustice change his climate or his country, let him live in regions of savage rudeness or in more polished society, let him leave even the converse of men and try the life of a hermit; still will he find the bad effects of his habits follow him to the court or the camp, the city or the desert. From the torrid to the frozen zone, he will find his habits noxious, and sooner indeed may the Ethiopian change his skin than a man by altering his condition change his habits.

What reason then has he to suppose that a passage to futurity shall wash away all his stains?

Thus have I showed that, even supposing there was no God, yet that this affords no argument /5.28 against a future state, or why our conduct here should not affect our condition hereafter. I come to consider the

3) Conclusion; whether men would be happier in the present life if the belief of a God or a future state were removed than under the impressions of a wise and righteous maker and governor of the world. I think it unfair here to compare, as Mr Bayle has done, the consequences of atheism with those of the lowest kinds of superstition; as I plead not the case of superstition but of religion.[9] Suppose it true, however, as perhaps it may be, that these may create some notions even more pernicious than what will follow from atheism, yet this is not to the purpose. The abuse of the best things are always the worst. Men by abusing their reason depress themselves below the level of brutes. The abuse of meat and drink is attended with hurtful consequences, so is it with religion. I would compare the state of men in a world conducted by inexorable fate with the condition of men living in a world governed by a righteous being, living under impressions of the righteous administration of all things. And I apprehend I need not say much to show that the former is more uncomfortable than the /5.29 latter. The case of the world without a wise governor is like a ship without a pilot, or a compass, or any hand on board who knows anything about ships or sailing. The winds and tides and currents drive her hither and thither, and she can pursue no determinate or regulated voyage. So on the system of the atheist, necessity or fate or chance drive on everything in the like blind way without either intelligence or design. Now would we not justly consider the man as distracted who would choose to make a voyage in the former rather than under the command of an experienced master, and is not he equally mad who can suppose that it would be better for

---

[9] Pierre Bayle (1647–1706) defended the position that atheism had no deleterious effects on society. See Haakonssen's commentary in *Practical Ethics*, 298 n. 11.

men that all events were directed by chance than by an all wise governor? Religion teaches us to consider the supreme being as the kind father of the universe, who knows our frame and pities us as a father doth his children.[10] It is as bad, then, to wish to be from under his indulgent care, as if children should wish to be orphans. But any rational man is so far from this wish that he considers the existence of deity as necessary to his well-being as the Sun to the planetary system. He rejoices in a belief which is the life of his soul and the spring of all his joys. Men may be divided into two classes, /5.30 the *thinking* and the *unthinking*. Let us consider what influence the belief of atheism could have on each of these.

As to the thinking part of mankind, if they are seduced into a belief of atheism, it would tend only to plunge them into distress, anxiety, and despair. He would see himself liable to many evils which he could neither prevent nor remedy. He would see himself compassed with infirmities[11] which he could not remove, obnoxious to many dangers he could not provide against. Thus would misery present itself to him on every side and, after all, often would some secret impressions of a supreme being, who would yet call him to account, come across his mind and enhance all his griefs. I do not deny that, when in high spirits and hurried away by the pleasing gales of prosperity, he may banish remorse and all foreboding of futurity, but yet in his more serious moments, when brought down by calamities to which all are liable, and especially when he has a near prospect of his dissolution, then are his thoughts let loose upon him, and he is plunged into despair. If he could still retain his atheistical principles, how would he rejoice in the thoughts of annihilation. /5.31 But now he cannot enjoy even the comfort of this assurance.

As to the unthinking, again, the only effect it can have upon such is to take away all restraint, to render them bolder in vice and callous to every manly feeling. All wise legislators, therefore, have thought it proper to call in the idea of

---

[10] See Psalm 103:14.
[11] See Hebrews 5:2.

future justice as an adminicle[12] to civil government. There is no example of any government where care has not been taken of the religion of the subjects. All governments have thought it necessary, where any important affair depends on the testimony of witnesses, that the religion of an oath should interpose as a proof of the truth of the declaration. All princes and states too always confirm their treaties and contracts by the most solemn oaths. Such a general conviction of the necessity of religion to aid the civil government has led some to say that it was entirely a device of the legislator, and contrived by him merely the better to confirm his own authority and procure a ready obedience to his laws.[13] This way of proceeding is at least a tacit confession of its utility.

Having said these things of the consequences that may be drawn from atheism, and having /5.32 showed 1) that though there was no supreme being yet it does not follow that there is no future state, or 2) that our happiness or misery in a future state does not depend on our conduct here, and 3) that even in the present life the belief of atheism has a worse effect upon our happiness than a persuasion that all things are governed by a wise and righteous governor; I proceed now to offer some arguments for the existence of the deity. Many of these have been given by different authors. I shall give only those of most consequence, as I apprehend it is better to offer a few of most force than to trouble you with a great number.

1) Some authors have justly argued the necessity of a first cause from this, *that everything beginning to exist must have a cause*.[14] This principle I endeavoured to show you before was a first principle; a principle to which all who are come to years of understanding assent, and without which we could not act with common prudence for a single hour in life; a

---

[12] A document attesting to the existence or contents of a missing document.

[13] Reid undoubtedly has several targets in mind here, including Pierre Bayle, David Hume (1711-1776), and Bernard Mandeville (1670-1733). Again, see Haakonssen in *Practical Ethics*, 298.

[14] Reid lists this maxim among his first principles of necessary truth. See *Intellectual Powers*, 497.

principle which was held as undisputed till Mr Hume dared to doubt it. I had formerly occasion to consider his arguments and shall not now resume what was then said.[15] It is taken for granted, therefore, that {it} is either necessarily eternal without a cause to produce it, or if it begins to /5.33 exist, there must be a cause of that existence; some being able to produce it, and with regard to this being, it too must either be eternal, or if not then it must have a cause to produce it, some other being with power able to produce it. Thus we are necessarily led to a first cause of all or to an infinite succession of beings, one producing another without a cause. The last of these is evidently absurd; for an infinity of beings without a first cause cannot possibly be, because it would be a chain, every link of which would be an effect which stood in need of a cause, and what is true of a part is equally true of the whole. Thus are we unavoidably led to admit the existence of some external being, uncaused, necessarily existing, and by his power producing everything we see.

Lecture 74th

It is demonstrable, then, that if anything at all exists now, something must have existed from all eternity without a cause. For if we suppose there were two beings, let us call the one A and the other B, then if A created B, surely A could not be created by its own creature, and of consequence A must be without any cause to produce it. And the reasoning is the same /5.34 if to these we add a third being, or if we add three thousand or three thousand millions; still the same conclusion will hold. For there is no principle more evident than this, that two things cannot mutually be the cause of each other.

Further, the same reasoning leads us to consider that which was uncaused, eternal, and the cause of all other things, as possessed of life, power, and intelligence. It is impossible that that which in itself hath neither life nor

---

[15] Reid is referring to his previous lectures on Pneumatology, in which he considers the subject of first principles. For Hume's arguments see *Treatise* I.iii.14. For Reid's published responses to Hume, see *Intellectual Powers*, 497–503.

power nor intelligence should yet bestow them upon other beings. The same light of reason that convinces us that there can be no existence without a cause, convinces us that every cause is not able to produce every effect. It is as shocking to common sense to say that mere inanimate, senseless matter could confer sense and reason upon intelligent rational creatures as to say that things may begin to exist without a cause of that existence. I know only two ways which atheists have taken to elude the force of this argument. The first is, by maintaining that the world as it now is existed from all eternity without any cause to produce it, or second, by saying that there has been an eternal succession of effects and causes without any first causes. /5.35

With regard to the first, it has commonly been said that it was maintained by Aristotle. However, there are some doubts concerning this and his interpreters have followed different opinions.[16] But we see that even those ancients who reasoned best on the atheistic system gave up this point. Epicurus and Democritus,[17] though they would not admit that the world was made by power and intelligence, yet they acknowledged that it was not eternal.[18] And we find Lucretius arguing strenuously against its eternity. Why, says he, if the world is eternal, why have we no monuments of anything farther back than a few thousand years? Can we suppose that everything beyond that short period, short indeed when compared to eternity, could have perished without leaving any vestige behind?[19]

Though it is common to all nations to carry back their history to fabulous ages, through a pride of being reckoned the most ancient, yet it is certain that we have no records that can pretend to any evidence that reach farther back than the sacred Scriptures. The Chinese monuments, the best attested beyond comparison of all others carry back their account of

---

[16] See Aristotle, *Metaphysics*, XII.6-7.
[17] Democritus (c. 460-c. 370 BC).
[18] See Diogenes Laertius, *Lives of Eminent Philosophers*, IX.vii.44 and X.45.
[19] See Lucretius, *De Rerum Natura* [*On the Nature of Things*], V.324-30.

the settling of their nation by Fohi[20] till near the time of the deluge only. What goes beyond that is mere uncertainty, /5.36 without any evidence that can satisfy a reasonable man. Besides, it is evident in the things that we see, that they are finite, dependent, and changeable; one generation passeth away and another cometh.[21] These things are sufficient to show that the world is not eternal unless we suppose an eternal succession of effects and causes without a first cause which was the:

Second subterfuge of the atheists I mentioned. But this evidently appears to be a great absurdity. The absurdity of it hath been illustrated by several authors in different ways. Thus, we may suppose a chain hanging down from heaven, composed of many links, the first of which we see but lose sight of the last. Now were the question put, how is this chain supported? Would any man say that the first was supported by the second, the second by the third, and so on without end, and yet that the whole was supported by nothing? Is not this absurd? It is as absurd, then, to suppose one thing produced by another and that by another and so on, because they all taken together make one great dependent whole, and yet there is nothing left to create it. Another way of illustrating it is by supposing a file of blind men pass along, the last of whom had his hand on the shoulder of the one next {to} him, and his /5.37 again upon the third, and so on till we lost sight of them. Now were it asked, who leads them? All that we see are blind, yet they keep the road distinctly and go on in a determinate path. We would conclude from this that some person who sees leads the whole. But if anyone will say that every one leads another without the aid or direction on any seeing person, would we not see that the position was ridiculous and absurd? As well might we suppose that blindness multiplied a thousand times would make sight, that dependence multiplied would make

---

[20] Fohi (Fu Xi) is the mythical first king of China. References to a great flood in the time of Fu Xi led some seventeenth-century British theologians and naturalists to speculate that he and Noah were the same person. See, e.g., William Whiston, *A New Theory of the Earth*.

[21] Ecclesiastes 1:4a. Ironically, the second half of the verse—'But the earth abides forever'—cuts against the lecture's next sentence.

independence, or a cypher a real number. This argument, then, from the present existence of things to an eternal cause of all existence, seems to be grounded on the plainest principles of reasoning, and there is no exception made to it which can bear examination.

The other topic from which {we} proposed to argue the existence of a first cause or of a deity was from the appearance of wisdom and design which we see in the creation and in the structure of the universe, to infer that they were at first produced and still are governed by a wise and intelligent cause. This is the argument which of all others makes the deepest impression on thinking men, and indeed it has the peculiar advantage that the more we learn by philosophical /5.38 investigation, it thereby gathers strength, and every new discovery discovers new evidences of the most excellent contrivance in the constitution of things. When we are ignorant, we may often imagine that we perceive faults in the construction and management of things, but this is the effect only of our ignorance. When we attend to them more narrowly and perceive their uses more clearly, what were thought to be faults appear to be excellences. Some have conceived that the world would be more beautiful if there were no mountains, if all were verdant fields and flowery meads, and if there were no rivers or seas, but this is ridiculous.[22] Without mountains there could be no springs, without seas there could be no communication with distant countries or kingdoms, and we in consequence would always remain savages. And the same is the case with respect to all others; what we think faults in the constitution of the world is plainly an evidence of our own ignorance. As, therefore, the more we know the more we discover marks of wise contrivance in the formation of the universe, this shows the importance of improvement in the knowledge of nature, as we thereby bring more clearly to light the great author /5.39 of all. This is an argument which leads us to a very wide field, because every object we can contemplate exhibits to us marks of wisdom, and, as it generally makes a deep impression on men's minds, I shall dwell upon {it} a little. I

---

[22] See Lucretius, *De Rerum Natura* [*On the Nature of Things*], V.197–210.

shall, however, mention only some of the most obvious
{examples}, and shall begin with those that are most distant
from us.

The most distant objects which fall under our view are
the fixed stars. Their distance is such that our imagination
can hardly grasp it, yet we find that they are not only orna-
mental but useful to us who inhabit the globe of this Earth.
That we may form some conception of these bodies which
we call *fixed stars*, it is proper to take notice of some
principles of astronomy. In reality, philosophers have never
yet accurately determined the distance of the fixed stars; all
that they have done is to determine that it is not below such a
distance, but how much more they do not know. The way in
which they determine it is this; they can determine the
distance of the Sun, and, by comparing the distance of the
Sun with that of the fixed stars, they can thus form a kind of
conjecture how far distant they are. And till of late even the
distance of the Sun was /5.40 not determined accurately,
when by observing two transits of Venus, the one of which
was in {17}61 and the other in {17}69, they determined with
certainty that the parallax of the Sun—i.e., the appearance of
the Earth's semidiameter at the Sun—was not above 8½" nor
below 7½". This was made sufficiently accurate by innumerable observations of those two transits. From this, by calcula-
tion on geometrical principles, it was ascertained that it must
be 96 or 100,000[23] of miles, an amazing distance which
imagination is unable to grasp! But there is another means of
proving this by the velocity of the rays of light, which pass to
all objects on this Earth in a time imperceptible to us, yet, as

---

[23] Whether one takes the final '0' in this number as a slip of the pen or
not, Baird inaccurately records the distance here. The actual
distance, depending on the Earth's position in its elliptical orbit, is
between ninety-one and ninety-four million miles. Measurements in
Reid's time were roughly accurate, and in the Anonymous Edinburgh notes, the Anonymous Aberdeen notes, and the notes by
Robert Jack, the distance is recorded as 96 to 100 million miles. For
more on Reid's own attempt to calculate the Sun's distance during
the 1769 transit, see Wood's unpublished 1984 dissertation, 'Thomas
Reid, Natural Philosopher, A Study of Scottish Science and Philosophy in the Scottish Enlightenment', 93–4, and Reid's 'Wise Club'
lecture notes in AUL MS 2131/2/I/7.

all motion must {be} progressive, it must take up some time, and it has been proved to take between seven and eight minutes in its passage from the Sun to the Earth. But though the Sun is placed at such a vast distance, yet are the fixed stars inconceivably farther. Such is their distance that, viewed from them, the semidiameter of the Earth's orbit will seem only a point of a few degrees, so that they are distant from us millions of millions of miles. Nor are we able to conclude that they are all at one and the same distance, or what is their respective distances, for though they all appear to us placed in the surface of the same /5.41 concave sphere, yet this is owing to their being placed beyond the limits of distant vision, as we are not able to determine distances beyond a certain extent. It has been judged probable that those that appear least are only the more distant and not less, and that those of the brightest appearance and greatest apparent magnitude have this only from being nearer to us; that they may be placed at various distances though the immense void and are particular suns illuminating other planetary worlds. But those which have the largest appearance and the most luminous are still millions of millions of miles distant from us. How unbounded the dominion of the universal king who made and governs them all! But how amazed are we to find that these bodies placed at such a prodigious distance are yet useful to us; they are made perceivable to us by the little organ of the eye by means of the rays of light which move with such velocity and are so minute that several of them fall within the pupil of our eye, and are there refracted so as to form an image of the fixed stars. This amazing velocity of light, whether considered in its motion or the minuteness of its particles, is no less wonderful than the immense distance of the bodies seen by means of it. But we may {also observe} /5.42 that the fixed stars are far from being useless. They afford us light to travel both by sea and land; by them the heavens are marked out as it were by fixed points; without them navigation never would have been learned; without them astronomy never would have made any considerable progress. Hence the use of the fixed stars to us does not appear to be casual. They were made not for the sole purpose of glimmering faintly in a serene sky upon this Earth, but they exhibit marks of wisdom and design intending them for the most beneficial purposes.

Lecture 75th

But in our own planetary system we perceive still clearer marks of wisdom and design. It is evident that the Sun being placed in the centre was intended to illuminate all the other planets that move around him, in different times indeed, but observing the most regular order. The ancient Pythagoreans talked much of the harmony of the spheres, but had they known what is known now of the harmonic motions of /5.43 the planets they would have had much better ground to talk on.[24] It appears that their motions are regulated according to the strictest mathematical rules, which produces a very great regularity, notwithstanding the law of gravity, by which they act one upon another, as well as are acted on by the Sun. We know not, for we have no means to know, whether the power of gravity by which the Sun retains all the planets in their orbits extends as far as the fixed stars; perhaps they are placed beyond the sphere of this power, or perhaps they are placed at such a great distance that the effects of it are so much diminished that they will not be considerable while the world lasts. But, though we be ignorant of its power over the fixed stars, yet we know that it extends to very great distances. It extends not only to the Earth but to Saturn, and not only to Saturn but likewise to all the comets belonging to this system: all of which, both planets and comets, perform their revolutions in certain periods and in regular orbits of an elliptical kind, according to certain rules which are common to all, which were discovered by the sagacious Kepler before the reason of them was known.[25] He discovered that they describe equal areas in equal times, and that their areas were proportioned to their periodic times, that they all moved /5.44 in ellipses of which the Sun was in one of the foci, and he conjectured too that the square of the periodic times was in the same proportion as the cubes of the distances. This has

---

[24] See Diogenes Laertius, *Lives of Eminent Philosophers*, VIII.29.
[25] Johannes Kepler (1571–1630) introduced the idea of elliptical planetary orbits in his 1690 *Astronomia Nova* [*New Astronomy*].

since been found true by observation, and it is wonderful how happy that philosopher was in guessing at properties of nature, but still the reason of all was unknown to him.

¶ The discovery of this was reserved for the great Newton. He observed that all bodies on this Earth gravitated to it. He observed that this power also not only reached to the tops of the highest mountains, but even to the clouds by which they were prevented from {escaping} entirely from the Earth. Now, says he, why may not gravitation reach to the Moon? If it does to the Moon, it may be that which retains her in her orbit. The general laws of motion had been discovered before his time. It had been discovered that all bodies remain in a state of motion or of rest till they are disturbed by some impelling force, that change of motion is proportioned to the force and to the direction of the force impressed, and also that there is a reaction contrary and equal to the impelling power. These laws had been discovered before but never applied to the power of gravitation, but Newton found that the same law extended not only to the surface of the Earth, but to /₅.₄₅ all the planets.[26] It is evident from fact that this power decreases as you remove farther from the Earth. This has been found by experiment, because the motion of a pendulum is slower on the top of high mountains than at the surface of the Earth. It appears that this power decreases in regular proportion as the distance of the bodies gravitating to one another increases, and that it decreases reciprocally as the square of the distances. It is a power which belongs to all the planets. They gravitate to the Sun and the Sun to them. The Moon gravitates to the Earth and the Earth to the Moon, as appears by the tides. The secondaries of Saturn and Jupiter also gravitate to their primaries. Thus was this beautiful system carried on by this simple law, and carried on according to the exactest laws before the reasons of them were known. For Newton has demonstrated that supposing this power to take place, then the consequence would be that this together with a projectile force will make them describe

---

[26] See Isaac Newton (1643–1727), *Philosophiae Naturalis Principia Mathematica* [*The Mathematical Principles of Natural Philosophy*], Books I–II.

elliptical curves, and that by this law they would describe equal areas in equal times, and that the squares of the periodic times would be in proportion to the cubes of the distances. Thus we see the whole system regulated by exact mathematical rules. We see these producing the most accurate and constant operations.

¶ Now can we seek stronger marks /5.46 of wisdom and design in the universe than this? If a man sees the structure of a watch and sees that the whole is moved by one great spring, if he sees how such wheels move such pinions which again move other wheels, and if he finds that all of these are regulated by the balance, would any man that saw this pretend to say that it was the effect of chance and produced without any skilful agent?[27] But what is this to the planetary system in which wisdom and design so clearly appear? The planets of our system seem to have attained their name from their *wandering* appearance in their conjunctions, oppositions, elongations, progressions, and retrogradations.[28] In all these cases they thought the bodies of our system wandered, while the fixed stars seemed to remain in one place, but now men see all these wanderings reduced to accurate rules, and now philosophers with the greatest ease can predict for hundreds of years their precise place and various motions.

¶ This was particularly done in the last transits of Venus over the Sun, when she appeared like a spot upon the Sun's disk. This had been predicted by Kepler /5.47 long before, but the tables at that time were so inaccurate that even Kepler himself began to doubt that it would not happen. Yet an Englishman, who had attended to the subject much, was satisfied that it would happen and had the happiness to see it. Jeremy Horrocks, an Englishman, in 1639 was the first of

---

[27] A similar argument was later made (in)famous by William Paley's 1802 work, *Natural Theology, or Evidences of the Existence and Attributes of the Deity collected from the Appearances of Nature*. However, as Reid's use here evidences, the comparison of nature to a complex mechanical device in design arguments was widespread long before.

[28] Reid is referring to the etymology of the word 'planet', from the Greek *'plantan'* or 'wanderer'.

Adam's race who ever discovered this phenomenon.[29] We are sure that it had not been observed before because telescopes were not in use, and without them it can't be seen. However, his observations upon it were so accurate that this transit can now be foretold and has been seen since. I mention this only to show by how exact rules all the planets are regulated. If they were not, it would be impossible to predict their appearances, but their appearances are found in fact and by experience to be regulated by unvarying rules. Now chance acts by no rules; nothing regular is produced by chance. The learned Archbishop Tillotson hath well observed, as, by throwing carelessly in a heap an infinite number of types it is not to be expected that a fine polished poem would be made, or even a tolerably sensible discourse in prose, how much less can we suppose that this beautiful system of nature could be the work of blind chance, acting by no fixed rules?[30] Nor does this power of gravitation account /5.48 only for the comets and planets in general keeping their orbits round the Sun, but also for the irregularities in the Moon's motion, for which the ancient philosophers were obliged to invent so many cycles and epicycles, and which after all they could never truly explain. But by the gravitation of the Earth to the Moon {we} account for it easily and fully. We know not the number of comets belonging to our system, but we know that they are regulated by certain laws. These are so well known that some of their appearances have been foretold and have come according to that prediction; though it is difficult to determine it with accuracy till astronomy has been reiterated for a long series of years. One of them takes seventy-five years in its course, and it observes the time exactly.[31] Nothing, then, surely can afford stronger marks of wisdom and contrivance than our planetary system.

---

[29] Jeremiah Horrocks (1618–1641).
[30] John Tillotson (1630–1694). See *Works of Dr John Tillotson, Late Archbishop of Canterbury, Volume 8*, 'Sermon CXXXVII, The Wisdom of God in the Creation of the World'.
[31] Reid here refers to Halley's Comet, the periodicity of which was shown by Edmond Halley in his 1705 work, *Synopsis of the Astronomy of Comets*.

¶ And if we descend to the Earth we will perceive still stronger marks of design there. The figure of the Earth, as {is} best for various reasons, is nearly spherical, not altogether so; the parts at the equator are higher than at the poles, and the figure becomes what is called an *oblate spheroid*. It /5.49 commonly was thought to be an exact sphere, but were this the case then all the parts toward the equator would be overflowed with sea; the centrifugal force bringing {it} to the equator from the poles and leaving them dry.[32] The wisdom of nature appears here then in giving the Earth a figure corresponding to the nature of this power, by which we see that these parts have all their just proportion of sea and land, and so it is over all the globe. We find too an atmosphere surrounding the Earth, and which extends to forty or fifty miles height above the surface of the Earth.[33] This atmosphere was not made in vain. It is necessary both to animals and vegetables. Without breathing, animals could not exist, even those that do not appear to have lungs, yet all find air necessary; even fish could not live without air. And it appears equally necessary to vegetables as to animals, and being thus necessary to all, the wisdom of nature hath produced it in sufficient quantity to answer all these purposes. It invests us around like our garments, and we can go nowhere when we have it not. Some ancient atheists have argued that it was useless, but without it we could have no rain: the /5.50 vapour are carried up and supported by it till they fall down by the action of gravity; and without it we would have no rivers, no springs. Thus we see all the constitution of nature admirably fitted for the care of the various inhabitants of this globe.

¶ Some ancients also found fault, too, that there was so much sea. Why was it not all fruitful fields and thus supporting many more inhabitants?[34] But in this we see the folly of men when they begin to censure the works of God. We see it is necessary not only for furnishing supplies to rivers, but

---

[32] See entry for 'Earth' in the fourth edition of John Harris's *Lexicon Technicum* [*Technical Lexicon*].
[33] Ibid., see entry for 'Atmosphere'.
[34] See note 22.

also for navigation. The wisdom of nature intended us as social creatures, and our society was to be not only with those that are near, but the most distant parts of the world, and she therefore has furnished us with navigable rivers and with seas by which we may visit distinct regions and convey their improvements and productions to our own country. No man can trace the origin of navigation; where seas are there, nations have been found engaged in commerce.[35] And commerce is one of the greatest means of improvement among men. Hence, /5.51 as far back as we can trace ancient history, we find those the most improved who were soonest engaged in commerce. Thus, all who lived on the banks of navigable rivers or of seas were always first civilized, first improved in arts and sciences, whereas those who inhabit the heart or inland parts of a country are long rude. Thus, in the heart of Asia and Africa, there has been no improvement for thousands of years. On {the} other hand, we see that the Egyptians who lived on the banks of the Mediterranean, the Red Sea, and the Nile were early a commercial people and early flourished in the arts and sciences. So too the Arabians on the Red Sea. We see too the Chinese have many navigable rivers and are a polished people. Surely, then, it is not in vain that nature has given such a great proportion of water.

¶ Other ancient atheists have thought, too, that mountains were a useless deformity on the face of the globe; why such rugged rocks and horrible precipices, the dens often of wild beasts?[36] Would it not be better and more beautiful were it all a verdant plain? There too we see the weakness of man in pretending to censure the works of God. Were the Earth a plain then there could be no rivers, because /5.52 rivers run only where there is a descent. All springs fall upon the laps of hills, where moistening the Earth they descend till they come to some strata which they cannot penetrate, they run along them, and, bursting out, come down in copious streams. And without rivers to moisten it, how uncomfortable an habitation would the Earth make! Besides, it is evident that the mountains are fitted to maintain some

---

[35] See note 30.
[36] See note 22.

animals, and so too vegetables of certain kinds grow only on mountains. They contain also there metals which are so useful to man and various substances from which human industry has reaped great advantages. Some poets indeed have introduced metals, especially shining gold, as the cause of many evils to man.[37] However this may figure in poetry, there is no truth in it, no solidity in it. No doubt there have {been} many evils {which have} arisen from the use of it, but this is the abuse of the creation of God. They tend to promote our advantage, but the best things may be abused. And the placing {of} these minerals in mountains is a strong mark of design and wisdom, as they are thus prevented from encumbering the face of the Earth. In great houses there are / 5.53 always cellars to hold what is not immediately useful, so these may be called cellars in which to deposit the metals and minerals so useful to man. Now surely no man can call all this the effect of chance or say that there is not wisdom and contrivance in it.

¶ Thus there we see evident marks of design in the inanimate part of the creation; that part of the creation which is unorganized and hath neither animal nor vegetable life. But if we attend to the vegetable we find marks of wisdom still more striking. Vegetables differ from unorganized bodies in various respects. In vegetables there is some kind of organization to be seen, and all the parts of a plant have a certain relation to the whole which is not discoverable in the minerals and metals. Thus a stone may be broken or divided ever so much, but still each of these divisions is a stone. But with plants it is otherwise. They have a certain unity by destroying which you destroy the plant. We do not know in what vegetation consists. We know indeed that every plant is filled with tubes to carry up sap, and that by this means the tree gradually extends itself, but how this effect is produced surpasses the power of philosophy to explain. / 5.54

Lecture 76th

The structure and organization of vegetables is indeed wonderful. They bend their tender fibrous roots into the

---

[37] Lucretius, *De Rerum Natura* [*On the Nature of Things*], V.1113–1118.

Earth and creep along in quest of support, while the branches invariably ascend to the light and flourish in the open air. Besides, it has been discovered by some late botanists that many of the plants have what is called *a sleep*, that is, at certain times they shut themselves in, as it were, to rest, and at others they open their leaves wide to receive the influences of the Sun and the dew. They are capable of an irritation by heat and moisture, it appears by which they acquire life, whereas they were dead in the seeds. These seeds, it is found, can be without life for a very long time, sometimes for years and even for centuries, yet when they meet with a proper degree of moisture and heat, their powers disclose and they burst forth in all their parts. We know not what produces this organization which distinguishes them from inanimate matter and bodies where the life is gone, far less do we know how they grow and how they propagate their kind. But we see /5.55 that they are admirably fitted for all these ends and that they are carried on by regular laws. The variety of them is great, but we evidently see the intention of nature in giving that variety corresponding to the variety of climate, soil, heat, and moisture. Some we see affect the mountains, some the valleys, some one season and some another, one hot, another cold, and by this means is the face of the Earth always covered with verdure, and no soil is to be found without it. Even the rugged rocks produce a great variety of beautiful and useful mosses. It appears to have been the intention of nature in this variety to satisfy the uses and accommodation of men and the inferior animals.

¶ There is no science which has been cultivated with more assiduity in modern times than botany, yet the botanist has not been able to ascertain exactly the number of the various genera of plants, though to all probability they have been fixed from the beginning of the world.[38] We find that this

---

[38] Although the French botanist Georges-Louis Leclerc, Comte de Buffon hypothesized the phenomenon of species extinction in his *Histoire Naturelle* [*Natural History*], published between 1749 and 1804, its occurrence was not well accepted until Georges Cuvier published his work on fossilized remains in 1796. For more on Reid's providential naturalism with regard to speciation and biological

branch of knowledge was attended to by the ancients and was carried to considerable degrees of improvement by the labours of {?}³⁹, though in the days of Hippocrates⁴⁰ it was in a low state. But as their descriptions are so inaccurate as hardly to be understood, we are often at a loss to know the plants by the description they have given of it. /$_{5.56}$ Indeed, the only descriptions that can last and be understood by posterity are those that are founded on some systematic and accurate division and arrangement of the whole genera and species, a plan which they never adopted. This, however, has been adopted in modern times, and the descriptions now given are such as must be understood in all future ages. Future ages will thus too be able to decide with more certainty whether the same genera and species have always continued or if any have been lost. But as far as we can learn, it cannot be shown that any one of them hath perished or that any new one has been produced. All of them seem to have been endowed with particular qualities by the great creator, of producing each after his kind, but none have a power of producing new kinds. It is supposed that in all there may be about twelve or thirteen thousand genera of plants added to our former stock on this subject by the late discoveries in the South Sea.⁴¹ All these have distinct characters, by which they may be distinguished from any other and may be described so as to be known by this description.

¶ Now surely all this cannot be the /$_{5.57}$ effect of chance. They all observe established rules by which it appears that

---

taxonomy, and particularly his response to Buffon, see Wood's comments in 'Introduction', *Animate Creation*, 4–12.

[39] There is no evidence in the other lectures or student notes indicating which name fills the blank. Given what Baird records in 5.62, however, Aristotle seems likely.

[40] Hippocrates of Kos (c. 460–c. 370 BC).

[41] Reid is likely referring to the botanical discoveries made by Joseph Banks during the 1768–71 voyage of James Cook. Cook was originally commissioned by the Royal Society to observe the 1769 transit of Venus from the Southern hemisphere and map the coastline of Australia.

an all-wise cause first formed and still carries them on in their operations. We see some of them fitted for food to man and the other animals, others for medicine, others for clothing. There is no use of human life {that} can be thought of for which some of them are not properly fitted. And even those plants which are poison to some are wholesome food to others. Further—as they are the common aliment of all, both men and brutes, for all either live on vegetables or on some animals that are supported by vegetables, it was proper that there should be such a quantity as is sufficient to support the life of all the inhabitants of the Earth, and this accordingly nature has done. Some of them require no care of ours in order to rear them, others again require culture to bring them to perfection, and it evidently appears to have been an employment intended by nature for man, that he should cultivate the various plants of the Earth, discover their qualities, and thus fit them for his use. The first appearance of this culture was the Garden of Eden, and it still continues {as} an important employment to supply us with the necessary supports of human life.[42] /5.58

Further, they are all fitted with powers to propagate their kind that none may perish. In the manner of producing the seed and of disseminating it, we find a great variety. In some the seed is strongly guarded by an oily coat which defends it {from} external injuries and admits moisture that is sufficient for its growth, but no more. Some of them are wafted through the air by down, others are thrown at a distance by the elastic spring of the seed, some are carried away {by} birds, and so on. Some of them we see are of a large, some of a small size. How uncomfortable would life be without trees sufficient for houses, ships, and various utensils that render life agreeable? As far back too as we can trace the history of man, they appear to have used some kind of vegetable for clothing, as flax, hemp, etc. It may here be observed that there is in vegetables an unaccountable disposition, that when the seed is planted in the Earth, whatever is its position, still the roots push downwards and the {stems}[43]

---

[42] See Genesis 2:15.
[43] Baird wrote 'roots' again.

upward, but by what attraction or repulsion this is produced we cannot learn. We see that in the seed there are two opposite ends from which the stem and the roots issue out, and yet though the stem is placed downwards, yet it will turn round and pushes upward. On the other hand, though the roots be up, yet will they bend downward and search into the earth.

¶ Nay, /5.59 we may observe that if a root is planted amidst earths of different kinds, its fibres spread around, avoiding the bad and seeking the best. Now we have no reason to ascribe to vegetables either sensation or thought, in this they are guided by that power implanted in them that is necessary to propagate their kind and provide against the species being lost. Neither are we able to explain the manner in which they draw their nourishment from the Earth, every one drawing that which is proper to itself. For this purpose they have a wonderfully curious structure. Their roots are divided into very small fibres which receive the sap from the ground, which is conveyed in sap vessels and is afterwards curiously altered and assimilated to the nature of the plant by vessels of various kinds. This has been fully and accurately observed in modern times by Malpighi and Dr Grew.[44] These two gentlemen formed the design of examining the structure of vegetables about the same {time}. Being both members of the Royal Society, they transmitted their discoveries to them by whom they were published, and though they carried on their researches separately, yet their descriptions so remarkably agree as to add the greater authority to both. The engravings of these two philosophers show that the works of nature are continued at once in a beautiful and useful manner. It may be observed that particular parts manifest /5.60 an intention with regard to the whole. Now every intention supposes design and intelligence. Everyone sees that the roots are designed to furnish the plant with nourishment and to fix it firmly in the ground. The leaves also, in time of a drought, draw in moisture from the air. No man can doubt that the bark was intended for a covering to the tree, and it serves admirably for this purpose, and the inmost bark is the part

---

[44] Marcello Malpighi (1628–1694) and Nehemiah Grew (1641–1712).

from which the growth arises, it being a film of the inmost bark that swells from year to year and makes an addition to the body of the tree. We see some of the seeds enclosed in a shell so hard that we can {only} penetrate it with difficulty. We would be apt to think, then, that it must rot in that shell, but nature has provided against this, for always opposite to that point from which the root issues it is so soft that the root itself is able to force a passage through it. Thus we see that nature has provided against every difficulty, for that shell which to us seemed hardly penetrable is easily perforated by the slender fibre of a seed.

¶ Some plants, too, we see are not able to support themselves. They must be supported by other things. Thus they cling to trees and walls, whatever can bear them. Of this kind are ivy, vines, and hops. For this peculiarity nature has provided in their structure; some of them are furnished with a kind /$_{5.61}$ {of} claspers which creep round the body that supports them; such are the hops and the vine. Others again exude from themselves a sort of dung which glues them to the body that bears them, as the ivy sticks to the rocks, and thus adheres so firmly as to resist all the violence of the winds. It would be endless to mention all the marks of wisdom and design which appear in the vegetable creation. What I have said may suffice to show that they cannot be attributed to chance.

¶ I shall now consider a little the marks of wisdom to be seen in the animal creation. Here I shall divide what I have to say into three parts: the marks of wisdom and design 1) in the structure of the lower animals, 2) in the structure of the human body, {and} 3) in the human mind.

In animals the qualities of both inanimate matter and vegetables join, but they have something of a superior nature to vegetation still. All of them have some perception of external objects, and some of them too have a degree of memory or something very like it. Thus a horse will know the way home again and will keep {to it}, even though it is so dark as that the rider himself should not know it. They appear too to have some trains of thought, though we cannot discover their laws. We see among animals a great variety in different cases, each keeping the way presented to it by nature. Some are viviparous and suckle their young. Some again are oviparous and hatch their young by incubation. Yet all agree in breeding them carefully after they are produced. /5.62 By this, nature takes care that, while the individuals are always perishing, yet that the species should not entirely perish. Accordingly, in all the variety we know—of quadrupeds, of birds, of fishes, insects, and reptiles—it cannot be shown that any one kind has perished altogether.[45] This, however, will be more certain in future ages because, by the industry of the moderns, they have been more accurately reduced to genera and have been most distinctly described by those who have applied to this branch of knowledge.

¶ It were to be wished that natural historians were more careful in describing their various instincts. They have been laborious in describing their structure, but surely the instincts by which they live and by which they are preserved and regulated are no less worthy of observation. These have been more or less observed in every age. Aristotle has treated this subject.[46] He made his collections and observations with candour and judgement, being furnished with expenses by his pupil Alexander. His descriptions are faithful where he himself made the observations, and where he did not he delivers it only as a hearsay or report. The descriptions he has given of what he saw are just and answer exactly at this day. So true is it that, though man may in several respects {be} said to be not the same as in his days, yet in brutes there is no difference. They are the same now as in the days of /5.63 Julius Caesar. They are not able to communicate their knowledge, and for this cause never can arrive at higher degrees of perfection, but by instincts they are fitted to preserve themselves and to continue the species. And, though some species are made the prey of others, yet we do not see that they ever perish, nature having made them more prolific in proportion to the devastation made upon them. There is no evidence that the brutes possess some of those powers which distinguish human creatures {such} as abstraction, moral perception, {and} reasoning, nor do they appear to have any power of self-government; they seem to be always directed

---

[45] See note 38.
[46] See e.g. *History of Animals*.

by what gives the strongest present impulse, nor do they appear to pursue any rules of action to the attainment of any end. It is true we see a kind of government among black cattle, but they appear to be governed by instinct rather than by fixed laws. And how prodigious so ever the variety of animals may be, yet have they always continued from age to age perfectly regular in their way of life, every species its own way. We may here take notice only of the way in which birds build their nests. How great a variety is there in their way of building, yet do all those of a species build in one way. They all build in a place which appears free from danger or disturbance, where they may quietly bring forth and safely rear their young. In this last, both the parents commonly join, but in some cases, where the care of one of them is sufficient, the other leaves off attending to them. And even there are some cases where the young need no aid, and there the parents leave them to shift for themselves. Thus the caterpillar. /5.64

¶ From all this we see what an infinite number of instincts belong to the brute creation and all precisely suited to their manner of life with great skill, and of this we can have no solution but in concluding that they were so ordered by the wisdom of him who ruleth over all nature.[47] If again we consider their bodies, we will find a vast variety, but at the same time the structure of each admirably suited to their way of life. Thus we see that some animals, such as quadrupeds, who can easily turn their head, have their eyes placed in the side of the head, but others, {such as insects,} who have not this power of turning their head, have eyes all round and behind as well as before. Some flies and bees too have two crusts like hemispheres on the sides of their head, in each of which are inserted a great number of eyes, in each of which there is a distinct picture formed, each of which have a distinct optic nerve, and thus they see in every direction. In spiders, some have four eyes and some have six. In the mole, they are all covered with hair so as to be safe in pushing through the earth and are so small as to be hardly discernible, yet are sufficient to warn them when they are

---

[47] See Psalm 103:19.

above ground. And in those animals that have occasion to push among trees and brushwood, the eye is defended with what is called a *membrana nictitans*.

¶ In the other senses too there is the same beautiful variety and wise contrivance. One being endowed, where their situations require it, with a wonderful acuteness of sight, another of taste, and so on, by which they may distinguish wholesome from poisonous food. For this reason, depending on *their* taste, when people are shipwrecked in warm climates and /$_{5.65}$ come to woods where varieties of fruit present themselves, they think they may safely eat those in which they see marks of the birds beginning to feed upon, but those that are untouched they suspect as noxious. It is evident that some of the animals are intended for the use of others—to serve them as prey—but still some were intended for the use of man. The ox was intended to assist him in his laborious employments, the horse, the dog, and the elephant were all designed for the service of man, and they have generally such instincts as fit them for this purpose. The dog especially seems intended to be his companion. If we can trust to Colben, a traveller, there are great numbers of dogs that run wild in troops without a master, and, though they prey on every kind of beast, yet they never prey upon man. Nay, so great is their reverence for them that they will allow him to carry off what prey they have caught without hurting him.[48]

Lecture 77th

But it would be impossible to enumerate every mark of wisdom to be met with in the animal creation, for every part shows it. These I have mentioned seem to be regulated by fixed laws. They manifest certain ends to which they are proportioned means, and must satisfy every candid mind that he who made them is divine, and that chance never could produce them. I shall now consider the marks of wisdom to be met with in the body of man.

---

[48] Peter Kolbe was a Dutch explorer whose 1719 work, *Caput Bonae Spei Hodiernum* [*Today's Cape of Good Hope*], gave an exaggerated account of the fauna found near the Cape of Good Hope.

It is impossible not to see /5.66 that man was intended to take care of his own preservation by food and drink and by alternate labour and repose, and we see that his constitution is fitted for this purpose. As it is necessary that his body should be supplied with food, this is taken into the mouth, which we find adapted to this end, to prepare it for digestion in the stomach. The mouth is furnished with the tongue, teeth, and glands, all of them admirably contrived for their several ends. The teeth {are given} in order to grind and comminute it, while mixing with a fluid secreted by the glands, {until} it is fitted to pass through the gullet without {injuring}[49] it. We see likewise that these teeth are not perfectly formed in infants. This would be inconvenient for the mothers in suckling them. They are only a pellucid mucilage in that socket or cavity in the jawbone, which afterwards receives them and holds them so firmly. By degrees they grow into a greater consistency, as {a} small opaque speck appears in the middle, and they gradually harden and push up till they penetrate the gum. It may be remarked that all our other bones are covered with a covering called the *periosteum*, which is necessary to nourish them, but the teeth have it not. For though they had it, it would soon be worn down and destroyed and so be of no use. They appear of different forms and are designed for different purposes, some to cut and others to ground the food we eat. Hence they are divided into two kinds by the /5.67 anatomists. The *incisors* and *molars*, each of which we see are fitted for the ends intended. And that man surely must either be stupidly blind or obstinately perverse who does not see that all the structure of the mouth is[50] the most proper of any that could be thought of, to receive our food and {for} preparing it for being digested.

¶ The preparations too made for swallowing our food are admirable. Were we left to do this by our own art we would of necessity starve, but we see it done without any care of ours. The stomach also is evidently intended for digesting our food, being by its structure fitted for the purpose, and

---

[49] Baird wrote 'entering'.
[50] Baird wrote 'mouth is not'.

having certain glands in order to assist it. We know likewise that the bile is thrown and mixes with the contents of the stomach and guts so as to help the digestion. There are innumerable small vessels which are called *lacteali*, fitted to receive what enters into them while the rest is carried down and goes off. What is separated by these vessels is carried by other vessels and mixes with the blood in the left subclavian vein where, by means unknown to us, it is assimilated with the blood and makes that fluid which is so necessary to our existence. The system of the veins and arteries have also a most wonderful construction. The blood, being collected together by the veins and brought to the right auricle of the heart, is from thence conveyed by the pulmonary vein to the lungs—through which many branches of that vein are spread—where, mixing with air, it is fitted for our support. From thence it returns to the left auricle of the heart, and from thence is thrown into a great artery. /5.68

The muscles of the heart have a strength proportional to the work they are to bear. They contract and dilate alternately with great force without any intention on our part. But, as we know from the principles of philosophy that the blood acts equally in all directions, we would be apt to think that it would return back, but nature is never deficient in any of her operations. She has guarded against this by valves which afford an easy passage out to the blood but hinder it effectively from returning, so that it is still protruded forward, and, the arteries being constructed with valves of a similar kind, it is thus carried to the utmost extremities of the body. This circulation of the blood was unknown to the ancients. We owe the discovery to the famous Dr Harvey, physician to Charles I.[51] It is now universally adopted and is sufficiently evident in man and also the other animals that seem to have blood. In all, we observe a fluid which, though not red, yet supplies the place of it. The construction of the vessels through which this fluid circulates is exquisite and wisely contrived. No hydraulic or hydrostatic machine could better serve their purposes. And as we are ready to admire

---

[51] William Harvey (1578–1657) described of the circulation of blood in *De Motu Cordis* [*On the Motion of the Heart*].

any contrivance for conveying water from one place to another and the like, so ought we to admire the invention of nature in adapting the vessels of the heart, the arteries, etc. to the circulation of the blood. /5.69 But from this common mass of blood there are other fluids to be secreted by the glands, the whole mystery of which we are unable to discern. As there is a system of veins and arteries for circulating the blood which divide into smaller and smaller branches till they reach the farthest extremities of the body, so nature, in case they should be hurt by bruises or even destroyed by amputation perhaps, has provided against these contingencies by making communications in many places between the arteries and the veins and between the arteries themselves. These communications, if an amputation {occurs}, are at first small, but they widen by degrees and the circulation goes on freely as before.

¶ Another mark of wisdom in the structure of the body is the system of veins and nerves. These we know are the instruments both of sensation and of muscular motion, though we know not how they perform their offices. The brain, from which many of them issue, is admirably guarded by the bones of the head, which enclose it and defend it from external injury. These are at a small distance from each other in infants and are capable of a small degree of compression, but by degrees become so indented in one another and become so firm as to form a firm covering to the brain. This is also guarded by two coats called the *dura mater* and the *pia mater*, and from these two coats proceed films which go along with all the nerves that proceed from the brain. But, besides the brain, /5.70 there are nerves which proceed also from the *spinal marrow*. These too are guarded by the backbone from injuries, but as the back is often obliged to be bent, it is formed that it may yield without hurting the *marrow*. From these two, the brain and spinal marrow, do all the nerves proceed in pairs. It is commonly thought there are about thirty-nine or forty pairs of them, for in some particular person there may {be} a small difference, yet in general they are similar, so that the descriptions given in anatomical books are commonly found to answer. The nerves extend to all parts of the body, so that a pin point cannot be set down without touching some of them, and they are so distributed because they are the instruments of sensation, so that if a nerve is cut it has no more feeling than if it were not a part of the body. They are therefore divided into smaller and smaller branches till they become imperceptible to the sight. How they perform their office, anatomists and physiologists never have been able to discover. They do not appear to have any fluid in them like the veins. They are, rather, solid, though of a soft and medullary substance. But though we know /5.71 not the manner how they perform their office, yet by the effects we see that they are fitted for it. From the nerves, the power is conveyed to the muscles by which they contract and dilate and so produce all the motions of the body.

¶ The muscles are of a fleshy substance, being more so in the middle, and a kind of tendons round it, by which they are drawn together and perform their motions. The famous Borelli, an Italian philosopher, calculated the strength necessary in our muscular exertions.[52] Their strength indeed must be prodigiously great because, by a law of mechanics, the nearer a force is to the fulcrum or centre of motion, the greater must it be, and for the conveniency of the body, and to prevent it from being too bulky, the force exerted by the muscle must be very near the centre of motion. The muscles of the arm, for instance, must be within an inch and a half of their centre of motion, and yet the force to be raised may be two feet distance, so that the strength of the muscle must be to the force as two feet is to an inch to an inch and a half. In this Borelli calculated the force necessary for all the muscles, /5.72 and we see that nature has adapted them exactly to it. They are not insufficient for the force they require, for there are no instances of them being broken. They have been shown by anatomists to be admirably fitted for giving motion to the body. How they are contrived is beyond our comprehension, but when a muscle acts we know that it swells in breadth and contracts in length, and thus the motion is produced. We know that this power is

---

[52] Givovanni Alfonso Borelli (1609–1679) published his findings on biomechanics in a two-volume work *De Motu Animalium* [*Of the Motion of Animals*].

communicated to them by the nerves, but of the manner of its operation we are entirely ignorant—so far is the wisdom of God beyond the wisdom of man. That these muscles may move easily without injuring themselves or one another, they are all surrounded with a membrane which is commonly moistened with fat, that at once lubricates them, but also fills up all the interstices so as to add beauty to the whole. When this is taken away and the muscle made bare, the /5.73 body appears a most horrid spectacle.

¶ We may observe that the whole body, in order to be preserved in its curious organization, must have one common cover, and here nature has also shown her wisdom and design in making a skin, which is a tough membrane capable of great contraction and dilation, so that whether a person is fat or lean, young or old, it affords a close cover. This skin is preserved by a *cuticula*, or scarf skin, and, as this is much exposed to injuries, it is renewed when rubbed off. It consists of scales that are easily perceived by a microscope. It is this cuticula that is raised by a blistering plaister, and we then see how tender the real skin and how impossible it would be to live without this.

¶ But we must not omit that, besides the nerves that are for the muscular motions, there are others for the various senses, one pair called the optic, which are the instruments of seeing; another called the /5.74 {olfactory}, which is the instrument of smelling; the auditory for hearing, and other small fibres of nerves which go {to} the various parts of the body and are the instruments of touch. The nerves are collected in the greatest number at the points of the fingers. We are at {as} a great loss to say how these nerves perform their functions as those that are intended for the muscles. We see no difference in their construction, and yet we see that one kind are fitted for giving sensation and perception, and the other only for giving motions. There are holes in the skull and spine exactly fitted for the transmission of the nerves to all parts of the body. The optic nerve enters the bottom of the orbit of the eye and is fixed in the globe of the eye. When it is cut or obstructed there is no distinct vision, though this eye be perfectly sound. The same happens of all the other nerves, though we are ignorant what impulse is necessary towards their communicating sensation and perception to the mind.

Besides the nerves for sensation, there are also external organs of admirable contrivance.

¶ The eye is an organ admirably fitted for vision. It is necessary that a picture of the object should be formed on the coat called the *tunica retina*. How this conveys the image to the brain anatomists know not, but this they know, that when the image is not properly formed, the vision /5.75 is hurt or destroyed. It would be difficult, perhaps, to make those who don't understand anatomy comprehend all that is known of this little organ. I shall not therefore enter on the task, but those who know the least discernment will discern that it is intended for seeing and therefore that the rays of light are fitted for it and it for them with admirable skill. Nothing can be more surprising than that by a small ball fixed in a socket we can perceive the fixed stars and the various objects around us by means of the refraction of the rays of light. These rays move with such rapidity as are adapted to this end. The other organs of sense contain no less marks of wisdom, though we are more at a loss with regard to the use of their several parts.

¶ The external ear is well fitted to receive the undulations of the external air that produce sound. These are conveyed to the *membrana tympanica*. In the inside there are several small bones that receive the impression made by the motion of it, and so it is conveyed to the auditory nerve which is spread over the inner ear. The nerve for smell is also spread over the internal part of the nose, and the nerves intended for {taste}[53] are diffused over the tongue, palate, and circumambient parts. Every part there is fitted for its proper use. If, therefore, upon seeing a curious engine, we conceive /5.76 that it had a wise and skilful maker, must we not in a much higher degree apply these qualities to {the} contriver and maker of the curious fabric of the human body? This argument is elegantly summed up by the sacred writer. He that made the eye, shall he not see? He that made the ear, shall he not hear? He that gave a man understanding, shall he not under-

---

[53] Baird wrote 'smell'.

stand?⁵⁴ No argument can be more forcible to any candid and ingenious mind.

¶ I might also take notice of the structure of the bones, these supports of the human body, so admirably constructed for use. While the body is in the {womb},⁵⁵ the bones are soft and flexible, without any of that strength and solidity which they afterwards acquire. But as they are intended for supports, they gradually acquire a firmness of texture which is in no other part of the body. They have various articulations, some of {them} resembling a ball and a socket, fit for turning in all directions as, for instance, those that join the arm to the shoulder and the thigh bone to the *os sacrum*. Of the other *joints* there are different forms, all suited to their ends, and by all of these joined together we are fitted for walking, running, jumping, stooping, and the like, which we do with great ease and facility. Besides these articulations for motion, there are other parts not /5.77 intended to be moved, where the bones are not jointed, but firmly joined to one another in a manner something like what the carpenters call *dovetailing*. This is the case with the two parts of the skull. In some, articulations the motions are intended to be small, such as the back, and accordingly the bones of it are fitted so as to move a very little. In some cases again we see that motion is performed merely by the bones being joined by a cartilage or intermediate substance between bones and flesh. In this manner are the ribs joined to the breast bone. We may observe too that all the bones which touch one another are smooth and lubricous at the ends, so as to make their motion more easy; all of their structure exactly answering to the laws of motion. It is worth noticing before we conclude that the famous philosopher and physician {Galen},⁵⁶ having been brought up in the Epicurean tenets of a fortuitous concourse of atoms and that there was no providence, no care of a deity, when he had occasion to consider the structure of the

---

⁵⁴ See Psalm 94:9.
⁵⁵ Baird wrote 'foetus'.
⁵⁶ Galen of Pergamum (129–c. 216). Baird erroneously wrote 'Galileo'. As the Anonymous Aberdeen notes say 'Galen' in a parallel passage, either Reid misspoke or (more likely) Baird misheard. See also *Intellectual Powers*, 510, for a parallel reference.

human body, was soon converted from this principle and convinced of the existence of a wise and discerning being. /5.78

Lecture 78th

To what I have already said I may now add that provision which nature has made for the cure of diseases. As we are liable to many accidents which are apt to produce disorders in our bodies, the wisdom of nature hath likewise provided for the cure of these. When any of our bones are broken there is a fluid which issues out. At first it is of a cartilaginous nature, by degrees, however, it hardens and becomes as firm as before. And all that is done by the physician is not to disrupt nature in her operations. It is the same with the cure of our other diseases. It is the operation {of nature}, not of medicine. All that {medicine} does is to exclude the action of the air or whatever may prevent nature in her process. This seems to have been the conception which Hippocrates and the ancients had of medicine, that it only was useful in aiding nature without pretending to assume the merit to itself. We see too, when extraneous bodies are anywhere admitted into the body, they are frequently expelled in a very wonderful manner. Of this /5.79 there are innumerable instances in the history of medicine. But I now proceed to the last branch of this division, viz. the marks of intelligence and wisdom to be found in the structure of the human mind.

In the structure of the human mind we may perceive various intentions and, at the same time, observe means fitted to answer these intentions. And

1) It is evident that man was intended to take care of his own preservation, to avoid those hurts that would impair his health or endanger his life, and also that he should seek what is necessary to support his life. For this purpose the infant is provided with various instincts to take care of its life. It sucks when it is hungry and swallows its food, which by art it could not learn to do. It is by the instruction of nature. When it ails, too, it cries by instinct, and these cries are understood by the mother or those around, and their bowels are moved to give it all the assistance in their power. Nature has taken care that all our diseases should be attended with acute

pains, which lead us to avoid or remedy them. As food and drink are necessary to supply the waste of the body, so the appetites of hunger and thirst are given us to fulfil their end, to admonish us when /5.80 they should be gratified, and without these we could not know when, what, how much, or how often to eat or drink. As alternate labour and alternate rest are necessary to our health and even to our life, so nature has given us a disposition to alternate exercise and repose, by admonishing us when we have continued too long in either. The love of life and an aversion to whatever has a tendency to destroy it is implanted in all animals, in order to induce them to take care of their life, and so we find that there is no animal but what uses all the means in its power to preserve or prolong its life.

2) Another instance of wisdom in the structure of the mind is an intention that the race should be continued. This we see too in the other animals as well as man, and they are all accordingly fitted with appetites to answer to that end. In the human race, the love of the sexes and the parental affection serves this end. In all ages, whether men are wise or foolish, virtuous or vicious, we can see no reason /5.81 why the race should ever cease. In all situations, nature has provided against this, and indeed, if it was otherwise, the race must very soon perish, as individuals are only short-lived and temporary beings. For this purpose too nature hath furnished the mother with milk and has taught the infant by instinct to suck it. Whether we consider the weakness or the wants of children, it is evidently impossible that they could support themselves without the tender care of the parents, particularly of the mother, who often deprives herself of rest and all the conveniences of life to supply its wants. And this takes place not only among wise and enlightened nations, they might perhaps do it from a principle of duty, but it takes place among all kinds of men. The different disposition of the sexes, too, seems to have designed them for family society. This has been taken notice of in very ancient times. Thus in the *Oeconomics* [Economics] of Xenophon we find

Socrates display this very elegantly and agreeably.[57] Nature has given to the female sex that timidity and delicacy that is proper for the management of domestic affairs and the rearing of the tender offspring; to the other sex that fortitude /5.82 and courage necessary to procure subsistence for the family and {for other tasks} which require greater labours and robustness.

3) Nature evidently intended man for society. Solitude and seclusion appear unnatural and contrary to the constitution of his nature. We see that all men in all ages have lived in this way, if we except a few individuals who, either from affectation of singularity, or a wish to be thought remarkable for sanctity, or perhaps from false notions of religion, have lived by themselves. But the intention is that we should live in society, and this intention is to be seen not in man only but in some of the lower animals. Some of these, we observe, are gregarious, others are solitary. Foxes, lions, bears, etc. associate only during the time that is requisite for copulation and the rearing of their young. Black cattle etc., on the other hand, are naturally gregarious and are always found in society. Now man is evidently of the last kind; he is a gregarious animal. In all ages, the principles of his nature have led him to this state. /5.83 Even the most rude and barbarous are always found in tribes or clans. Accordingly we see that he is fitted for this situation:

1) By language, which is peculiar to man. For though there are some signs by which the lower animals can communicate their feelings in some degree—thus a dog can easily, by his appearance, warn another whether he approaches him with a friendly or hostile design—yet these signs are few. They are all natural signs, understood from their nature, and it is not in their power to enlarge them. But man, besides the use of natural signs, is able by them to form other artificial signs, and by these communicate to others not his present feelings only, but his past knowledge. And thus, by receiving the experience and knowledge of others to assist

---

[57] Xenophon of Athens (c. 340–c. 350 BC) was one of Socrates' students, and composed several Socratic dialogues, including his *Oeconomicus* [*Economics*].

his own, men are perpetually improving in civility and useful science. And this seems to be peculiar to men only, for it is not to be found among the brutes. They never improve. They are the same now as in former times, and will remain the same to the end of the world. By language, then, it appears that we are intended for society, as it could have no existence without it. /5.84

2) Men are led by natural instinct to imitate the actions of those around them. Now this has an evident relation to society. For did we not live in society we would have none to imitate. I might here take notice of the social affections, of which there could be no exercise without society, such as gratitude for favours received, compassion at the distress of others, ambition of superiority and power, friendship, esteem, and benevolence, all of which serve as many ties to bind men together in social union. Nay, even those affections which we call malevolent show that we were intended for society, as without it we could have no occasion to exercise them.

4)[58] Nature intended man to improve in knowledge and the useful arts. 1) We see that he is fitted for this by his very constitution. We observe in children a great curiosity to enlarge their knowledge: they pry into whatever is unknown; everything that is new delights them; they examine it on every side; and are thus daily acquiring new ideas. Children are led to this by instinct, and indeed if it were not thus /5.85 they never would acquire any knowledge at all. 2) What tends to our improvement in knowledge and the arts is that credulity incident to children, by which they receive with implicit submission whatever is taught them. One could be apt to think at first sight that we ought only to believe what we see just reason to believe when we have sufficient arguments to induce our belief. But were this the case with children, the consequence would be that they would lose much of what tends to improve their faculties and enlarge their knowledge. One of the most remarkable parts of our constitution is the power of acquiring habits, by which, by doing a thing frequently, we acquire a facility of

---

[58] This '4)' evidently follows the '3)' on the previous page.

doing it. This is a power so familiar to us that we require no account of it, but if we attend to it, we will find it altogether unaccountable, though we see the ends for which it is intended. Inanimate machines, by going in a road frequently, never learn to move more easily in their road, but man is so made that what at first was difficult, by repetition becomes easy. By this much time is spared for our acquiring other habits and arts. If children by repetition did not acquire a faculty of doing /5.86 them, they would never walk tolerably or speak properly all their days. The same may be said of all the other arts: of writing, dancing, fencing, etc. Habit is the foundation of them all.

Further, man was intended to improve in his social affections. For this purpose nature has annexed a pleasant sensation to the exercise of them. There is a tranquillity attending them which is the comfort of life and invites us to the practice of them as our highest happiness. On the other hand, to our malevolent affections there is an uneasy sensation annexed which admonishes us against the indulgence of them, except where they are absolutely necessary.

Further, nature has intended us for political society. Though there be some very savage tribes which give small marks of this, yet it is manifest that we were designed for this. For, some submission and subordination is necessary in order both to defend us against injuries we might receive from those of our own community or of a different one. Even in the violent savages, as in the Canadian /5.87 tribes, we find that though they know neither fixed laws nor magistrates, yet it is always understood that when an injury {is done} to any of them by one of the same tribe, then he is entitled to revenge the quarrel, and if from any of another tribe, then the whole tribe think themselves bound to assist him in procuring retaliation. And when they go a-hunting or to war, there is always a kind of subordination which, though rude, yet is sufficient for them. But as men improve in politeness, their wants increase, {and} a stricter union becomes necessary.

¶ The indications of nature which show that we were intended for this state are 1) we see that men are endowed with various and different talents. Hence we see that all are not equally fitted for every profession. This difference is not to be observed in the other animals. We see a greater difference between a man and another than between any two of them. As in a building we see stones of various figures and fit for different ends, some for cornerstones, some for lintels, some for windows, and so on; so in society various persons are endowed with different talents and are fitted for different offices in that society. And if they are endowed with these, nature surely intended that /5.88 they should have an opportunity to exercise them. If all lived separately and in solitude, then all would have the same things to do, so that the same abilities would be required in all, whereas, in society, the deficiencies of one are supplied by another, and all find a profession to suit his talents. Besides, 2) in large societies we find that there are few who have either the wish or the talents to govern. The *many* are tame and easily led by a superior address. If all had the same ambition for power and pre-eminence, then it would be impossible that societies should subsist. Their rivalship would effectually hinder it. But if we see that the greatest part are easily made obedient to an ambitious few, then from this we may collect that nature intended them for government and political society.

The last intimation of nature which I shall mention is that men were designed to have the means of improvement in virtue and moral goodness. That we have temptations to do wrong is no doubt true. It does not /5.89 appear to have been the intention of nature that we should be free from temptation. This is a state of probation — but still we have sufficient inducements to improve in virtue. For this end, every man is endowed with natural conscience, which points out to him in most cases what is right and what is wrong. Self approbation follows the performance of virtuous actions, but no man can perform any crimes of an atrocious nature without remorse. Every man sees that wisdom, prudence, justice, temperance, and fortitude tend to real happiness, and if at any time he yields to the force of temptation and acts contrary to the direction of conscience, he always finds remorse follows it more than sufficient to counterbalance all the pleasure he felt in deviating from his duty. Everyone then has the means of improvement, though some perhaps from various circumstances, as, good education, good example, etc. may have it in a higher degree than others. From all this it is clear that, in the structure of the human mind, there appear various intentions and there are, we have seen, means fitted to answer their intentions, which shows wisdom and skill in the contrivance of our constitution. /5.90

Having now at some length pointed out these marks of wisdom and design which appear in various parts of the universe, and showed thus that they arose from wise contrivance, I come next to consider the account which the atheists give of the origin of all things and examine its probability in comparison of what has been already advanced.

Lecture 79th

Before I proceed directly to the subject proposed in the conclusion of my last lecture, it may be proper to make some remarks with regard to the argument which I last insisted on, viz., that from the marks of wisdom and design to be met with in the universe we infer it is the work of a wise and intelligent cause. It is worthy of notice that intelligence, wisdom, and skill are not objects of our external senses, nor indeed objects of consciousness in any person but ourselves, and it may be observed that, even in ourselves, we are, properly speaking, {not} conscious of any either natural or acquired habit which we possess. We /5.91 are conscious only of their effects when they are exerted. A man's wisdom can be known only by its effects, by the signs of it in his conduct —his eloquence by the signs of it in his discourse. In the same manner, we judge of his courage, and strength of mind, and of all his other virtues—it is only by their effects that we can discern those qualities of his mind. Yet it may be observed that we judge of these talents with as little hesitation as if they were objects of our senses. One we pronounce to be a perfect idiot, incapable of doing anything that will be valid in law—another to have understanding and to be accountable for his actions—one we pronounce to be open, another cunning—one ignorant, another knowing. Every man of common understanding forms such judgements of those he converses with, he can no more avoid it than he can seeing objects that are placed before his eyes. Yet, in all these, the talent is not *immediately* perceived; it is discerned only by the effects it produces. From this it is evident that it is no less a part of the human constitution to judge of powers by their effects than of corporeal objects by the senses.

¶ We see that such judgements are common to all men and absolutely necessary in the affairs of life. Now every judgement of their kind is only an application of that general rule, that from marks of intelligence /5.92 and wisdom in effects, a wise and intelligent cause may be inferred. From a wise conduct we infer wisdom in the cause, and from a brave conduct we infer bravery. This we do with perfect security — it is done by all — they cannot avoid it. It is necessary too in the conduct of life; it is therefore to be received as a first principle.[59] Some, however, have thought that we learn this by reasoning or by experience. I apprehend it can be got from neither of these. We may observe that philosophers who can reason excellently on subjects that admit of reason, upon this subject appeal only to the common sense of mankind, and in some cases offer instances to make the absurdity of the opposite glaring, and sometimes using the weapons of art and raillery, which in cases of this kind is very proper and often successful. Cicero, in his tract *De Natura Dedorum* [*On the Nature of the Gods*], speaks thus — can any thing done by chance have all the marks of design? If a man throws dice and both turn up aces, if he should throw 400 times would chance throw up 400 aces? Colours thrown carelessly upon a canvas may have some rude appearance of a human face, but would they form a picture beautiful as the pagan Venus? A hog grubbing the earth with his snout may turn up something like the letter A, but would he turn up /5.93 the words of a complete sentence?[60] Thus, in order to show the absurdity of supposing what has the marks of design could arise from chance, he gives a variety of examples where the absurdity is palpable without reasoning on the matter. And we find other authors arguing in the same way.

¶ The ingenious Mr Hutchinson endeavours to prove it by reasoning, and he is the only author I have met with who has

---

[59] See *Intellectual Powers*, 503.
[60] None of these exact examples are used by Cicero, but see II.87–8 & 93–4 for close approximations.

made the attempt.[61] Without pretending to say whether the reasoning is just or not, I shall only observe that he has drawn arguments from chance to show that a regular arrangement of parts must proceed from design, that they could not proceed from chance. It may be remarked that the doctrine of chances is a branch of mathematics not yet a hundred years old, but the truth of this principle has gained the assent of all since the beginning of the world and could therefore receive little strength from that reasoning.

¶ Let us next consider whether it may not arise from experience, that from marks of design in effects, we ascribe them to a designing cause. That this truth is not derived from experience is evident for two reasons. 1) Because this is a necessary truth, and no experience can discover a truth to be necessary. Thus, though it is consistent with our experience that twice three /5.94 makes six and the Sun always rises in the east and sets in the west, yet between these two all must perceive this distinction: that the first is a necessary truth and has been and will continue {to be} true independent of our experience or of any cause, but the latter is not a necessary truth. It is contingent and depends on the will of the maker of the world. If two things appear to us constantly conjoined, and if our experience of them is uniform, this still gives no reason to conclude that they are necessarily connected or that they cannot be disjoined. In a word, experience informs us only of what has been, not of what shall be.

¶ Further, experience may show us a constant conjunction between two things in those cases when both things are perceived, but if one only is perceived, experience never can show it constantly conjoined with the other. For example, thought is connected with the thinking principle, but how do we know that thought may not exist without a mind? These, no doubt, we find connected, but if a man says he knows it by experience he deceives himself. Mind is not an object of consciousness, however — one only of them is perceived; we can't say then that they are constantly conjoined. We conclude, therefore, that the necessary connection of thought and the thinking principle is not learned by /5.95 experience.

---

[61] See note 3.

The same reasoning applies to the inference of design in a cause from marks of it in its effect.[62] The one is an object of consciousness, but not the other. Experience then cannot show a necessary connection. Thus it appears then that, from marks of design and wisdom, to infer intelligence in the cause is a first principle learned neither by reasoning nor by experience; it is self-evident and assented to by all men. It is on this principle, then, that my argument is grounded.

¶ There are clear marks of wisdom and design in the formation and government of the world, must they not arise then from a designing cause? And this argument has this peculiar advantage, that it gathers additional strength with every improvement in knowledge, every discovery in philosophy. We are told of Alphonzo, a Moorish king, that, when his philosophers explained to him their notions of our planetary system, he said 'that he could have made a better one himself'.[63] But the system they gave him was not the work of God, it was the fiction of men. But since the present new theory was introduced, no one has presumed to show how it could be better. Indeed, when we attend to the marks of wisdom and intelligence that appear all around, every discovery proves a new hymn of praise to him who is the creator and governor of the world. /5.96

¶ This argument has commonly been called the argument from *final causes*, and we shall accordingly use it without enquiring into the propriety of it. If reduced to the form of a syllogism, these are the two premises. 1) That an intelligent cause may be inferred from marks of wisdom in the effects. 2) There are clear marks of wisdom and design in the works of nature. The conclusion is thus — the works of nature are effects of a designing and wise cause. Now it is evident that we must either deny the premises or admit of the conclusion. The second of them I have endeavoured already at some length to prove, and I have also showed that the first is got neither by reasoning nor experience, that it is instinctive and believed by all men. But we find that among the ancients that the first of these was admitted, that those things which bear

---

[62] The preceding three words are unclear in the manuscript.
[63] See note 30.

the marks of wisdom and design could proceed only from an intelligent cause and not from chance, but they denied that any evidences of these were to be seen in the construction of things. We may learn this from what we find put into the mouth of one of that atheistical sect in the third book of Cicero's *De Natura Deorum*. But modern improvements in philosophy have shown the folly and weakness of the assertion, and none now have the effrontery to deny that clear marks of wisdom are to be seen in the works of creation. /5.97 This appeared evident to the famous Galen, who wrote a book, *De Usu Partium* [*On the Use of the Parts (of the Body)*], though he was educated an Epicurean, purposely to show that all could not proceed from chance.

¶ Those in modern times have seen the weakness of this and have that stronghold as untenable,[64] but they have assaulted the other of the premises I mentioned, viz., that we can infer design and wisdom in the cause from discovering it in the effects. In his dispute against the principle, Descartes, though he surely was not an atheist, has led the way, and his motive for it probably was this: that having invented some new arguments himself for the existence of the deity, he wished to disparage all others in order to bring the greater credit to his own, or because he was offended perhaps with the Peripatetics for mixing final causes in their solution of the phenomena of nature.[65] A *physical cause* is different from a *final cause* — the physical cause points out the laws of nature from which the phenomena flow, thus, for example, we can show that the physical cause of water rising in a pump is the weight of the atmosphere, but the *final cause* again points out the end which nature had in view. Thus, the end of the eye for seeing, the foot for walking, and so on. These final causes Descartes thought we could /5.98 not know. He thought the philosopher had nothing to do with them, and to attempt to explain them, he considered as presumptuous and arrogant. In this tract he was not followed by many who admired him greatly in other things. Particularly by the pious Dr Henry

---

[64] Baird's writing is clear enough here, but his meaning is not.
[65] René Descartes (1596-1650). See his *Meditations on First Philosophy*, 'Third Meditation'.

More of Cambridge and Fénelon Bishop of Cambray, who has wrote a book on the existence of God, and his arguments are mostly drawn from the art of nature, as he calls it, or those tokens of wisdom and design which appear in all parts of nature.[66] Since the time of Descartes, however, we find that some have adopted his sentiments who may be suspected of a tendency to atheism.

¶ Of those we may reckon Maupertuis[67] and Buffon,[68] but the most direct {argument} against this principle has been made by Mr Hume, who puts an argument against it in the mouth of an Epicurean on which he seems to lay great stress. It is this, that the production of the universe is a singular effect, to which there is no similar instance, therefore we could draw no conclusion from it, whether it is made by wisdom and intelligence or without.[69] I shall consider a little the form of this objection. The amount of it is this, /5.99 that if we were accustomed to see worlds produced some by wisdom and others without it, and saw always such worlds as ours produced by a wise cause, the conclusion would then be that this {world} of ours was made by wise contrivance, but as we have no experience of this kind, therefore we can conclude nothing about the matter. This conclusion of his is built on the supposition of past experience, finding two things constantly united. But this I showed to be a mistake. No man ever saw wisdom, and if he does not conclude from the marks of it, he can form no conclusions respecting any of his fellow creatures. How should I know that any of this audience have understanding? It is only by the effects of it on their conduct and behaviour, and this leads me to suppose that such behaviour proceeds only from understanding. But, says Hume, unless you know it by experience, you know nothing of it. If this is the case, I never could know it at all. Hence it appears that whoever maintains that there is no force in the argument from final causes denies the existence

---

[66] Henry More (1614–1687) and François Fénelon (1651–1715). The book Reid refers to is Fénelon's *Demonstration de l'existence de Dieu* [*A Demonstration of the Existence God*].
[67] Pierre Louis Maupertuis (1698–1759).
[68] See note 38.
[69] Hume, *Enquiry Concerning Human Understanding*, XI.112–3.

of any intelligent being but himself. He has the same evidence for wisdom and intelligence in God as in a father, a /5.100 brother, or a friend. He infers it in both from its effects, and these effects he discovers in the one as well as the other.

Having thus vindicated the argument from any exceptions that have been brought against it, I now proceed as I proposed to consider a little the causes which atheists assign for the universe and the production of all this beautiful system.

Some of them attribute it to chance as the ancient Epicureans did, but we may observe that chance cannot be the cause of anything, and when we say a thing happens by chance it is a word expressive only of our own ignorance of the cause. Chance can never be the efficient cause of anything. When a man throws a dice we say it is a chance which side turns up. Now, what is the meaning of this? Chance can never be a cause, {so} it means only that we are unable to discover the cause, for no man can measure the force with which he throws a dice with such accuracy as to tell what side will turn up; and it is so in all[70] /5.101 we attribute to chance. When a thousand tickets are put into a box and mixed and turned over by the motion of the lottery wheel, a boy puts in his hand and we say it is chance whither he pulls out a prize or a blank. What is the meaning of this? It is that no man knows what it will be, whether the one or the other, but there is no part of it but has its cause.

¶ To assign chance then as a cause of anything is absurd, and where the atheist tells you the universe was produced by chance, he means only that it was produced he does not know how. This, however, does not hinder it from being owing to some cause, and that cause we have already showed is eternal. Besides, nothing which we ascribe to chance is regular. If a man, says Tillotson, throws down a heap of types on the ground, it is a chance how they fall, but chance could not form them into a poem like the *Iliad* or the *Æneid*, or even into a discourse in prose.[71] Some again have attributed all things to *necessity*. But if we attend to the

---

[70] The preceding three words are unclear in the manuscript.
[71] See note 30.

meaning of the words, we will see necessity cannot be the cause of anything. When we speak vaguely of causes, indeed, we say some of them are *necessary*, others /5.102 *voluntary*. Though a cause in the philosophical sense of the word signifies only an agent by his own will producing the effect, yet in vulgar language we apply it to any instruments or means used to the production of the effort. So we say the pressure of the air is the cause of the mercury rising in the barometer, and the necessary cause of this is the weight of the air which is as necessary as the effect it produces, and this is produced by its gravitation, which also must have a cause, and thus may we go on till we rise to the first cause of all. A necessary cause, then, is an effect produced by another cause till we are landed in a first cause of all, which is not necessary but a real efficient cause. We showed before the absurdity of supposing an infinite series of causes, and shall not now resume what was then said.

Another refers the universe to nature. They tell you nature does so and so and that it produced all things. A late French philosopher[72] has wrote a treatise in support of this doctrine entitled *System de la Nature* [*The System of Nature*], in which he ascribes everything to nature. But what does he mean by nature? It is a phrase as improper as *chance* or *necessity*. /5.103 It is common indeed to say a thing is done by nature to distinguish it from what is done by art. Thus we say a cabinet is the work of art not of nature. A tree, again, is the work of nature not of art. In this way we are accustomed to consider nature as something opposite to art. We consider it as producing some things, and art others. But here, by nature, we must mean it is either produced by the laws of nature or by the author of nature. Here the phrase is intelligible, but as an efficient cause it has no meaning. A law of nature never could produce anything without an intelligent being to put them in execution. As in civil law, it is not the law which tries a man, but the judge acting according to those laws and executing them. So the rules of grammar never would produce a finished oration of themselves, without someone to form the sentences according to them. In like

---

[72] Paul Henri Thiry, Baron d'Holbach (1723–1789).

manner, a law of nature supposes a lawgiver, a being who established and operates according to them. We see, then, it is vain to have recourse to this subterfuge, to say that all was produced by nature. The term is as unmeaning as if we said it was produced by chance or necessity.

Having now insisted so long on this argument, I think it needless to insist at long length upon others.[73] /5.104 Some have argued the matter from the unanimous consent of all men in all ages, except those who are so sunk in barbarity as hardly to merit the name of human creatures, and also from this—that every part of the creation bears marks of a recent formation. These and several others you will find in authors who have handled the subject, but though I would be very far from disparaging those arguments as useless, yet I would despair of convincing a man by these who resists the force of this. Such a man is hardened beyond the powers of arguments. I now proceed to consider the nature and attributes of the deity.

Lecture 80th

This is a subject too high to be grasped by our weak and limited capacities. When we consider attentively the works of nature, we see clear indications of power, wisdom, and goodness, yet we see still much remains into which we cannot penetrate, and of which we must be forever ignorant. If this is true, then, in this case, may it not be expected that our notions of the great author of all will be /5.105 imperfect and inadequate as our notions of his works. The divine nature indeed is a more proper object for the humble veneration of the pious heart than of curious disquisition to the most elevated understanding. The pride of philosophy, however, has spurred on some to excogitate how the world might have been created and how governed.

¶ It was from this intemperate desire of comprehending the laws of the universe that many among the ancients excogitated or invented their theogonies and cosmogonies, and among the moderns too gave rise to their theories of the

---

[73] The Anonymous Aberdeen notes also mentions, but does not provide, an argument from miracles.

Earth and of the universal government of things, which appear indeed rather as the reveries of fanciful men than as truth. I may venture to affirm that all these theogonies and cosmogonies which are not legitimately deduced from observation will always appear as unlike the works of God as the castles built by children, which the next moment they toss over with their foot, to the most regular and finished piece of architecture, and we have reason, therefore, to think that our notions of the attributes of deity will be as imperfect as the notions we can form of his works. This consideration, then, ought to make us diffident in the conceptions we form of the divine nature.

¶ We have no means of forming conceptions in any degree adequate to the object. The supreme being operates before us and behind us, on our right hand and on our left, and even within us /5.106 but we see him not. In rude ages, we see men generally ascribe to him a form like that of their own, with organs and appetites similar to their own. When men improve in refinement and knowledge, a little reflection leads them to form more {perfect} ideas of deity, as of a more spiritual nature. But though they do not ascribe to him a bodily figure or the organs and appetites incident to {the} human body, yet they find themselves under a necessity of assigning to him something analogous to the human mind, such as understanding, will, and moral character. All our original notions of mind and its attributes are got by a consciousness of its operations in ourselves, and so we can form no concept of any attribute in the supreme being to which there is not something analogous in ourselves. As a blind man can form no conceptions of colour, or a deaf man of sounds, so neither can we form a notion of anything belonging to the divine mind of which we have no consciousness in our own. And perhaps there may be attributes belonging to the divine nature of which we can form no more a conception than a blind man does of colours.[74]

¶ It may be proper, then, to point out the topics from which we commonly reason on this subject before we proceed to

---

[74] See Newton, *Philosophiae Naturalis Principia Mathematica* [*The Mathematical Principles of Natural Philosophy*], General Scholium.

consider particularly his nature and attributes, and these /5.107 I think may be reduced to three heads. 1) From the appearance of such attributes in the operations of nature we may collect that they exist in the deity. Thus, from the appearance of wisdom in the structure of things we may collect his wisdom, and from the tokens or appearances of good contrivances—of such contrivances as tends to the good and happiness of his creation—we may collect his goodness. This is precisely like collecting the characters of men from their ordinary conduct, and it is indeed the chief source from which, by reason, we collect the attributes of the divine nature—from the tenor of his conduct in the administration of things, as far as they fall under our view. 2) We may reason with regard to some of the divine attributes from his necessary existence. As it is evident that this is an attribute belonging to the deity, so it lays a foundation for our reasoning to some of his other attributes. This is a mode of existence quite different from that of those beings that are merely contingent, and perhaps draws consequences[75] with it which by no means result from *it*. 3) In like manner we argue from his unlimited perfections. If it appears that we should ascribe to deity every perfection in the highest degree, we may from hence deduce more accurate notions of some of his attributes.

¶ These, I think, are the different topics from which authors have reasoned with regard to the attributes of deity, notwithstanding /5.108 some have advanced it as a fixed point that we can reason only from the first of these topics, viz., from the appearance of his attributes in the operations of nature we may collect they exist in him. This, Mr Hume lays down as a first principle, and thence draws it as a consequence that we ought to ascribe to the deity no higher degree of wisdom and goodness than what appears in the construction of his works, and from this he endeavours to conclude that we ought to ascribe to him not those qualities in an unlimited degree, but only in a certain inferred limited proportion.[76] The argument is grounded on this: it is to be observed that we can reason

---

[75] This word is unclear in the manuscript.
[76] See e.g. Hume's *Enquiry Concerning Human Understanding*, XI.105.

with respect to the nature and attributes of deity from no other topic but from the appearances of these attributes in the contrivance and government of things.

Having premised these things, I may remark that the attributes of the supreme being are commonly distinguished into two classes: his *natural* attributes and his *moral* attributes. I shall begin with the first. By natural attributes we understand those in which his will is not concerned. By the moral attributes, those which give direction to his will and conduct. /5.109

Of the natural attributes of deity, the first we take notice of is his eternity—that is, his being without beginning or end of existence, or as the sacred writer prettily expresses it, 'from everlasting to everlasting God'.[77] Our notions of his eternity are derived from the notions we form of duration. We have an immediate distinctive belief of duration in every act of memory, for it is essential[78] to this that it relate to something past and that some interval of duration has interposed between it and the present. Every man, in every act of remembrance, has a conception of duration, but there is something peculiar in this conception of duration, that, though we can assign limits to our own duration, to the duration of any created being, yet we can assign none to duration itself. *We* had a beginning, but duration did not begin with us. There was a time when we were not, but then duration was. So it is with every being made by God—put their beginning as far back as you please, still if they had a beginning, there must have been a time when they were not, and therefore duration did not begin with it. We see, then, though the whole creation had a beginning, yet duration could have none. /5.110 Its nature will not permit us to believe that it had a beginning, and neither can it have any end. We see no impossibility in supposing all created things annihilated in a moment, and others created in their stead, but this would be impossible if duration did not continue to flow equally when no created being existed. Thus we see that duration considered in itself is necessary—it had no

---

[77] Psalm 90:2 and 103:17.
[78] This word is unclear in the manuscript.

beginning and will have no end, and we cannot suppose it limited without a contradiction. Things which have a beginning occupy only a small part, which bear no more proportion to duration than finite to infinite. If we conceive a right line drawn out without beginning or end, any part of it that could be measured by inch or feet or even miles would bear no proportion to the whole. Such a part must have a beginning and an end. It can have no proportion, then, as arithmeticians say; it cannot be an aliquot part of the whole, which has neither beginning nor end.

Another thing remarkable in the nature of duration is that as it is unlimited, so it is *necessarily existing*. We cannot say so of our own /5.111 selves. For though we have existed for a certain time, yet there is no absurdity in supposing that there was a time when we did not exist or when we will not exist. It depended on the will of God, and he might give us existence or might not give it. It is a contingent event which may be or may not be. But can we say so of absolute duration? By no means. It involves an absurdity in supposing that there was a time in which it did not exist or will not exist. Having premised these things with regard to the duration, I apprehend that there is no argument necessary {to} show that the deity is, was, and will be in all points of duration. His existence is commensurate with duration, and there is no point of it in which he will not exist. And perhaps, after all, this conception of the deity is inadequate and puerile. It is, however, the only one which our weak and limited faculties can reach. Some of the Schoolmen thought to form a more adequate notion of duration by calling it 'a moment continued forever without alteration',[79] but this definition involves an absurdity in it and, instead of throwing light on the subject, rather darkens it; for to suppose any point of duration to stand still involves a contradiction {in} it and is inconsistent with every notion of duration which we can form.

---

[79] I have been unable to trace this reference, but it is an apt summation of the answer given by Thomas Aquinas (1225–1274) in *Summa Theologica* Ia, Q 10.

¶ It may be observed that all men, even atheists themselves, allow that something must have been /5.112 eternal, and indeed this is evident from the first principle which I have already mentioned, that nothing can begin to exist without a cause, and for the same reason it will follow that what is uncaused and not produced by the power and wisdom of some other being must be eternal. Against any existence from eternity, some objections have been brought, but they conclude equally against duration itself. These objections amount to this, that in the infinity of duration which is past, there must be a certain number of years, but there must {be} twelve times as many months as years and three hundred and sixty-five times as many days as months, which is to make one infinity twelve times or three hundred and sixty-five times as great as another. But this, if it shows anything, leads us {to} think duration had a beginning, which is absurd. The fallacy of the reasoning lies in this—that we apply years and months and days to measure that which from its very nature admits of no measure—infinity is immeasurable. Sometimes we apply infinite to express any large indeterminate number. In this sense it is intelligible, and in this sense eternity may be said to contain an infinity of years, that is, that no number of years can equal eternity. But if we use *infinite* to express any determinate /5.113 number, then it is absurd and involves a contradiction no less than if we should talk of a square circle.

Another attribute of deity is his necessary existence, that is, it is impossible he could not be. Every being that exists is either contingent or necessary. These two ways, when opposed to each other, are contradictory, and therefore one or {the} other is applicable to every being. We call that *contingent* which either might or might not be and that *necessary* which must be. Whatever either might or might not be depends on the will of some agent with power to bring it to pass or not. A power to produce evidently implies a power also not to produce. Hence it follows that, whatever be {the} cause of any existence, its existence is contingent and depends on the will of the agent whether it should exist or not. That we do exist is most certain—but that existence is contingent, the supreme being gave it and he can take it away when he pleases—it depends on his will. But are we to suppose that the supreme being himself exists in the same manner? This evidently would be absurd. He derives his power and his existence from no other being. Therefore he is not contingent but necessary. As necessary existence is a mode of existence of which no other being but the supreme being is possessed, no wonder that it is too big for our weak faculties /5.114 and that we find it difficult to conceive it.

¶ In order to assist our conceptions, we may illustrate the distinction of necessary and contingent existence by the distinction between truths, which are also divided into necessary and contingent. Some truths we perceive manifestly to be necessary, such are all the truths of mathematics, as this, that equals added to unequals makes the whole unequal, etc. These we perceive are necessary. They must be true in all times and in all places without variation or change. They depend not for their truth on the will of any being. But there are truths of another kind, which are contingent, thus, the Sun has always continued to rise in the east and set in the west. This is a truth confirmed by uniform experience, nevertheless it is not a necessary truth. There is no contradiction in supposing the course of the Sun to be quite opposite, to rise in the west and to set in the east. It depends entirely on the will of the supreme being that the one course takes place and not the other. Thus have we seen the distinction between necessary and contingent truths—that the one is true in all times and in all places and depends not on the will of any being, that, on the other /5.115 hand, contingent truths depend on the will and power of the being who produced them. Now, there is a similitude, though imperfect, here to necessary and contingent existences. That is necessary existence which cannot not be, which must be, and which depends not on the will of any being. That, again, is contingent existence, which arose from a cause, which depends upon that power, and may cease to be if that cause alters.

The next natural attribute of the deity which I shall consider is his *immensity*—that is, that he is everywhere present. Of a thing so far above us, our conceptions must be inadequate. A child has only a dark and indistinct conception of those nobler powers in man which have not yet unfolded themselves in his infant breast, so our notions of the divine perfections and attributes must always be imperfect and puerile. Now we see them only darkly as through a glass and judge of them as children do of matters beyond their comprehension.[80] We can attribute nothing to deity of which there is not some faint ray or resemblance in ourselves. Whatever we perceive of real excellence in ourselves, in our own mind, which is the work of God, it must be in /5.116 the author of it. For no reasoning can be more convincing than this used by the Psalmist, 'He that made the ear, shall he not hear? He that made the eye, shall he not see? He that gave man understanding, shall himself not understand?'[81] So if he has given man {and} the work of his hands[82] a certain sphere of action, shall not he himself act in a sphere far more extensive and uncircumscribed by no narrow bounds. We have, however, I apprehend, a more distinct notion how body occupies space than how the mind does. By the sense of touch we receive certain notions of the places of body. We know that two bodies can't occupy the same place at the same time. We know too that body is in its nature finite, limited, and composed of parts totally independent of each other, yet space is in its nature unlimited and indivisible. We cannot call space a substance—neither can we call it relation—neither any modification of any substance, yet it is something of which we have a distinct conception. The subject is intricate—there is something in the nature of space which overpowers and is sufficient to humble the most elevated /5.117 understandings when they see they cannot comprehend its nature. Without then making any farther reflections upon it myself, I shall lay before {you} the sentiments of one of the most profound and penetrating geniuses ever the world produced, I mean Sir Isaac Newton. They are to be found in the {*General*} *Scholium* annexed to his *Principia*: 'He is eternal and infinite, omnipotent and omniscient; that is, his duration reaches from eternity to eternity; his presence from infinity to infinity; he governs all things and knows all

---

[80] See 1 Corinthians 13:11-12.
[81] See note 54.
[82] See Psalm 119:1, which makes clear that the work referred to is God's, not man's.

things that are or can be done'.⁸³ No human authority can be greater than this, and they are the result of that deep reflection on the works of nature which makes him the lasting honour of his age and country. His great merit has been admirably and concisely displayed by Mr Pope in these two lines

> Nature and Nature's laws were hid in night;
> God said, Let Newton be, and all was Light!⁸⁴ /5.118

Lecture 81st

We are at a loss in what sense to ascribe place to the mind; the Schoolmen maintain that it was *'all in all and all in every part'*.⁸⁵ But this is so far from throwing light upon the subject that it darkens it. We rather, then, should acknowledge our ignorance and confess this to be one of the many things beyond the reach of the human faculties. They must have a manner of existing in place totally unlike to the body — a certain sphere in which they act, and we cannot conceive action without an agent. Since, then, we find in ourselves a limited sphere of action and that we exist in a limited space, it may {be} asked: what sphere of action or what place can we ascribe to that being who is himself uncaused and the cause of all things, who is from everlasting to everlasting,⁸⁶ and who has unlimited duration with his existence, and whose existence is no less necessary than endless duration and unlimited space? Shall we consider such a one as /5.119 confined by any limits? I conceive the most natural notion we can form is agreeable to what we have been endeavouring to establish, that unlimited space is the sphere of his power and that it is filled by his immensity as duration is by

---

[83] Baird writes 'Deus eternus est et infinitus, omnipresens and omniscius etc. _____ cognosiumus'. It seems clear from the garbled Latin and missing words that Baird did not clearly hear what Reid said. I have supplied Andrew Motte's 1729 English translation of the passage Reid was most likely quoting.

[84] The unused epitaph for Newton's tomb in Westminster Abbey, by Alexander Pope (1688–1744).

[85] Baird writes *'Totus in toto and totus in omni partie'*, a slightly garbled variation on *'totus in toto et totus in qualibet parte'*.

[86] See note 77.

his eternity. But, to reason more closely—the arguments which reason suggests on this subject are chiefly two. 1) We see marks of his wisdom and power in all the parts of the universe which fall under our view. 2) We may infer his immensity from his *necessary existence.*

1) There are manifest indications of his power and presence through every part of his wide extended dominions. For, all being was fist created by an act of his will and power, and surely could not be exerted when the agent was not. He laid the foundation of the Earth and the heavens, nay, the heaven of heavens is the work of his hands.[87] The most distant of the fixed stars also was made by him. Now, when we consider their distance, yet that their light though twelve thousand miles {distant}[88] are made visible to us, that they are in magnitude and lustre not inferior to our Sun, and, if we judge by analogy, who are as distant /$_{5.120}$ from one another as from us, and each having his *primaries* and *secondaries* revolving round him; if to this we add the immense number we see even by the naked eye, and the still greater number by the telescopes, when, I say, we consider the supreme being as exerting his power and presence through that prodigious extent of space, what measure can we set to his being, or to what limits of space can we suppose him confined?

¶ Further, we are not to suppose the divine operation to cease merely on giving existence to these objects. We see many changes and revolutions {in} nature which require the finger of omnipotence to perform them, though to us they appear regulated by fixed laws. But we should observe that the laws by which a being acts is one thing, and the being who acts agreeable to those laws is a different thing. It requires power and authority to act agreeable to laws, as well as to act without them. The being who acts without them we consider as possessed of no wisdom nor goodness, but he who acts by them we consider as possessed of wisdom and goodness and power nevertheless. /$_{5.121}$ Now, the laws of nature—regular, constant, and uniform—not only

---

[87] See Psalm 19:1.
[88] An erroneous figure. See note 23.

display his goodness and wisdom but require also his constant operation, and therefore require his presence in all parts of duration. We formerly took notice of the laws of nature in the vegetable and animal kingdom as excellent and regular—in the manner of propagating their species, so various in the different kinds and so uniform in the individuals of each kind—in their manner of growth and of drawing nourishment—in the uniformity of their structure—and in a remarkable manner we perceived his operation in the instincts of animals and in the gradual evolutions of the powers of the human mind. In the inanimate kingdom too, there are many laws of nature no less uniform and constant as the cohesion of the particles of matter—their corpuscular attraction—various chemical affinities—all of {them} affecting only at small distances, but affecting every particle of {matter}. There are other powers, as magnetism—it appears indeed at a greater distance but affects only one kind of matter—there are others still more extensive than this—thus, gravitation acts not only on every particle of matter on the surface of our Earth but to every part of the solar system, and /5.122 by it every particle in that system acts on and is itself acted on by every other particle. Whether this power extends to the fixed stars we know not, but this we know, that the rays of light coming from them are subject to the same laws of refraction and reflection with the light in our own planets. The same laws of nature thus operate through all uniformly and regularly.

2) There is an absurdity in supposing limits to a being, either in time or place, who exists *necessarily*. For this necessity is the same at all times and at all places, and therefore we cannot suppose a being necessarily existing in one place which is not necessarily existing in another place. Though our notion of this kind of existence, as I observed before, is imperfect and inadequate, yet we can have a clearer conception of it by attending to the distinction of truths into *necessary* and *contingent*, and this is an evident property of truths which are necessary, that they are true in all places and at all times, and could not possibly be otherwise. /5.123 We conceive space and duration to exist necessarily, and therefore conceive them unlimited from their very nature, and we can as easily conceive them not to

exist as not to exist always and everywhere. What exists necessarily, then, exists everywhere and at all times, having no relation to one thing or one place which it has {not} to another.

Another attribute we have reason to ascribe to the deity is *unlimited power*. His power is manifested 1) in the works of creation. The power exerted in creation is beyond our conception, for all human power consists in supplying causes to effects—things active to things passive—but cannot produce a single particle of matter not before existing, nor can ever annihilate a single particle that God has made. Indeed, all the operations of nature which we see consist in various combinations, compositions, and decompositions of what is already made, without either creation of new or annihilation of old. But it was not so from all eternity—matter is a thing so imperfect that to ascribe an eternity of existence to it is absurd; all must be ascribed to the deity, the great first cause of all. /5.124

2) His power is manifested in governing the world. To suppose, with Leibniz,[89] that everything when created was endowed with such internal powers as to produce all the changes that afterwards happen in them is to exclude all divine management together. But we have no reason to think that the world is governed in this way, without the interposition of the supreme being.[90] Nature leads us to conceive {of} the maker of the universe as its constant governor, and leads us to apply to him as the hearer of prayer and the kind protector of his rational offspring. The weak and imperfect power of man is soon exhausted, but the power of the Almighty is subject to no lassitude or fatigue. We must not include, however, in our notion of his omnipotence, the doing {of} things impossible. This notion we find was advanced by Descartes, on purpose to support some parts of his system.[91] He would not say, be it that deity could {not} do

---

[89] Gottfried Wilhelm Leibniz (1646–1716).
[90] See *A Collection of Papers, Which passed between the late Learned Mr Leibnitz, and Dr Clarke, in the Years 1715 and 1716*; especially 'Mr Leibnitz's Second Paper', §8–9.
[91] See Descartes, *Meditations*, 'Reply to Sixth Objections', §6.

things impossible; this is a mistake into which that philosopher, it is probable,[92] would not have fallen had it not been that to support a favourite theory. For to do what /5.125 is impossible is a contradiction in the nature of things. We may as well conceive a thing to be and not to be at the same time. There are certain things which we perceive are necessarily true. Now, to suppose them subject to any power, even infinite power, is absurd, for what is necessarily true is always true. Another thing we cannot suppose the divine power to extend to is his moral nature. It is absurd to suppose that he has the power of depriving himself of any of his perfections, as, his goodness, wisdom, justice, etc. It is no less absurd to suppose his power to extend to his moral nature. When talking of a good or virtuous man, we say that it is impossible he should cheat as do an immoral thing; this expression is perhaps too strong when applied to man, but it holds with respect to the deity and is to be considered not as an impeachment of his power but an expression of his rectitude—not a defect in his nature but a perfection of moral goodness.

Another attribute of the deity is *unlimited perfection*. This, indeed, is rather a general declaration of his attributes than of any one in particular, but it was necessary to take notice of it, as from it we may argue some other of his perfections. /5.126 It may be observed that there are some notions of the mind which are general and abstract, yet are formed in every individual of the species, and that, too, very early. Of this kind are our notions of *good* and *ill*, and, what is nearly allied to these, of *perfection* and *imperfection*. We give the name of perfection to that which every good man values in himself or in others, and what he wishes not to lose. Although men, from different degrees of moral refinement, may differ in their estimation of the value of things external, yet we find a very great unanimity in what qualities of the mind are properly called excellences or perfections. Thus everybody agrees that ignorance and folly are imperfections, that knowledge and wisdom are perfections. All agree that power is perfection and impotence an imperfection, that self-

---

[92] The preceding three words are unclear in the manuscript.

command is a perfection and being a slave to passion or appetite is an imperfection. To do what we know to be wrong and what we will afterwards repent and be sorry for is an imperfection. To pursue steadily what is proper and right is a perfection. Indeed, I believe there is nothing in which men /5.127 are more generally agreed than in the application of the terms of perfection and imperfection to the qualities of the mind. This shows us that these terms are not words without meaning, nor do they depend for their truth on the variable tastes of individuals, but that there is some common standard by which they may be measured. Whatever implies defect, weakness, or disappointment, or misery we call imperfection. Whatever is the object of esteem, love, veneration, or admiration we consider as a perfection.

¶ Having thus laid down our notion of perfection and imperfection, what reason have we to ascribe to the supreme being every perfection in the highest degree? 1) It ought to be considered that every perfection or real excellence which we perceive in the creation belongs in a much higher degree in the creator, and perhaps in deity there may be perfections of which we have no more a conception than a blind man of colours.[93] If this is true, however, as undoubtedly it is, that every perfection in the effect is to be found in the cause, then we conclude that every real excellence we observe in God's creation are only faint rays of more eminent perfections to be found in the creator of all. But 2) reason teaches us not only /5.128 {to ascribe} to the supreme being perfection only in a superior degree, but even in the highest degree. We, his creatures, are possessed {of} only that portion which he willed to bestow upon us. It is bounded by narrow limits. But what bounds can be set to his perfections, who is necessarily existent, and who is unlimited?

Another natural attribute of deity is *perfect knowledge and wisdom*. The arguments reason suggests here are chiefly these two. 1) The marks of wisdom and design to be seen in the works of creation. In all the parts of nature—in water, air, earth, and sea—in the disposition of things upon the Earth's surface—in the wonderful variety of vegetables and the no

---

[93] See note 74.

less wonderful variety of animals—in the structure and instincts of animals—in the structure of the human body and mind—in all these we found marks of a wise artificer, and the more we know of his works, the more our admiration of his wisdom was raised. As a man ignorant of clockwork, when he looks at the outside, admires the regularity with which this observes the hours and minutes and seconds and can't help thinking that it required knowledge and contrivance /5.129 to execute it, but when he is allowed to look into it and see the beauty and exquisite contrivance of the parts of the whole, how will his admiration of the skill of the mater be raised? It is so with our admiration of the skill of the great artist who formed the universe. The various parts of the vast machine excite our surprise and wonder, but we are still more struck {by} the skill and wisdom which executed so stupendous a fabric. The wisdom and knowledge of others around us are discovered only by the signs of them—in their conduct and actions. Now we have the same evidence of the wisdom of the deity, and in a much higher degree.

¶ It may be observed 2) the supreme being knows all his creatures and all their qualities; as it was him who first created them and who still governs them. The artificer knows his own workmanship. 3) We have reason to ascribe knowledge and wisdom to deity because it is a perfection. I formerly endeavoured to show you that we have reason to ascribe every perfection to that being who is himself uncaused, independent, and necessarily existing. Now, no one can deny that knowledge is a perfection and a natural object of esteem, respect, and love, and, as it is found in some degree in the creation, it must be ascribed in an unlimited degree to the creator. All the knowledge which man now possesses or every will possess, nay, /5.130 all that the most exalted seraphs know, is the gift of God. Is it not just reasoning, then, to say, 'he that giveth understanding shall himself not understand'?[94] Besides, in all ages and in all countries we find men disposed to ascribe such knowledge to the deity. This is manifest not only from writings of the

---

[94] See note 54.

heathens, but from the universal use of an oath in all solemn transactions. Now why would they appeal to deity if they did not believe that he knew their actions? This is a clear proof of a belief of a deity who is the avenger of treachery and that from him nothing can be concealed. Indeed, without knowledge and wisdom there could be nothing that deserves the name of perfection. If we dare to hazard a conjecture according to our weak faculties concerning the objects of the knowledge of the deity, we must conclude he knows himself, his creatures, and all their constitutions; that he knows all that has existed, that now exists, or that ever will exist; that he knows every relation of those things of which we now see only so small a part, and also, that he knows all the events of *necessary* causes, as well as of *free* agents.

¶ Some, however, have conceived that the future actions of free agents can {not} be known unless they flow from necessary causes, but this never has been proved. We have indeed /5.131 no notion of any such power in ourselves, and are at a loss, therefore, to conceive it to belong to another, even to deity, but this surely is no reason why it should not belong to him. It never can be shown to be impossible why future free action should not be foreseen, and till this is done we have no reason but to ascribe it to the supreme being. And the cause of our being unwilling to allow it even to him is that we do not possess it ourselves.

¶ If this, however, is therefore[95] a sufficient ground to deny it to him, why not also his creative power? We know how things already existing may be formed into various combinations, but how to give existence to what did not exist before we know not. Are we therefore to deny that power to deity? Surely not. In the same manner we know not how the future actions of his agents can be foreknown, and we know not how it is brought about, but we have this ground to think that it belongs to deity, that *we* by *our* memory know actions that are past, yet there is no argument to show the impossibility of foreseeing future actions which will not equally apply to memory, and were it not that we ourselves are endowed with memory, I apprehend, we would be apt to

---

[95] This word is unclear in the manuscript.

think that *it* would be as impossible as the foreknowledge of future actions.

¶ Some other philosophers, unwilling to deny this power altogether to the deity, attempt to account for it, but their attempts seem /$_{5.132}$ vain and impossible. Dr Clarke does it in this way, that we ourselves, when we know the characters of men, can form some conjecture how they will act in a given situation, so as we must allow to the supreme being a more perfect acquaintance with the character of men, hence he will have a more certain knowledge how they will act in any case.[96] This is, I apprehend, reducing the divine prescience to an infinitely sagacious guess. Besides, it is supposing that men always act according to their character, which is by no means true. Some of the Schoolmen, particularly the Jesuits, in order to account for this knowledge, invented what they called a *scientia media*,[97] that is, not only a perfect knowledge of all that depends on necessary causes, but also of all events that can happen in any possible situation.[98] With regard to this *scientia media*, there were numberless disputes in the School which it is {not} my design to enter upon here. We must also ascribe to the supreme being the possession of his knowledge without acquiring it by labour, exercise, or slow degrees; a knowledge liable to no error or disappointment, but which is certain and unerring, and which is the result of his own nature and perfection. /$_{5.133}$

Lecture 82nd

In all the natural attributes of deity, though we find something analogous to them in the human mind, yet we are to consider them as far removed from all that imperfection with which they are attended. In particular, in the case of *knowledge*, as formerly noticed, we are not to suppose the knowledge of deity acquired by slow degrees or painful application, or by inferring one thing from another; this is altogether inconsistent with the perfection of the divine

---

[96] See Clarke, *Demonstration of the Being and Attributes of God*, X.
[97] i.e. 'middle knowledge'.
[98] The origin of this doctrine is typically ascribed to the Jesuit priest and scholar Luis de Molina (1535–1600).

nature. It must be supposed to extend to all things, past, present, or future, nay even to the thoughts of our hearts, and it is not provable or conjectural but certain and unerring. This consideration of the divine knowledge ought surely to have a powerful influence on our conduct. We know very well how great an influence the presence of any character we respect has upon the human mind. Much more ought this to have, if we deeply considered and firmly believed that we were always in the presence of God, and our hearts are always open to him with whom we have to do.[99] It shows the folly of all hypocrisy and disguise, as we cannot be concealed from him with whom we are most concerned. It ought to stifle also all vainglory and desire of men's applause, while at the same /5.134 {time} it should render us careless of their censure or contempt. Let us be more concerned to appear just and innocent in his sight who is the best judge of our merit, and who will call us to account.

Another natural attribute of deity of which we ought to take notice is his *spirituality*, which expresses not so properly what it is as what it is not. It signifies that his nature is far removed from body or matter, that it is not confined to place as material things are, in short, that it has none of the qualities of matter: we see, however, in men a great proneness to attribute a visible form to the deity, especially the human form, as thinking it the most dignified with which they are acquainted. This seems to be owing to the weakness of the human mind, by which we conceive of other things as like ourselves and are prone to judge by analogy. But of the absurdity of this there is sufficient evidence if we would consider with any degree of care that the supreme being who is eternal, omnipresent, omniscient, and the final cause of all can never be material. All matter is finite from its very nature, it is divided into parts and consists of a variety of parts, each of which are distinct and independent of the rest and therefore /5.135 is incapable of thought, for thought never can result from a composition of different beings. And as the operations of the mind are one and indivisible, so this forms a strong argument that everything endowed with thought

---

[99] See Hebrews 4:13.

must be immaterial. Though the evidence for this is clear and convincing, yet have men conceived otherwise of the supreme being, and such gross conceptions must be considered as the cause of that general spread of idolatry among the heathens. Weak and foolish men conceived the deity to inhabit only in their temples, but his presence is bounded by no such scanty limits, for in *every* place will the prayer of the humble and acceptable worshiper be heard by him.

Nay, they even imagined that if they worshiped on the tops of high mountains their prayer would be better heard, as they were the nearer to heaven than in the valleys. Strange! that reason should be so corrupted as to form such mean ideas of the great cause of all, yet so it is, that we see they were generally spread over the heathen world. But everyone who has rational notions of the deity must conceive that he dwells not alone in temples made with hands,[100] but that universal nature is his temple, and that his ear is forever open to the cry of his saints[101] wherever they are placed. It is a natural and a /5.136 just inference which our Saviour makes from this, that they who worship him must worship him in spirit and truth[102] and that {it is} the homage of the humble and devout which is most acceptable to him.

Another attribute of the deity is his *unity*, that is, he is *one* and not a number or plurality. We see how grossly the heathens erred in this, imagining all the universe full of deities, which was entirely owing to their mistaken notions of the divine nature. For had they carefully attended to the attributes which we have already run over, they might have seen that they could not belong to a plurality but to one. This may be argued from: 1) the form and uniform contrivance of the universe. All appear under one government, subject to the same causes, and therefore there must be one lawgiver. I had occasion to mention before, a ray of light coming from the fixed stars to our system, that is, from the most distant part of nature which falls under our view, is governed by the same laws of refraction, reflection, and inflection as those

---

[100] See Acts 7:48 and 17:8.
[101] See Psalm 34:16.
[102] John 4:24.

produced on the surface of the Earth or our planets. We see the law of gravitation, by which /5.137 various bodies on the surface of our Earth gravitate to the Earth, extends also to the Moon, and not only to the Moon, but also to the planets of our system, by which they gravitate to the Sun and to one another. Thus, from the most distant to the nearest parts of nature, all appear one great system, under one governor, and subject to the same laws, and not according to that absurd idea of the heathens, who conceive a vast variety of gods, each of which had their separate departments, and that they often differed in their design and intentions, nay sometimes quarrelled and fought as it is represented in Homer.[103] But there is no such discord under the government of the deity. The whole is under one governor and subject to {the} same laws. Besides, if we consider this as a perfection which our reason tells us to ascribe to deity, then it is impossible to conceive it as belonging to more beings than one. We have already shown that the deity is eternal and immense and unlimited in all his perfections. Now it is impossible to conceive a number of beings endowed with these. In all cases when we consider number, there must be something to distinguish the individuals of that number /5.138 from each other; they must be distinguished by time, or place, or their nature, or some other circumstances. Take away all these, the plurality is lost and they really coincide with each other. This reasoning applies to the divine nature. We cannot suppose two beings endowed with those qualities to be distinguished either in time or place, or by their nature, or indeed any other circumstance.

I shall only take notice of another natural attribute of deity, viz., that he is *immutably happy*. Even the Epicureans gave an eternity of happiness to their deities, but this they conceived to consist in an enjoyment of pleasure without any concern in the affairs of mortals.[104] This suited the tenets of Epicurus, who placed their happiness in the enjoyments of sense, but reason would lead us to consider it a perfection inherent in the divine nature, and that he who made all and

---

[103] Homer (9th or 8th century BC), author of the *Iliad* and the *Odyssey*.
[104] See Diogenes Laertius, *Lives of Eminent Philosophers*, X.121.

is possessed of all power must be happy in himself. He is therefore called in Scripture the blessed God—*makarios*, *eulogétos*[105]—meaning, properly, an object of praise or adoration.

¶ One cannot but take notice here, from the account now given of the natural attributes of God, of the perfect correspondence of what we find dictated /5.139 by reason and the accounts given by the inspired writers. We see in the Old Testament that Jehovah, the Lord God who revealed himself to the people of Israel, is everywhere represented as possessed of these qualities of eternity, immensity, power, perfection, spirituality, etc. which from the light of reason we have now ascribed to him. And the same we find in the New Testament. And indeed it hardly can be supposed that such rational notions could be formed by a people so ignorant and gross as the Jews were, and while the neighbouring nations were all deeply sunk in idolatry.

Having said these things of the *natural* attributes of God, I shall now consider his moral attributes. There is no branch of knowledge which it concerns us more to know than the moral attributes of the supreme being. For, on these depend all our hopes from him, and from a knowledge of these will flow our behaviour toward him and the devotion we pay him. If we do not conceive the supreme being possessed of moral perfections in the highest degree, all our services to him will be the effect of fear and not of true devotion. This devotion can arise only from a belief that he is the best, as well as greatest of beings, and that our perfect virtue consists in resembling him as far as our weak faculties allow. By his moral attributes we mean those which relate to his actions and his conduct, by which his will and his /5.140 operations are directed. He has an active as well as intellectual nature. The world was made by him, and he still upholds and governs {it}. And action consists in the exercise of power, and without the desire of acting, the power would be given to no purpose. Therefore, to every creature to which God has

---

[105] Both of these words mean 'blessed' or 'happy' in Greek, and are used frequently in the Septuagint and Greek New Testament to refer to God.

given power, he has given, at the same time, the principles of action to prompt them to the exercise of that power. Thus the instincts, appetites, and passions of animals all draw them on to action and the exercise of their power. But besides these inducements to action, man is possessed of a much nobler faculty: the moral faculty by which he distinguishes right and wrong in conduct and distinguishes what he should pursue from what he should avoid.

¶ As by the eye he perceived colours, by the ear, sounds, and by the memory, past events, so by this faculty he perceives what is right and wrong — what is a subject of approbation, what of censure or indignation. This I shall have occasion to explain more fully afterwards. I shall then show that the qualities of right and wrong which we perceive by the moral faculty are really qualities inherent in the moral agent in which we conceive them to be, and not /5.141 merely, as some hold, sensations in the percipient.[106] Now, however, we must take it for granted that there is a real and intrinsic difference between moral qualities: that gratitude, friendship, etc. are in their own nature more worthy than perfidy, ingratitude, etc. Every man who consults his own breast must be convinced of this. If then there is a moral character in man, let us consider if we have reason to ascribe it to the deity.

¶ Is there anything in the deity analogous to moral character in man? Here it ought to be observed that there are various principles of action in man which appear suited only to our dependent nature and to {a} state attended with imperfection. These we never can suppose to belong to the supreme being. Thus, we never possibly can ascribe to him those instincts of which we see common[107] in men and the lower animals, which lead them blindly to certain actions necessary for such imperfect creatures as we are, but to a being so perfect as the supreme being cannot belong. Neither can we ascribe to him those impulses which men receive from *passions*, these were given to man to supply the defects

---

[106] In Reid's lectures, ethics follows natural theology. See also *Active Powers*, 294–9.
[107] This word is unclear in the manuscript.

of reason and the moral faculty. It is only what belongs to man as a rational creation that we must ascribe to deity. /5.142 Now it is manifest that our reason leads us to ascribe to him a perfect moral character. In order to confirm this I observe:

1) Every real excellence in the effect is to be found in the cause. No reasoning can be more forcible than this 'He that gave understanding shall not he understand?',[108] and the same reasoning leads us to attribute a perfect moral character to deity from what we discover in ourselves. He who made man capable of acquiring qualities worthy of esteem, respect, and confidence, must surely possess them himself in an infinite degree, free from all the imperfections which accompany them in our frail nature. Besides, shall we ascribe to him knowledge and power and yet deny him righteousness and truth? Indeed, there is no argument which can lead us to ascribe to him powers etc. which will not equally lead {us} to ascribe to him those moral qualities which render the being possessed of them truly excellent and amicable.

2) Another reason why we should ascribe a perfect moral character to the deity is from the moral government of the world. We see from the contrivance and /5.143 administration of things that virtue is countenanced and vice discouraged. Virtue is in itself rewarded by the approbation of our minds; an approbation is felt from the practice of virtue which forms the only sincere enjoyment attainable in this life. It inspires the mind with confidence in God and the hopes of a future reward; it affords a pleasure which never pales on reflection nor is ever followed by satiety or disgust. This can by no means be said of the other pleasures of our nature. They are either momentary in their duration and often, on recollection, yield ground for repentance and sorrow. Virtue again is countenanced by this, that it tends to enlarge our own power in the world, to produce respect and good offices for ourselves and {others}.[109] Vice, again, is punished in the general administration of things, as in itself it is attended with remorse and a dread of discovery, by the contempt of men and the lash of the civil law.

---

[108] See note 54.
[109] Baird wrote 'ours', but this appears to be a slip of the pen.

3) The voice of conscience leads us to ascribe a perfect moral character to the deity. There is no sentiment more natural to man than this, 'shall not the judge of all the Earth do right?'.[110] I had occasion to observe before /5.144 {that} trust in the virtue of God was the firm support of injured virtue and led all men to the expectation of a future state where a more perfect retribution would take place. This sentiment of the justice of the supreme administration is surely what every man feels in himself. I hope there are none so bad, who commit any bad action without having some temptation to commit it, some prospect of interest, some bodily appetite or something or other which influences them; even the worst will do virtue when there is no temptation to the contrary. Now we cannot suppose the supreme being to have any temptation to do wrong—every creature is his—and all are in his hands; justly has an inspired writer said, *'God tempts not any man neither is he tempted'*.[111]

Having thus briefly showed that we have reason to ascribe a perfect moral character to deity, as well as natural attributes, I come now to consider what notion it is most reasonable to form of the nature of this moral character. Here I observe that the only notion we can form of his moral character is by ascribing to him what appears most excellent in ourselves, separated from all the weakness and imperfection /5.145 of human nature. We ought to observe that there are some virtues grounded on our state as dependent creatures, liable to danger, error, and misconduct, such as repentance, contrition, etc. These are suited to the state of man, not to the state of the supreme being, and can have no place in him who is exempted from error, danger, disappointment, or mistake. We are, then, only to ascribe to him such as imply no weakness or defect, such as: 1) goodness, mercy, and forbearance; 2) truth and veracity; 3) regard to virtue and dislike to vice; {and} 4) justice and equity in the administration of things.

1) Goodness, mercy, and forbearance, are evidently implied in a perfect moral character, for without it we can

---

[110] Genesis 18:25.
[111] James 1:13.

conceive no moral character whatever. It appears from all the works of creation which are full of his goodness that the laws by which the universe {is governed} are good and, indeed, as far as we can trace them, they are fitted to promote the interest of his creatures and to give all that degree of happiness of which their several natures are capable. These laws indeed are general, and sometimes through accident may produce harm, yet the state of man required the world to be managed by general laws. If fire should sometimes burn and sometimes not, if water sometimes bear him and sometimes not, and so on of other parts /5.146 of nature, it would be impossible without the longest experience to acquire any prudence in our conduct. These general laws are necessary and are well contrived for the purposes of the various animals which are capable of happiness or misery. Thus the harms which attend any hurt are necessary calls to prevent us from neglecting to remedy what might endanger our health or our life. So the pains that follow the appetites of hunger and thirst are necessary to procure {a} supply of meat and drink which we might otherwise forget. All their general laws serve as proof {of} the goodness of the deity, as they evidently tend to the wellbeing of his creatures and the enjoyment of that happiness of which every nature is capable.

2) Another moral attribute of God is his *truth and veracity*. There is no attribute belonging to the supreme being to which we more readily assent {than} this, and on which we more firmly rely. Some authors pretend to maintain that, in reasoning with regard to the attributes of God, we ought to reason from no topic but from the appearances we observe in the universe.[112] Now, it cannot be said that we have experience by means of our reason of his truth and veracity. They only have any experience of his truth and veracity to whom a revelation of his will has been made and who discern the truth and veracity /5.147 in a conduct suited to that revelation, but they who are left merely to reason can have no such experience. Yet are all men found to believe in the veracity of the supreme being.

---

[112] See note 76.

Lecture 83rd

We daily experience his goodness, but of his veracity we have no such experience, yet is the belief of his veracity found to be inseparable from a belief of his existence. Even human authority previous to experience has a weight with us, and let us suppose that the divine being should please to communicate anything to us by a revelation. I ask if any person could doubt of its truth? Is it possible anyone could think it all a lie? No man can entertain such a thought. And the reason of this seems to be that truth and veracity we conceive as inseparable from a perfect moral character.

3) Love to virtue and dislike to vice is another moral attribute of the deity. This is likewise in a perfect moral character, for it is impossible to conceive a being endowed with any considerable degree of virtue unless he regards the former and dislikes the latter. /5.148

4) Justice. The writers on jurisprudence have distinguished justice into two kinds, *commutative* and *distributive*.[113] The first regards our transactions with men when we consider ourselves as on a level with them, as in making a contract, carrying on traffic, etc. But the second is the justice of a judge or governor in dispensing rewards and punishments in exact proportion to the merit and demerit of a person. Now, if we ascribe justice to the deity at all, it evidently must be distributive justice, that is, a disposition to deal with all his creatures without partiality or prejudice; making all allowances for those whom his providence has placed in a more disadvantageous situation. And in the final distribution of rewards and punishments, justice requires that he should not accept the person of anyone in preference to another of equal merit, and that every alleviation and every aggravation should have its full force; that the punishment should be proportioned to the degree of atrocity in the crime and at the same time that the rigour of punishment should be tempered by clemency as far as /5.149 goodness will permit. This, I think, is the best notion we can form of the moral government of God, and this is to be ascribed to the supreme being, and it is that character which is everywhere

---

[113] See, e.g., Aristotle, *Nicomachean Ethics*, V.2.

attributed to him in the sacred Scriptures, where we are told, that 'he is no respecter of persons, but that in every nation he that fears him and does righteousness shall be accepted of him'.[114]

¶ But there are some peculiarities here, and which ought to be attended to when we form a notion of the divine nature. 1) Though it is a dictate both of reason and of conscience that an immoral conduct ought to be punished, yet they afford us no precept to determine the measure of that punishment. That criminal conduct deserves punishment is the voice of all men's conscience. 'No one', says Plato, 'either of Gods or men dares to say that punishment is not due to the unjust'.[115] It is an indignation at this which makes all so ready to give their assistance in apprehending malefactors and in bringing them to punishment. In human courts, to be sure, the judge cannot pass sentence as to the real demerit of the /5.150 criminal. There is {therefore} another rule which they use to observe: they are to judge how far the crime is hurtful to society or prejudicial to the interest of the civil government. They can judge by no other standard; they know not the heart, nor what measure of temptation he had, {nor} from what principles he acted. Of this the supreme being is the only judge. To him every heart is open and every circumstance that tends either to alleviate or to aggravate the guilt. There are many crimes heinous in their own nature which a human judge cannot punish at all, as they are not absolutely necessary to preserve the peace of society. Thus, ingratitude is in itself highly criminal, but it is not punishable by human laws if there is no injustice done: not that it is not considered as criminal, but because it is not considered as necessary to the preservation of human society. Xenophon indeed tells us that, under Cyrus, the Persians, by their laws, punished ingratitude severely.[116] By many, however, this account of the Persian constitution[117] is considered as mostly fiction,

---

[114] Acts 10:34.
[115] *Euthyphro*. Following this quotation in English, Baird writes it in slightly garbled Greek.
[116] Xenophon of Athens, *Cyropaedia*, I.ii.7.
[117] This word is unclear in the manuscript.

and it is certainly true that never has any instance occurred in any well-regulated government where ingratitude /5.151 was held an object of the civil law.

¶ {2)} Further, reason does not dictate to us how far clemency should extend to the penitent offenders. Justice certainly requires that an offender who repents and reforms ought to be otherwise dealt with than one who continues obstinate and impenitent, but how far this should be carried, whether they should be remitted altogether, or in what way or upon what terms they should be accepted, reason does not enable us to determine. I have thus endeavoured to show that we have reason to ascribe a perfect moral character to the deity and shall now consider some systems that have been advanced by authors of reputation concerning the attributes of the deity and which contradict what I have now held forth as the fact.

1) I shall consider what has been said by Mr Hume, not indeed in his own person, but in that of an Epicurean friend, whose sentiments he has held forth to us in his essay {*Of a Particular*} *Providence and a Future State* and adorned with all the strength of his reasoning and his eloquence, without either adopting or censuring it. He thinks that we have no reason to {ascribe to} the supreme being wisdom, power, or intelligence in a higher degree than what we see /5.152 manifested in his works; a conclusion evidently grounded on this, that a cause is exactly proportioned to its effect. As, therefore, these marks of wisdom etc. are limited, so we must conclude that their cause, that is, the perfections of the deity, are limited. 'When we infer any particular cause from an effect, we must proportion the one to the other, and can never be allowed to ascribe to the cause any qualities but what are exactly sufficient to produce the effect'.[118] It is allowed, then, that the deity 'possesses that degree of wisdom, power, and benevolence' which appears in his workmanship, but 'nothing farther can be proved, except we call in the assistance of exaggeration and flattery to supply the defects of argument and reasoning'.[119]

---

[118] *Enquiry Concerning Human Understanding*, XI.105.
[119] See ibid., XI.106. The quotation is not exact.

¶ I may observe here that this notion upon which the argument is grounded, that a cause is exactly proportioned to the effect and limited to the effect, may perhaps be true of natural causes, but as to intelligent causes which operate freely and voluntarily, this maxim is not founded on reason. I had occasion to observe formerly that this word *cause* is very ambiguous. Sometimes it signifies only some concomitant circumstances, and sometimes even the /5.153 name of the cause is given to the law of nature itself. This is an improper sense, but though from the use of language we cannot avoid it, yet ought we to be cautious lest we be imposed on by the ambiguity of terms. In the proper and strict sense of the word, we understand by cause, an agent with power to produce the effect and will to produce it. When we say cold is the cause of freezing in water, *cold* is here used in a vague and improper sense. Cold is only a negation of heat and cannot be the cause of anything. But that is a cause of an effect which has power to produce it. We say too, heat is the cause of the liquor rising in the thermometer. Here heat is used in a vague sense. But when we apply this maxim to intelligent beings, that the cause is proportioned to the effect, it will be found to hold neither in reason nor in the common judgement of mind.

¶ Suppose I should ask a man, on a journey, pray which is the road to Edinburgh? And he returns me a pertinent answer. Here the understanding of the man is the cause, the answer is the effect. Now, perhaps I never spoke to the man before; I know nothing about him. Am I therefore /5.154 to conclude that his understanding just enabled him to answer my question and neither more nor less? Surely this would be absurd. The natural conclusion is that he has such a degree, how much more I do not know. Again, if I converse with anyone half an hour upon ancient history and find that his knowledge is accurate, full, and well digested, shall I say that this man knows no more than what I have heard him express? By no means. I am to conclude that he knows not only what he has expressed but much more. So it {is} with regard to his goodness. If I had stood in need of the benevolent assistance of a friend, and that I found him always prompt to bestow his favours, do {I} conclude that he has merely that degree which he has manifested to me, and that I have exhausted all his stock? It appears then, that this maxim of Mr Hume's, when applied to voluntary causes, is neither self-evident nor consistent with our reasoning about causes in common life.

¶ But still it may be said that we can consider the supreme being as possessed only of that degree of skill, of power, and wisdom, etc. which we see displayed /5.155 in his works. This indeed is Mr Hume's reasoning, but it is evidently grounded on the supposition that there is no argument for the perfections of deity except what is drawn {from} those indications of perfection which we see in his works. This, no doubt, is one topic from which we do reason on the subject, but it is not the only one, as Hume supposes it to be. I concur that there is real force in our reasoning from the necessary *existence of deity* and his *unlimited perfections*. It has already been showed by clear arguments that that being who exists without a cause or a beginning exists necessarily, so that it is impossible for him not to exist or not to have such a degree of power, wisdom, and goodness as is manifested in his works. Now can it be said that necessary existence has a connection with one degree of power which it has not with another? When we consider a being possessed of necessary existence, we can see no connection he has with one portion of time more than another, that therefore his duration is from everlasting to everlasting.[120] We conceive him to have no greater connection with one part of space than another, that therefore {he} is omnipresent. In like manner, when we conceive {of him} as endowed with one degree, we must consider {him} as possessed of every degree, /5.156 as there is no connection between necessary existence and one degree which is not with another. This reasoning applies to all the other attributes of God.

¶ I endeavoured to show formerly that he was endowed with *unlimited perfection* from the consideration of his necessary existence. We cannot avoid ascribing different degrees of perfection to different objects, thus, we prefer a plant to a clod of earth, an animal to a plant, a rational to an irrational animal; and a being endowed with the highest

---

[120] See note 77.

degree of perfection is the most perfect we can conceive. Now if there really is such a thing as perfection and imperfection, we cannot help thinking that there is more perfection in the cause than in the effect, nor would the deity have given us ideas of perfection beyond what he really himself possesses. We may observe that this reasoning of Mr Hume's tends greatly to lessen the perfections of deity—to reduce them from infinite to finite and bring them on a level with our own, at least, to set them not so far above us as that a comparison may be drawn between the excellences of men and the excellency of God. Shocking thought! Presumptuous man! Does thou think with the short line of thy understanding to search the /5.157 unfathomable wisdom of God? It is difficult indeed to say whither pride, impiety, or presumption are most conspicuous in the man who makes the bold attempt. The man who boasted understanding is unable to discover how one particle of matter adheres to another. Indeed, the idea is so singular that I once imagined that either Mr Hume or his Epicurean friend must have been inventors of it, but I found that Milton, long before Hume's time, has attributed it to Lucifer, who gives the same reason to encourage his associates in rebellion against their maker, but they were convinced of their error by this event

> So much the stronger proved
> He with his thunder; and till then who knew
> The force of these dire arms? whom I now
> of force believe almighty, since no less
> Than such could have o'erpower'd such force as ours.[121]

I now proceed to consider another {view} concerning the moral attributes of deity which has come from a different quarter but {is} equally unfriendly to religion and virtue. I mean Lord Bolingbroke.[122] It had been advanced indeed by Mr Hobbes[123] before, and we find it adopted by Mr Hume in a /5.158 posthumous work of his on natural religion. He

---

[121] From John Milton (1608–1674), *Paradise Lost*, Book I, but not in strict order.
[122] Henry St. John, Viscount Bolingbroke (1678–1751).
[123] Thomas Hobbes (1588–1679).

admits that there must be a first cause possessed of power, wisdom, and the other natural attributes we have ascribed to him, but maintained that we know nothing of his moral attributes or the principles of his action; when we talk of his goodness, mercy, or justice, we use, says he, words without meaning.[124] This system strikes at the root of all religion, for if the moral attributes of deity are taken away, we can have no foundation for all the homage we pay him, or for all the hopes we have from him. He who believes that the Lord is just in all his ways and holy in all his works,[125] that justice and judgement are the habitations of his throne,[126] and that mercy and truth forever go before his face,[127] will of consequence believe that real virtue and real excellence consist solely in our resemblance to him, a consideration which gives them an authority they could not otherwise have. But this system cuts all the sinews of virtuous conduct, robs it of all its splendour, and rests it on a very weak and slippery foundation. We certainly, however, have the same reason to ascribe justice and goodness to the deity as power and intelligence, nor is there the least ground to think his moral attributes /5.159 more incomprehensible than his natural attributes. We acknowledge that our ideas of all the attributes and of the being of deity are inadequate, but this is no reason why we should not have as distinct a notion of his goodness, justice, and truth as of his power and intelligence. There are some vestiges of both in the human mind, and of the one our notions are as clear as of the other.

Lecture 84th

We can have no greater degree of testimony for the truth of anything than the testimony of our senses and of these faculties which God has given us; by these we discover that some propositions are true and others are false, and he who {has} a conviction of the imperfection of his faculties {and} presumes to call in question their information must remain a

---

[124] Hume, *Dialogues Concerning Natural Religion.* See esp. Part III.
[125] Psalm 145:7.
[126] Psalm 89:14.
[127] Psalm 97:2.

sceptic forever. There is no remedy for it. Now, our judgement of right and wrong is as certain {as} our judgement of true and false, and to suppose that the supreme being has another standard of measuring these than we, that he thinks morally ill what we think morally good and the contrary, is as absurd as to say /5.160 that he has a different conception of what is true and false. For it is no less evident that goodness, justice, humanity, etc. are intrinsically better than their contrary than that two and two make four. It must surely be allowed that a being of infinite understanding and intelligence can discern these moral relations as well as we. If the differences between moral right and wrong are distinguished by the human mind, {they are} much more so by him whose understanding is infinite. It is an eternal and immutable truth that virtue in its own nature is amicably respectable and deserving approbation; that vice, on the contrary, is an object of disapprobation, dislike, and demerit. When we judge so, we judge according to the truth, the supreme being must be allowed always to judge according to the truth, therefore they must appear so to him as to the human mind.

Having considered these two theories which tend wholly to overturn the attributes of the deity, I now proceed to consider some hypotheses whose authors in themselves were not unfriendly to religion, but which have been advanced in order to render our notions of the divine attributes more conceivable and to give such impressions of them /5.161 as are most agreeable to truth. The first of these I shall take notice of is what is commonly called the *Beltistan* theory.[128] Of this I shall now give some short account and offer a few remarks upon it. Whoever wants it once fully explained may consult Leibniz, in his *Theodicé* [*Theodicy*], who has adopted it. It has been also adopted by others, as that which gave the best account of the origin of evil and the most amiable representations of the divine perfections and administration. According to this system, the supreme being from all eternity, by his

---

[128] I have been unable to trace this reference, but 'Beltistan' may refer to the Baltistan, or 'Little Tibet', region of China. Leibniz became interested in Neo-Confucian ideas after meeting Joachim Bouvet, a Jesuit missionary to China.

infinite understanding, saw all the possible constitutions of {the} world which could be and their various qualities. Among all the possible systems that could be, he would choose that in which there was the greatest sum of happiness upon the whole. He then, from his infinite understanding and his perfect goodness, constituted the present system of that which contained the greatest possible sum of happiness on the whole, and that all the divine attributes consist in directing all things to produce the greatest degree of good on the whole.

¶ This system leads {one} to form a particular notion of the divine attributes. It is conceived that, though /5.162 we give different names to the moral attributes of deity such as justice, truth, and righteousness, yet that they may all be resolved into one and are only different modifications of his goodness or benevolence. That, therefore, we have no reason to ascribe any moral attributes to deity but his benevolence, that is, a disposition to promote the greatest degree of happiness on the whole in the universe. Some others since Leibniz have followed this system, and particularly a divine among the dissenters in England, whose name is commonly thought to be *Boyce*, in a pamphlet entitled *Divine Benevolence*, in which he has endeavoured to show that all the moral attributes we ascribe to deity are only modifications of benevolence, or benevolence considered in particular light.[129] We see that, according to this system, there is supposed in deity no love of virtue or dislike of vice than as they tend to promote the happiness or misery of the beings in the world; that a desire of promoting the happiness of all is the only principle of his action and gave rise to his laws and the government which he exercises. By this system, it is thought, the best account of the origin of evil, both natural and moral, can /5.163 be given. They think that all the evil we see in the world is a necessary ingredient in a system in which we see the greatest possible good; it was proper, then, to admit it, and if

---

[129] *Divine Benevolence, or an Attempt to Prove That the Principal End of the Divine Providence and Government is the Happiness of his Creatures* by Thomas Bayes (1702-1761), the famous mathematician. Baird has apparently misheard the name.

we remove it an equal proportion of happiness is at the same time removed.

¶ We cannot help thinking this a theory of the divine attributes; but it is a theory which, though well intended, has no sufficient arguments to enforce it, nor does it, after all, give us any clearer notions of the attributes of God than we had before. For 1) as we can only form a just notion of moral character in deity from what appears most perfect in moral characters among human creatures when separated from all the imperfections with which they are attended in us, so I conceive that *goodness* alone is far from making a perfect moral character in man. We cannot conceive a moral character without a regard to virtue and a dislike to vice. To make the only principle of action in man to produce the happiness of others is to degrade his nature. This, though a necessary branch of virtue, is not the whole of it. There is no reason why the whole attributes of the deity then should be resolved into one. 2) Though by this system we have the /$_{5.164}$ greatest possible sum of happiness, yet does it carry very uncomfortable prospects along with it and which appear very far from being agreeable to the truth. For it supposes that in this system *evil* has a necessary and fatal connection with *good*, and that it could not be removed even by divine power. This is to suppose a fate superior to the human being, which necessarily connects evil with the greatest possible sum of happiness. Likewise, we see that this system leads to the necessity of all human actions, which indeed was maintained by Leibniz and the other patrons of this system because it was necessary that every part should be so adjusted as to produce the greatest degree of happiness on the whole.

¶ Now, if an author affirms that the greatest possible sum of good could not be without that degree of evil, we observe then they admit that there is a necessary and fatal connection between the one and the other. If, however, they do not adopt this system of a fatal necessity, if they admit these moral attributes which we conceive as real perfections, then we have no reason to believe that evil is necessarily connected with good, nor is it necessary to reduce all his moral /$_{5.165}$ attributes to one class. Perfect virtue in man consists not in a desire to promote the happiness of the universe without any regard to truth, any love of virtue, or dislike of vice. Now, we form our notions of the divine by the human character. If, then, we ascribe these to a perfect human character, they must be attributed equally to the deity.

¶ Some again conceive that the attributing {of} different moral attributes to the deity is inconsistent with the simplicity and unity of nature which we ought to ascribe to an infinitely perfect being. But in this there is little force. Our conceptions of the supreme being are undoubtedly inadequate, but such as these notions are, they are the result of our faculties, and their imperfection must remain with us till our faculties are enlarged. We find too the sacred writers ascribing to deity not only perfect goodness and benevolence, but also of a being of perfect purity who cannot behold iniquity; a God of truth in whom is no iniquity.[130] These representations lead us to conceive of a moral character in the supreme being as we conceive it in a human being, but without the imperfections of humanity. Indeed, if this was not the case, and if those attributes to which we give names in man had not the same meanings when we {apply} /5.166 them to God, we would speak without understanding and could reason no ways without regard to them.

There have been others who, through a love of simplicity and to reduce the divine attributes to what they think consistent with the unity {of the} divine nature, have included all under divine rectitude and divine wisdom. But it does not appear that, by reducing them all under one word,[131] we make the notion of them any clearer. Before I leave this subject we may consider a little the origin of evil, a subject which has given rise to many theories, some of them absurd and others which tend to darken it rather than throw light upon it. All the evil we see in the world may be considered in two different lights. 1) As giving rise to objections by some who are unfriendly to religion against a good government of the world, and as a topic from which atheists draw arguments against a good administration of the world. 2) As a phenomenon giving occasion to the wit and ingenuity of

---

[130] Deuteronomy 32:4.
[131] This word is unclear in the manuscript.

philosophers and divines to exercise themselves in accounting for its origin and why {it is} permitted under a good government.

All evil has by some been reduced {to} three classes: 1) the evils of imperfection, 2) evil which they call natural evil, {and} 3) moral evil. /5.167 1) By evil of imperfection no more is meant than this, that in the creatures we observe there is not that degree of perfection which they might have had. That is, that a man might have been much more perfect, he might have been an angel, a brute might have {been} a rational being, and a plant might have been a brute animal. This, however, is not an evil, it is only a lesser degree of good. 2) There is *natural evil*, that is, that suffering and pain which we see endured by beings in the universe. 3) *Moral evil*, that is, the violation of the laws of virtue by moral and reasonable agents.

¶ When this evil and imperfection is offered as an objection against administration of things we ought to observe 1) that objections which have equal force against any possible system which can be conceived have no force at all and are therefore to be rejected. Now with regard to the evil of imperfection, it appears impossible that any system can be made free from this objection. It therefore can have no force. Suppose a world twice, nay, two thousand times more perfect than ours, still the objection remains, still they could have been more perfect.

¶ Again as to *natural evils*, if they are brought as an objection /5.168 {against} a good administration of things, it may be observed {2)} that they answer many good ends. We see that it is by natural evil that men are trained up to wisdom and prudence in their conduct. Whether men could have been trained to that degree of wisdom, prudence, and virtue without these means we are not competent judges and cannot possibly determine, but from the present construction of things we see they are necessary to our acquiring any prudence or wisdom, or patience or resignation. Besides that, as far as we perceive, they are necessary consequences of good general laws. I showed before that it was necessary for the constitution of rational creatures that they should be governed by general laws, for without these they never could perceive any means to the attainment of an end. And in a world governed by general laws, occasionally evils will happen. If gravitation is a good general law and necessary to the preservation of our world, yet, by this, ruinous houses may fall and crush the inhabitants. It may be observed 3) that we cannot determine what proportion of this evil bears to the sum of the enjoyment of God's creatures. We see only a small part and can't judge of the whole of the universe. If a man who was a stranger to Britain should land upon any corner of it and from that form an /5.169 opinion of the whole, how uncertain must his judgement be?

¶ Next, *moral evil*. This means the misconduct of {a} rational being and has also been objected to a good administration of all things by the atheists. In order to judge of this, let us consider what properly can be said to be God's doing and what is not to be considered in that light. If, on one hand, we suppose man not to be a free agent, then every event, good or bad, is to be considered as God's doing, and the actions of the worst men are equally imputable to deity as the rising or setting of the Sun. But if, on the other hand, we suppose God to have given man a certain sphere of powers, then the actions done in consequence of this are men's doing and not God's. There is no maxim more evident than this, that the action of one agent cannot be the action of another. If men then are voluntary agents, no argument can be drawn from them either for or against the supreme administration. What then can properly be said to be God's doing from which we may judge of his moral character? Here I observe 1) every creature is made by God and has its qualities from him, therefore these are to be accounted to him. 2) What are the necessary consequences of that constitution are also properly his doing and operation. This is no less agreeable to reason than to the sacred Scriptures. He made the Sun, Moon, and stars, he made a place called sea, he feeds the young lions, and hears the savage cry.[132] /5.170 And all of these he does either by means of some subordinate agent or by his own immediate power. 3) To him we must ascribe the lot in which we are placed by his providence, with all its advantages and disadvantages. By such a connection with fellow men we are

---

[132] See Psalm 104:21.

indeed liable to be sometimes hurt; this is a consequence of our situation. But such injurious actions are not to {be} attributed to God; he indeed gave the power, but they proceed from an abuse of that power. All moral evil, then, is not properly the doing of God but of men who, by abusing their power, are liable to misery and are then justly punished for their misconduct.

It appears, then, that the objection against a good administration of all things, brought either from the evils of imperfection, natural evil, or moral evil, have no force, and now I proceed to consider evil as affording room for exercising the wit and ingenuity of philosophers and divines to account for its origin, and why it was permitted to exist in the world. This I shall speak of in my next lecture. /5.171

Lecture 85th

That the system, called the Beltistan, was invented for the purpose of enabling us to comprehend more easily the moral attributes of deity, the origin of evil, and the end for which it was permitted to prevail, is not to be doubted. But we must always judge that these authors, who pretend to unravel all the mysteries of divine providence, and like Ariadne's thread[133] pretend to lead us through all the turning and winding of this great labyrinth, however much they deserve praise for their zeal, deserve little for their prudence or modesty. To comprehend the plan of the universe and all the laws by which it is governed exceeds the utmost extent of human genius. Presumptuous man that thou art! Wouldst thou vainly wish to be privy counsellor to the Almighty, thou who art unable to comprehend half of the wisdom displayed in the meanest works of God? Consider the puny worm that crawls beneath thy feet and licks the dust of the Earth, doest thou know the end for which it was made? The useful purposes it serves to thee and to other animals? Canst thou unfold its structure? No man can. Here the art of the skilful anatomist is baffled; the physiologist and the

---

[133] A reference to the thread which, according to Greek mythology, Ariadne gave to Theseus so that he could escape the Minotaur's labyrinth.

philosopher are put to shame. Shall we then vainly attempt to comprehend the whole, /5.172 who know not how one particle of matter adheres to another and how one body communicates motion {to} another? As soon may a mite comprehend the structure of an orrery or unfold a system of legislature, as we the structure and plan of the universe. We see indeed in everything around us, in the curious structure of all of our bodies and minds, means excellently adapted to certain ends. We see a profusion of wisdom and power displayed, but all that falls under our view is only an inconsiderable part of the whole. A man who should read a few pages of the *Iliad* of Homer would have good reason to conclude that he was a very great poet, but from such a small specimen no man that was not a fool would pretend to describe the plan of the whole or the manner in which it was conducted.

¶ In the like manner, from the little we know of the works of God, we have good reason to ascribe to him goodness, wisdom, and power, but there is neither wisdom nor modesty in ourselves when from the little we see we think to describe the plan of the whole. In this respect, the Beltistan theory and all others formed to explain the ends of phenomena we see in the universe may be compared to the various theories {of} the /5.173 Earth which we have had by different authors. Many attempts have been made to explain the present appearance of things, of mountains, valleys, minerals, the different strata and layers of earths, those extraneous bodies, animal and vegetable, found at great depths in the Earth, and so on. Many ingenious authors have exercised their wit to invent a hypothesis to solve all these appearances. Accordingly, we find some attributing all to the universal deluge,[134] in which everything was displaced, torn up and tossed about, and hence that mixture of marine bodies on the tops of mountains etc. which is to be found. Others again think the Mosaic deluge insufficient for this purpose and ascribe mountains and all these phenomena to the eruptions of earthquakes and volcanoes. Some again are of {the} opinion that the whole Earth was originally covered

---

[134] See Genesis 6–7.

with sea, and, as some places gradually wore away, then others were left higher and became mountains. Others account for them by a gradual decrease of the waters, by which more and more ground was gradually left dry. Such are some of the conjectures about these appearances, and what do they amount to? They are only the dreams of speculative men. Hence it is that every new theorist easily confutes the system of his predecessor and erects one equally flimsy in its stead, which falls also /5.174 before them that come after him.

¶ Now if this is the case in this instance, how can we expect to discover the plan of the universe, of which we know so little and make so small a part? Hypotheses indeed of any kind, as I have often mentioned to you, brought to explain the appearances of things, are only the whims of a fanciful imagination, and have always {a} higher probability of being found false and futile than {true}.[135] As well may a child understand the various beauties or defects of the British constitution, or settle the balance of power in Europe, as we comprehend the plan of the great empire of God. In a word, so weak and contracted {is} our understanding that, even in a human production, we meet with objections which we cannot answer and difficulties which we are unable to resolve. In the measure of nature's works, we are presented with difficulties which the short line of our understanding cannot sound. What presumption, then, is it to attempt to discover the end for which the universe was formed and all the different parts made subservient to the whole. In what we see, no doubt, we perceive manifest indications of wisdom and power and goodness, from whence we may conclude that these attributes belong to the author of all, but how ridiculous to think of comprehending the ends of the whole when we cannot /5.175 comprehend the end of one of the meanest creatures.

---

[135] By 'hypothesis' Reid does not mean a falsifiable scientific explanation, based on observations and subject to empirical investigation. Rather, he means 'conjectures in philosophical matters... founded on slight probabilities'. *Intellectual Powers*, 48. See also Newton, *Philosophiae Naturalis Principia Mathematica* [*The Mathematical Principles of Natural Philosophy*], General Scholium.

¶ I observed before that one, from reading a few pages of the *Iliad*, might have room to admit the abilities of the poet, but surely he who presumed from that with regard to the plan of the whole would justly be stigmatized as a fool. And if we cannot comprehend the works of men, how shall we pretend to comprehend the works of God? In what we see there are proofs of wisdom and power, but all is far above our comprehension. He who takes it for granted that he is equal to the arduous task of unfolding the laws of the universe will infallibly make blundering work of it, and, instead of solving objections by his theory, he will rather create more, and indeed we find that the objections of unreligious men are commonly made to these theories, which are not formed from a just observation of nature, but are the creatures of fancy and therefore more easily demolished.

Thus have I offered what I had to say with regard to the attributes of the supreme being and shall only make one observation upon the whole; and that is, that as the generality of men are little fitted for reasoning on subjects of this kind, as very strange perversions of sentiment concerning the truths of natural religion have prevailed among /5.176 the heathens. Though from what we have now seen, all things appear to be under one government and subject to the same laws, yet was the opinion of a plurality universal among them. The immensity, eternity, and unlimited perfection of the supreme being are necessarily connected with his necessary existence, yet the deities of heathens were all conceived to have had a beginning, to have each his different department assigned him, and to be limited with the follies[136] and even vices of humanity. Such were their gross conceptions of the Gods, nor was all the philosophy of the polished Greeks and Romans able to root them out. We must observe at the same time that {there} was one nation, I mean the Jews, who had more rational notions of the supreme being and of his attributes, notions perfectly agreeable to the dictates of reason as we have explained them. Now we can hardly suppose that a nation, barbarous as the

---

[136] This word is unclear in the manuscript.

Jews were, should have their reasoning powers more refined on this subject than their neighbours, without a revelation from the father of lights.[137] This, then, may teach us of how /5.177 great importance it is for {us} to attain proper notions of the deity and his attributes, since so many of mankind have wandered so far from the truth and so contrary to what reason would dictate to them.

I now proceed to consider the works of God, which is the last branch of this division of our course. These have commonly, by writers, been referred to *two* heads. 1) creation of things, and 2) his subsequent government of them.

1) With regard to *creation*, that is, the giving existence to what had no existence before, we do not find this to have been the opinion of the heathen philosophers. We do not find that they conceived there was any such power as the giving existence to what had no existence before. They conceived that as there must be an eternal contriver and artificer of the universe, so there must be an eternal matter, necessarily existing, of which all things were made. The Platonists and Pythagoreans are allowed to have formed the justest and most rational conceptions of the deity. Yet we find that all of these sects maintain these {three} eternal first principles: 1) an eternal cause the maker of all things, 2) an eternal matter of which all things were /5.178 made, 3) an eternal idea or model according to which all things were made.[138] What seems to have led them to this error is that creation is a work totally dissimilar to anything which is within the compass of human power. The supreme being has given us the power of compounding and decompounding what already exists, but in us there is no vestige of the power of creation. We in no instance can give being to what had it not before. All the works of human power extend neither to creation nor annihilation, and their operation being so far beyond our own power, we are unwilling, therefore, to allow it even to

---

[137] See note 1.
[138] Reid may here be drawing on Ralph Cudworth's 1678 work, *True Intellectual System of the Universe*, Volume I, which depicts Pythagoras and Plato as proto-Christians. For Pythagoras especially, cf. Diogenes Laertius, *Lives of Eminent Philosophers*, VIII.i.25–29.

the deity. But this is weak reasoning, and if we duly exert our powers of reason, we will see it more probable that finite things must have their existence from the hand of the first cause of all. Indeed, from the properties of matter it appears impossible that it should be eternal or necessarily existing. What exists necessarily must exist everywhere and in all points of duration, but omnipresence and ubiquity belong not to matter. From its nature it is limited to one place, it cannot then be necessarily existing. And if we acknowledge that the supreme being gave existence to beings of a superior nature, even to rational /5.179 beings, it appears silly to attribute necessary existence to the meanest of all the creatures of God.

March 2nd, 1780

/6.1

Lecture 86th, March 3rd, 1780

When speaking of creation we may take notice of a theory which has been advanced by some theologians, with a good design no doubt, but which seems to draw dangerous consequences along with it. It is this, that the preservation of God's creatures is a perpetual and constant recreation, and that therefore from the very nature of created beings they must every moment fall into annihilation if not thus reproduced, as it were.[139] This is no doubt intended to represent more forcibly to us our entire dependence on the supreme being, but it must not be taken in too strict a sense, otherwise our personal identity would be lost, for if what exists this moment is annihilated, then what exists the next moment is not the same with that which is now {no} more, nor can it be accountable for *its* actions. Indeed, it is impossible that we can form a notion of what is necessary to continue creatures in existence. We know not what it is, as we know not the power which gave it being, but we cannot, I apprehend, reasonably conclude that it is the same with creation. A very

---

[139] See Francisco Suarez (1548–1617), *On Creation, Conservation, and Concurrence*.

ingenious /₆.₂ philosopher, as well as pious divine, gives us his sentiment on this subject. I mean Dr Isaac Watts.[140] You will find them in his *Philosophical Essays*, Essay 11th §4, to which I refer you. What he says there is perfectly agreeable to reason and good sense, and I shall only add that this notion of preservation being a continual creation is destructive of all personal identity and, of consequence, of the accountableness of human actions.

¶ I shall now consider the government of the supreme being which has been distinguished into two heads. Viz., 1) his natural government and {2)} his moral. On this subject we ought to speak with reserve and modesty, and draw conclusions only from what our faculties are fully able to reach, without pretending to form any connection with regard to the plan of the whole.

¶ According to the theory of Leibniz, the world was so made as to need no operation of the deity for its government; that everything had such power implanted in it at its first construction, that produced all its subsequent changes without any interposition of the supreme being, and therefore, he concludes, every interposition of the deity as a miracle.[141] This is a theory which has had many admirers, /₆.₃ but seems to have no foundation in truth or in reason. It may be observed that he differs from the common meaning affixed to the word *miracle* when he considers every interposition of deity as a miracle. It is not every interposition of deity that constitutes an action *miraculeux*, it is only action done in express violation of the usual fixed laws of nature, in order to attest a divine {omnipotence}.[142] Thus the raising from the dead a man who has been four days in his grave and whose body is become putrid by a simple word, this is a miracle as it is contrary to the laws of nature. But that *every* interposition of deity is a miracle cannot be admitted. We see, indeed, that this world is governed by general laws, but do

---

[140] Isaac Watts (1674–1748), often called 'The Father of English Hymnody'.
[141] See *A Collection of Papers, Which passed between the late Learned Mr Leibnitz, and Dr Clarke, in the Years 1715 and 1716*; especially 'Mr Leibnitz's Second Paper', §12.
[142] Baird wrote 'omniscience'.

not laws require an agent to execute them and to produce effects according to them? Laws are not agents, they are only rules according to which an agent operates; the laws of nature, then, suppose an agent to operate according to these laws, but whether the supreme being executes these immediately or by subordinate beings is beyond the reach of our comprehension.

¶ Besides, it cannot even be shown that this system of Leibniz is even possible. He endeavours to illustrate it from the structure of a clock. If, says he, a workman should make a block that perpetually goes on of itself without needing any further interposition, any mending or reparation, /6.4 this surely would be a more perfect machine than one that required the hand of the artificer to be continually employed in regulating its motions and preventing it from going wrong. Now, all the works of God are surely perfect. The universe, then, being the work of God, must be perfect and therefore need no future interposition of his power to direct or support it.[143] This similitude Leibniz relied on as very conclusive, but if examined carefully it will be found to lack much.

¶ The workman indeed fabricated the materials and arranged them in a certain order, but was he the author of these materials, or did he give them powers by which the work is carried on? Did he give to matter that cohesive power between the particles which is necessary to the clock's being formed? Did he give it that tendency to descend or gravitate to the Earth, by which the motion is caused, and which, if it ceases, the machine immediately must stop? All that he does is only to apply certain powers. Between these two there is no similitude, neither is there a greater beauty in this system than if we believed that all things are governed by a supreme being or by some subordinate /6.5 agent employed by him. Why should it be thought unworthy of deity to preserve by his care these creatures he formed at first by his power? Indeed, it is neither unsuitable to the

---

[143] *A Collection of Papers, Which passed between the late Learned Mr Leibnitz, and Dr Clarke, in the Years 1715 and 1716*; especially 'Mr Leibnitz's First Paper', §4.

principles of philosophy or the sacred Scriptures, which everywhere represent him as the kind preserver of all his works.

¶ With regard to the rules of the natural government of God, it appears 1) he governs all things by general laws, as far as we can judge. We may, however, conceive the supreme being to have produced all things occasionally, but this is inconsistent with his moral government of his rational creatures. For were not all carried on by fast fixed laws, *they* never could acquire any prudence, wisdom, or foresight. It is by general laws, therefore, that the supreme being governs, and in so doing his wisdom and goodness are conspicuous. These are called *physical laws* in order to distinguish them from what are called *moral laws*, by which is meant, those rules which ought to regulate the conduct of rational and moral agents. The former were appointed by the Almighty himself, and are executed by him. They are therefore seldom violated, and as I just now observed, were not the world governed by this, men could never acquire any prudence in their conduct through life, though he could as easily have done it /$_{6.6}$ by particular volitions.

¶ 2) These general laws which interest us most are made obvious to the experience of all, and are soon perceived by all: thus, that fire will burn them, that water will drown, that bodies all gravitate. Such then as are necessary to be known are obvious to all, but there are others again more hidden which are left to the sagacity of man to investigate by his reason and industry. These, which are commonly called laws of nature and which are the first principles of natural philosophy, no more properly deserve that title than many of those laws which are obvious to the vulgar, only the one is more hidden than the other. Those which are necessary to all are made obvious to all, but those again which are less necessary, though of use to enlarge human knowledge and human powers, are left to be discovered by our own sagacity and labours. These indeed have already gone great lengths; by these we have discovered why planets roll in their orbits and the comets are retained in their circles, and how far human genius may carry us no man {can} say. There is still ample room for the exercise of our talents from the beginning to the end /$_{6.7}$ of our existence, and every new discovery we make tends to widen the sphere of our power and activity. For it is by means of our knowledge of the laws of nature that we can bring about any end by using the properest means. It is by a knowledge of these laws relating to the fruits of the Earth that the husbandman knows when to plow and when to sow. By a knowledge of these the navigator boldly traverses the wide ocean, and, in a word, it is by a knowledge of these that every human art is carried on. The more, then, this knowledge is increased, the more will our power in these be enlarged. In the investigation of these, our talents find a manly and rational exercise, and our labour seldom fails to be rewarded by the advantages that follow.

¶ 3) In the government of God, we see brutes and infants directed by other inferior principles which supply the want of reason; by instincts, appetites, and passions. Were not the child directed by instinct, it must inevitably perish. Of itself, it could never know that food was necessary to its preservation, far less that that food was contained in the breast of the mother and to be sucked out by its mouth. Yet in all this, it is directed by instinct. Nothing shows more evidently the wisdom and superintendence of a supreme being than such instincts. We are unable indeed to discern the proximate cause of these, but their effects we see, and find that they /$_{6.8}$ are admirably fitted for this purpose, for which they were intended. Likewise, we may observe that men are directed by many inferior principles which supply the room of reason and assist us in our progress in virtue and moral goodness. That men were intended to make progress in virtue is obvious, but the progress which is made by the greatest number is small and inconsiderable. Society, of consequence, could not subsist if men were not directed by other principles of actions to the same course to which virtue itself would naturally lead them. We see thus that society may subsist not only among those which are virtuous, but even among those that are really bad, till they are corrupted in such a degree as we have few examples of in the history of the world. Men by means of their social passions, of natural affection, etc., though possessed of very little virtue, are yet prompted to that very tract which virtue, if followed, would point out.

¶ It is the duty of the parent to rear, educate, and protect their children, but were this done only from principles of virtue, I am afraid that, in the greatest number, we would find it neglected. To prevent this, we find implanted in every breast a natural affection, an inborn *storge*,[144] as the Greeks called it, which operates on all and produces these effects which virtue ought to produce. So, /6.9 in like manner, the social affections of gratitude, compassion, natural affection to relations, and the love of our country operate equally on the good and the bad and supply the defects of virtue. By these is society supported, and that whether the members of it are good or bad, virtuous or vicious, wise or foolish.

¶ We see too principles implanted in the mind which tend to our improvement, in acts, knowledge, and good habits. Of these we may take notice of that principle of *activity* in children which is instinctive and necessary for their acquiring habits and for their improvement in knowledge. Even the perfect use of our senses is to be acquired by habit and practice. Children thus, by their desire of seeing every object with their eyes and handling with their hands, improve them greatly, and before they come to years of understanding have skill in[145] perception. I took an opportunity formerly also to show that even our *perceptions* were mostly acquired, and we see that nature has fitted us with instincts fitted to acquire them.[146]

¶ *Credulity* too is evidently implanted in our nature for our improvement. It is a natural law of our nature, that, even before we ourselves know the importance of knowledge, we listen with patience to what is told us and swallow it down with security, /6.10 by which means we acquire knowledge before we could learn it by our own discoveries. The *imitative* principle in man was also intended too for progress in improvement. By this he is led to imitate what is done by others, and thus easily acquires habits of great importance to him. We know from experiments that have been made that it

---

[144] 'Familial love'.
[145] The two preceding words are unclear in the manuscript.
[146] Reid is referring to his previous lectures on pneumatology. See *Intellectual Powers*, 235–47.

is even possible to teach deaf people to speak and pronounce articulate sounds, though they have it not in their power to imitate them as others, by instructing them how to form the particular organs for the various sounds. This is no doubt a great art and requires great labour and attention. But the same difficulty would be found in everyone who learns articulate sounds and language if it were not from the power of imitating these sounds by others.

¶ We may observe also that these principles given for self defence, called *malevolent passions*, though intended to promote our improvement and happiness in society, yet from their very nature have checks to prevent their excess. They are attended with an uneasy feeling which is an admonition to indulge them no farther than what is necessary for our own good and the good of those to whom we wish well. /6.11

¶ We see by the constitution of things too that industry is encouraged as necessary to our subsistence. It is undoubtedly intended that man should earn his bread by the sweat of his brows,[147] that he should provide the necessities of life by his labour, and for this we see him well adapted. And while we are prompted to action by the infamy, poverty, and contempt which follows indolence and sloth, we are warned at the same {time} by a languor and lassitude which attends too violent exertions of our powers to take alternate repose. From all these observations, we may remark that there are some obvious general rules of God's natural government which are admirably fitted to the condition of man in this world.

Having said these things with regard to the *natural government*, I come now to the *moral government* of God. In the former he acts as a man does with his property. He disposes it in every particular as his wisdom and skill direct him. Therefore, whatever is done in the natural world may properly be ascribed to God as his doing, such are the motion of the Moon, of all the planets, the ebbing and flowing of the seas, and so on. These all are the operations of the deity, and the general rules according /6.12 to which they are produced are called *physical laws*. They are the rules to

---

[147] See Genesis 3:19.

which he adheres and which of consequence are never transgressed. But in his *moral government* he acts like a legislator who proposes rules of conduct to his subject and, as they obey or disobey them, so may they expect his favour or displeasure.

As to the inanimate creation, it is merely passive and can be subject to no laws. The brute animals, again, though they possess a small degree of power and will, yet are they incapable of duty or of following any general rules of conduct. Their actions are directed by blind impulse without being capable of distinguishing between right and wrong. The impulse which is strongest for the present always prevails, and as this is the constitution of their nature; they cannot be blamed. They may be noxious, but they cannot be criminal. They may be objects of like and dislike, not of approbation and disapprobation. But with man it is otherwise. Indeed, instinct and the blind impulse of our appetites and passions, as in the brute tribes, influence our actions in our infancy. By them we are governed, and therefore children and infants are not considered as /6.13 capable of obeying laws. They are not thought accountable for their actions. They cannot commit a crime. They are the subjects of discipline, not of blame or disapprobation. But when they come to years of understanding, they act from principles superior to appetites and passions. They are capable of considering the consequences of actions. They can propose ends to themselves and prosecute them by proper means. They can reflect on a course of life in others and observe the ends they pursue and consider the consequences of these pursuits. We can choose ends that are best on the whole. We blame ourselves when swayed by improper motives, {when} we are led to do what we will repent of and wish undone. On the other {hand}, nothing can give a virtuous man more sincere or lasting joy than a consciousness of having preserved his rectitude unsullied in opposition to every powerful inducement to abandon it. The consciousness of a wise and worthy conduct will always inspire with strength of mind. It encourages the heart of a man and makes his countenance to shine; and the more costly the sacrifice he has offered at the shrine of virtue, he will find his triumph the greater.

¶ It appears then, from this observation, that there is one kind of action which we consider /6.14 as deserving applause, another as unworthy. Nor is this distinction grounded on abstract disquisition, but flows from the nature of things. There is a right and a wrong, something worthy and deserving approbation, though there was no human being to perceive it, and other things foolish, base, and mean. This is the immediate dictate of our natural faculties, as well as the distinction between true and false. If we form an idea of a man capable of approving perfidy, injustice, rapine, theft, and so on, and of disapproving of what was anyhow good or excellent, we would soon determine that his judgement was as erroneous as if he should think twice three equal to fifteen. Now, the supreme being, infinitely wise and intelligent, discerns human conduct in its truest colours and discerns whatever in it is worthy of blame with all its aggravations and alleviations. His perfect moral character leads him to approve of what is truly worthy and to disapprove of what is improper. We must therefore conclude that God, in his government of rational creatures, has endowed them with the qualities of moral and rational agents.

¶ Here we may observe that man is evidently placed here in a state of trial and probation, where he has access to improve in art and knowledge, in virtue and a good /6.15 habits. The present state is intended as a school of discipline, and what we are to expect here is that proper means and inducements be set before us for our improvement, that proper incitements are held up to make us avoid vice and pursue virtue as alone possessing real dignity and alone worthy of our approbation. Of this a little reflection will satisfy us. Here our condition is such that the good things we enjoy and every evil which we suffer are in some measure put in our power. By this I mean that a man by his foolish conduct may deprive himself of every enjoyment of life by his folly and imprudence. He may bring on himself cruel and tormenting pains that may shorten his days. He may reduce himself to poverty, disgrace, and contempt, and make himself the object of public hatred and of public vengeance. In the same manner, all our good things are in some degree in our power, as by our wrong conduct we may deprive ourselves of them. This, then, surely is a very strong inducement to look to our conduct as our enjoyments depend on it.

¶ Further, our evils depend much on our conduct. I don't say *all* our evils. For the best men are designed to be trained to virtue and happiness /6.16 by suffering and trials, but of the common calamities of life, the greatest part are brought on by ourselves. For if we may trust to those who have made this subject their study, we will find that the greatest number of diseases are owing to our intemperance or to some wrong regimen, but health is generally enjoyed if we use temperance, proper exercise, and proper regimen. We see too that industry is commonly able to furnish the necessaries and the conveniences of life, and if, {by} providence, they are ever reduced to want and indigence, they are entitled to our compassion and will always find it, but poverty and all our ills are generally the consequence of idleness, intemperance, and bad economy. We see also how much our reputation depends on our conduct. If our conduct is worthy and irreproachable, whatever our station, we will meet with respect from those who know us. High rank may display virtue in brighter colours and with greater splendour, but in the meanest office will always be amicable and beloved. Thus we see that we are placed in a state of discipline, so that our good enjoyments and even our conduct depend /6.17 on our conduct.

¶ But we may observe further that man is placed in such a condition that his conduct also has great influence on his fellow creatures. So has the divine wisdom seen fit to connect men in society, as he intended them to live in society and mutually to assist each other. This circumstance interests us not only in our own conduct, but in that of others; we are concerned that they should behave properly. Men, therefore, in such a situation have strong inducements to virtue. Indeed, we may observe at the same time that the man who seriously intends to pursue a uniformly upright and worthy behaviour will find himself in a state of trial fitted for the exercise and improvement of his virtue. And such is our constitution that virtue is strengthened by exercise as well as our other habits are.

¶ Such then {are} the consequences of good or bad conduct. Great evils follow sloth, indolence, folly, etc., and that though not immediately, yet sometimes when the reason which caused it is forgotten, will it come. This is such an administration as might have been expected from the moral governor of the world. The encouragements of virtue and the discouragements of vice are as strong as we can suppose in the present state. We are /6.18 excited to virtue by the tendency it has to create power, esteem, and all the good enjoyments of life, from the inward satisfaction we feel in doing our duty, and the well-founded hopes of a future state. And as to the pains which even the virtuous sometimes are doomed to suffer, this is proper to a school of discipline, and it is by these they are improved in every duty, so that {they} have reason to say with the ancient servant of God *'It is good for me that I have been afflicted'*.[148] And all their sorrows here will be abundantly compensated hereafter. Thus it appears that in the moral government of the supreme being, as well as in his natural government, he acts in a manner suitable to the perfections which, by reason, we were enabled to attribute to him.

¶ We may observe, at the same time, that to form just notions of the deity by mere force of our natural powers requires a greater impartiality and abstract research than is to be met with in the bulk of men. Accustomed only to the objects of sense, though they may discover in the works of God evident marks of his being, power, and wisdom, yet rude men, if left to trace /6.19 out his attributes and perfections, will form conceptions gross and absurd, and far removed from the account I have now given you.

Lecture 87th

Hence we find that the doctrines of natural religion have been improved by the speculations of theologians and assisted by the representations of deity given in the sacred Scriptures. For nowhere do we find such a complete system of natural religion as in the Christian writers. The being of God is indeed so evident from his works and the conduct of his providence that no nation has been found so barbarous as to have *no* notion of a deity at all. Yet it is to be expected that

---

[148] Psalm 119:71.

rude men, if left to trace out his attributes by the mere force of their reason, would form very gross conceptions, widely different from the representations of Scripture and the dictates of sound reason. Mr Hume, in his treatise on natural religion, has endeavoured to show that men, especially in the early stages of society, with regard to their notions of religion, are prone to idolatry and to the conceiving {of} a plurality of deities.[149] And this, no doubt, is agreeable to fact, as far as we have access to /6.20 know, among every nation except the Jewish. Among all others the grossest notions have prevailed. Familiarized with objects of sense, they formed ideas of deities with a human figure and with human passions. They conceived {of} them as limited in their nature and by no means everywhere present in the universe. Each had his different department: one presided over the sea, another the earth, another the air, and so on. They had also deities that belonged to every family, their *Lares*,[150] these every one worshipped by different rites. They imagined the different heavenly bodies too had a different deity, and to such extravagance was this spirit of polytheism carried among the Greeks and Romans that they had deities to every wood and grove, and spring and river.

¶ But in all these notions there was nothing rational or that tended to improve the human mind. And it is highly probable that the enlightened writers on morality among the Greeks and Romans left out religion entirely from their system for this reason, that the notions of deity publicly established were so absurd and so little suited to promote the practice of virtue that they could expect no assistance from the principles of religion in establishing the /6.21 principles of morality. Of all their four cardinal virtues — prudence, temperance, justice, and fortitude — none have any relation to religion or point out the deity as an incitement to the practice of them. Nay, in some of these ancient systems we find them maintaining that the deities interposed not in the affairs of men, and that, however powerful, yet they had no hand

---

[149] Hume, *Natural History of Religion*, I–VIII.
[150] Ancient Roman guardian deities which protected certain locations or events.

either in the framing or the government of the world. As this is the case, therefore,[151] that without the aids of revelation our conceptions of deity are low, it appears a strange phenomenon that the Jews, who were not more polished and civilized than others, but rather a barbarous people, should have such ideas of deity, his attributes, and government as perfectly agreeable to what our reason dictates. They were not polytheists. They believed in one God, the maker of the world, who was eternal, omnipresent, omniscient, who had regard to virtue and a dislike at vice. Now, such refined notions of deity in a nation so rude as the Jews is hardly to be expected, unless by a divine revelation.

¶ It is even probable that the notions of a polytheism at first arose from a revelation, but were afterwards corrupted by the heathen nations. Idolatry was introduced, and the veneration paid to men of worth and distinguished /6.22 virtue was converted into the worship of them as a divinity. Fables, formed at first as pieces of moral instruction, by degrees gained credit and were received as real stories. The just sentiments of the deity were thus lost by the corruptions of human reason, the craft of the priest, or the cunning of the politician. We have seen that reason properly employed will point out the duties of natural religion, yet is it necessary to complete our notions of them that we be enlightened by a divine revelation.

Having thus laid before you the evidence we have for the existence and attributes of the supreme being, I cannot leave this subject without observing that it is of great importance, not only to the happiness of every individual, but to society in general, to have just and rational notions of the deity, his attributes, perfections, and providence deeply impressed on the mind. For,

1) There is no truth within the whole compass of human knowledge from which the mind can derive such comfort. Is it agreeable to a child to know that he has a careful father whose pleasure is to rear, educate, support, and protect it? The supreme being is the father of the /6.23 universe; the whole world is his care, and his reasonable creatures are his

---

[151] This word is unclear in the manuscript.

children, so we find him represented in the sacred writings and by an ancient heathen philosopher as quoted in one of the apostolical epistles.[152] We are his offspring and all nature is obedient to his command. His wisdom and power were employed in our creation, and still are in our preservation. He pities our weakness and infirmities as a father and a friend, and even to the wicked is he long suffering, patient, and ready to forgive. His ears are open to the cry of the young lions,[153] and much more to the humble and devout supplication of his rational creatures. In a word, all his administration is directed by perfect wisdom and with perfect justice. And though we are unable to comprehend the unbounded scheme of infinite goodness, yet of this we are sure, that neither envy, nor jealousy, nor any malignant passion can disturb his happiness or stain his perfections. At present, we cannot comprehend the plot of this great drama, and many scenes which show the skill and intelligence of the great poet may appear which we cannot account for, yet in this we may rest assured that at the conclusion, every difficulty will be resolved and every incident shine /6.24 forth as subservient to the design of the whole. That, whatever difficulties we may meet with in this {life} from the weakness of our faculties and the vast extent of the divine administration, yet a serious belief of the truths which our reason has pointed out cannot fail to fill every well-disposed mind with confidence and joy. The Sun is not more necessary to the beauty and harmony of the planetary system than the existence of the father of the universe to the comfort of every rational mind. Let the atheist rejoice in the conviction of owing his being to a fortuitous dance of atoms, and let him rest in the uncertain hope of a future world by the same capricious fate! Surely the theist has much more solid ground to rejoice; who considers himself as one of the offspring of God who loves him and protects him. For he who trusts in God need have no other fear.

---

[152] Although it is not an apostolic epistle, this may be a reference is to Paul's famous sermon on Mars Hill, recounted in Acts 17:22-34.
[153] See note 132.

'I fear God, and I have no other fears.'[154]

2) A firm belief of the existence of deity and of his providence is one of the strongest bonds of human society. By means of his social affections, we see that man was intended for society and for mutually benefitting each other. But there are some /6.25. men so wicked as to sacrifice all these to their lust of power or to some favourite passion. Now, the government of God provides some checks to prevent these from going such lengths as they otherwise would do. The contempt of good men {and} the civil laws are strong restraints upon criminals, but those other crimes of which the laws have no cognizance — which are above the law — against them the belief of deity and dread of a future judgement are powerful guards. But the belief of these are not only powerful restraints upon the *worst*, but unites the *best* more firmly in society. The man who considers all as the children of the same father will find every tie of humanity, justice, and benevolence strengthened by the consideration. And what more powerful incentive to promote the good and happiness of our fellow creatures than this, that in some degree we cooperate with the Almighty and merit his approbation, and that however our designs may be misconstrued by men, yet they will not be misrepresented by the great judge of all the Earth.[155] The atheist may complain that religion is the contrivance of the statesman, to strengthen his laws and give stability to government, {but} by this he acknowledges that it is one of the strongest bonds of society which could be contrived.

3) Just and rational sentiments of the deity are of high importance, as they guard us against superstition. /6.26 Two causes may be assigned for all the superstition which has appeared in the world. 1) Gross ignorance in the people, which has emboldened cunning men to perform tricks among them. The success of this is always in proportion to the ignorance among the people to whom it is first divulged, but it has no connection with religion. 2) False notions of

---

[154] Quoted in French and slightly adapted from *Athalié* [*Athaliah*] by Jean Racine (1639–1699).
[155] See Genesis 18:5 and Psalm 82:8.

deity, which have led men to believe that he is pleased with penances and burying themselves in cloisters, and sequestrating themselves from active life. Such notions, however, can have no tendency to make men better, and the only remedy against these is the acquiring {of} those notions which reason dictates to us and which revelation confirms.

Lastly, they have a powerful influence in promoting and strengthening virtue. True religion and virtue are natural allies and friends and cannot be disjoined without prejudice to both. Without a sense of religion, virtue would of itself be too weak to restrain the vices of men, and, {likewise,} religion without virtue would be mere hypocrisy or black superstition. The last has been allowed by all, but that virtue without religion is too weak to restrain the vices of men has been called in question by some, though, I apprehend, on insufficient grounds. Lord Shaftesbury /6.27 seems to be of {the} opinion that inculcating the rewards and punishments of another life as an inducement to virtue tends to promote a mercenary disposition, that the real and intrinsic excellence of virtue is the only inducement that ought to be proposed.[156] In this, however, his lordship is not consistent, for we find in his essay on virtue and morals[157] that he takes up a contrary opinion and acknowledges that rational sentiment of the deity will have a tendency to promote the practice of virtue in the world. Nor indeed can there be a truth more evident. Will not he who believes the existence of deity, and that he delights in virtue and abhors the worker of iniquity, endeavour to fulfil his pleasure and render himself agreeable to him by practising what he approves and avoiding what is displeasing to him? The example of the supreme being he sets before him as his pattern after which to copy, and when the allurements of vice are strong, the consideration of futurity are called in to balance them. And if, on the other

---

[156] See, e.g., Anthony Ashley Cooper, 3rd Earl of Shaftesbury (1671–1713), *Characteristics of Men, Manners, Opinions, Times*, Vol. II, 'The Moralists', II.iii.

[157] Properly, the 'Inquiry Concerning Virtue or Merit'. This work was first published, possibly without Shaftesbury's permission, in 1699. The Inquiry was later reworked and became the first part of Volume II of the *Characteristics* in 1711.

hand, the incitements to virtue are weak, the prospects of another world can add sufficient force to them.

Since, then, right notions of deity are of such importance, both to the individual and to society, it becomes all of us to think of them seriously and candidly, and endeavour to be established in a firm belief of them. I shall conclude all by recommending to your attention a passage in the works of Cicero *De Legibus* [*On the Laws*], lib 2.0.4. where that enlightened philosopher hath expressed his sentiments on the subject with perspicuity and eloquence. /6.28

**Concluded
March 3rd 1780**

Appendix I
Published Material

From: ***Essays on the Active Powers of Man***

Essay IV: Of the Liberty of Moral Agents

Chapter V
Liberty consistent with Government

When it is said that liberty would make us absolutely ungovernable by God or man; to understand the strength of this conclusion, it is necessary to know distinctly what is meant by *government*. There are two kinds of government, very different in their nature. The one we may, for distinction's sake, call *mechanical* government, the other *moral*. The first is the government of beings which have no active power, but are merely passive and acted upon; the second, of intelligent and active beings.

An instance of mechanical government may be that of a master or commander of a ship at sea. Supposing her skilfully built and furnished with everything proper for the destined voyage, to govern her properly for this purpose requires much art and attention. And, as every art has its rules or laws, so has this. But by whom are those laws to be obeyed, or those rules observed? Not by the ship, surely, for she is an inactive being, but by the governor. A sailor may say that she does not obey the rudder; and he has a distinct meaning when he says so, and is perfectly understood. But he means not obedience in the proper, but in a metaphorical sense. For, in the proper sense, the ship can no more obey the rudder than she can give a command. Every motion, both of the ship and rudder, is exactly proportioned to the force impressed, and in the direction of that force. The ship never disobeys the laws of motion, even in the metaphorical sense; and they are the only laws she can be subject to.

The sailor, perhaps, curses her for not obeying the rudder; but this is not the voice of reason, but of passion, like that of the losing gamester when he curses the dice. The ship is as innocent as the dice.

Whatever may happen during the voyage, whatever may be its issue, the ship, in the eye of reason, is neither an object of approbation nor of blame because she does not act, but is acted upon. If the material, in any part, be faulty; who put it to that use? If the form; who made it? If the rules of navigation were not observed; who transgressed them? If a storm occasioned any disaster, it was no more in the power of the ship than of the master.

Another instance to illustrate the nature of mechanical government may be that of the man who makes and exhibits a puppet show. The puppets, in all their diverting gesticulations, do not move, but are moved by an impulse secretly conveyed, which they cannot resist. If they do not play their parts properly, the fault is only in the maker or manager of the machinery. Too much or too little force was applied, or it was wrong{ly} directed. No reasonable man imputes either praise or blame to the puppets, but solely to their maker or their governor.

If we suppose for a moment, the puppets to be endowed with understanding and will, but without any degree of active power, this will make no change in the nature of their government. For understanding and will, without some degree of active power, can produce no effect. They might, upon this supposition, be called *intelligent machines*; but they would be machines still, as much subject to the laws of motion as inanimate matter, and therefore incapable of any other than mechanical government.

Let us next consider the nature of moral government. This is the government of persons who have reason and active power, and have laws prescribed to them for their conduct, by a legislator. Their obedience is obedience in the proper sense; it must therefore be their own act and deed, and consequently they must have power to obey or to disobey. To prescribe laws to them which they have not power to obey, or to require a service beyond their power, would be tyranny and injustice in the highest degree.

When the laws are equitable and prescribed by just authority, they produce moral obligation in those that are subject to them, and disobedience is a crime deserving punishment. But if the obedience be impossible, if the transgression be necessary, it is self-evident that there can be no moral obligation to what is impossible, that there can be no crime in yielding to necessity, and that there can be no justice in punishing a person for what it was not in his power to avoid. There are first principles in morals, and, to every unprejudiced mind, as self-evident as the axioms of mathematics. The whole science of morals must stand or fall with them.

Having thus explained the nature both of mechanical and of moral government, the only kinds of government I am able to conceive, it is easy to see how far liberty or necessity agrees with either.

On the one hand, I acknowledge that necessity agrees perfectly with mechanical government. This kind of government is most perfect when the governor is the sole agent; everything done is the doing of the governor only. The praise of everything well done is his solely; and his is the blame if there be anything ill done, because he is the sole agent.

It is true that, in common language, praise or dispraise is often metaphorically given to the work; but, in propriety, it belongs solely to the author. Every workman understands this perfectly, and takes to himself very justly the praise or dispraise of his own work.

On the other hand, it is no less evident that, on the supposition of necessity in the governed, there can be no moral government. There can be neither wisdom nor equity in prescribing laws that cannot be obeyed. There can be no moral obligation upon beings that have no active power. There can be no crime in not doing what it was impossible to do; nor can there be justice in punishing such omission.

If we apply these theoretical principles to the kinds of government which do actually exist, whether human or divine, we shall find that, among men, even mechanical government is imperfect.

Men do not make the matter they work upon. Its various kinds, and the qualities belonging to each kind, are the work of God. The laws of nature, to which it is subject, are the work of God. The motions of the atmosphere and of the sea, the heat and cold of the air, the rain, and wind, which are useful instruments in most human operations, are not in our power. So that, in all the mechanical productions of men, the work is more to be ascribed to God than to man.

Civil government among men is a species of moral government, but imperfect, as its lawgivers and its judges are. Human laws may be unwise or unjust; human judges may be partial or unskilful. But, in all equitable civil governments, the maxims of moral government above mentioned are acknowledged as rules which ought never to be violated. Indeed, the rules of justice are so evident to all men that the most tyrannical governments profess to be guided by them and endeavour to palliate what is contrary to them by the plea of necessity.

That a man cannot be under an obligation to what is impossible; that he cannot be criminal in yielding to necessity, nor justly punished for what he could not avoid, are maxims admitted, in all criminal courts, as fundamental rules of justice.

In opposition to this, it has been said by some of the most able defenders of necessity that human laws require no more to constitute a crime, but that it be voluntary; whence it is inferred that the criminality consists in the determination of the will, whether that determination be free or necessary. This, I think indeed, is the only possible plea by which criminality can be made consistent with necessity, and therefore it deserves to be considered.

I acknowledge that a crime must be voluntary; for, if it be not voluntary, it is no deed of the man, nor can be justly imputed to him; but it is no less necessary that the criminal have moral liberty. In men that are adult and of a sound mind, this liberty is presumed. But in every case where it cannot be presumed, no criminality is imputed, even to voluntary actions.

This is evident from the following instances: *First*, the actions of brutes appear to be voluntary; yet they are never conceived to be criminal, though they may be noxious.

Secondly, children in nonage act voluntarily, but they are not chargeable with crimes. *Thirdly,* madmen have both understanding and will, but they have not moral liberty, and therefore are not chargeable with crimes. *Fourthly,* even in men that are adult and of a sound mind, a motive that is thought irresistible by any ordinary degree of self-command, such as the rack or the dread of present death, either exculpates or very much alleviates a voluntary action, which, in other circumstances, would be highly criminal; whence it is evident that if the motive were absolutely irresistible, the exculpation would be complete. So far is it from being true in itself, or agreeable to the common sense of mankind, that the criminality of an action depends solely upon its being voluntary.

The government of brutes, so far as they are subject to man, is a species of mechanical government, or something very like to it, and has no resemblance to moral government. As inanimate matter is governed by our knowledge of the qualities which God has given to the various productions of nature, and our knowledge of the laws of nature which he has established; so brute-animals are governed by our knowledge of the natural instincts, appetites, affections, and passions, which God has given them. By a skilful application of these springs of their actions, they may be trained to many habits useful to man. After all, we find that, from causes unknown to us, not only some species, but some individuals of the same species, are more tractable than others.

Children under age are governed much in the same way as the most sagacious brutes. The opening of their intellectual and moral powers, which may be much aided by proper instruction and example, is that which makes them, by degrees, capable of moral government.

Reason teaches us to ascribe to the supreme being a government of the inanimate and inactive part of his creation, analogous to that mechanical government which men exercise, but infinitely more perfect. This, I think, is what we call God's *natural* government of the universe. In this part of the divine government, whatever is done is God's doing. He is the sole cause and the sole agent, whether he act immediately, or by instruments subordinate to him; and his will is always done. For instruments are not causes, they are not agents, though we sometimes improperly call them so.

It is therefore no less agreeable to reason than to the language of holy writ to impute to the deity whatever is done in the natural world. When we say of anything, that it is the work of nature, this is saying that it is the work of God, and can have no other meaning.

The natural world is a grand machine, contrived, made, and governed by the wisdom and power of the Almighty. And if there be, in this natural world, beings that have life, intelligence, and will, without any degree of active power, they can only be subject to the same kind of mechanical government. Their determinations, whether we call them good or ill, must be the actions of the supreme being, as much as the productions of the earth: for life, intelligence, and will, without active power, can do nothing, and therefore nothing can justly be imputed to it.

This grand machine of the natural world displays the power and wisdom of the artificer. But in it there can be no display of moral attributes which have a relation to moral conduct in his creatures, such as justice and equity in rewarding or punishing, the love of virtue, and abhorrence of wickedness. For, as everything in it is God's doing, there can be no vice to be punished or abhorred, no virtue in his creatures to be rewarded.

According to the system of necessity, the whole universe of creatures is this natural world; and of everything done in it, God is the sole agent. There can be no moral government, nor moral obligation. Laws, rewards, and punishments are only mechanical engines, and the will of the lawgiver is obeyed as much when his laws are transgressed as when they are observed. Such must be our notions of the government of the world upon the supposition of necessity. It must be purely mechanical, and there can be no moral government upon that hypothesis.

Let us consider, on the other hand, what notion of the divine government we are naturally led into by the supposition of liberty.

They who adopt this system conceive that in that small portion of the universe which falls under our view, as a great part has no active power, but moves, as it is moved, by necessity, and therefore must be subject to a mechanical government, so it has pleased the Almighty to bestow upon some of his creatures, particularly upon man, some degree of active power, and of reason, to direct him to the right use of his power.

What connection there may be, in the nature of things, between reason and active power, we know not. But we see evidently that, as reason without active power can do nothing, so active power without reason has no guide to direct it to any end.

These two conjoined make moral liberty, which, in how small a degree soever it is possessed, raises man to a superior rank in the creation of God. He is not merely a tool in the hand of the master, but a servant, in the proper sense, who has a certain trust, and is accountable for the discharge of it. Within the sphere of his power, he has a subordinate dominion or government, and therefore may be said to be made after the image of God,[1] the supreme governor. But as his dominion is subordinate, he is under a moral obligation to make a right use of it, as far as the reason which God has given him can direct him. When he does so, he is a just object of moral approbation; and no less an object of disapprobation and just punishment when he abuses the power with which he is entrusted. And he must finally render an account of the talent committed to him, to the supreme governor and righteous judge.

This is the moral government of God, which, far from being inconsistent with liberty, supposes liberty in those that are subject to it, and can extend no farther than that liberty extends; for accountableness can no more agree with necessity than light with darkness.

It ought likewise to be observed that, as active power in man and in every created being is the gift of God, it depends entirely on his pleasure for its existence, its degree and its continuance, and therefore can do nothing which he does not see fit to permit.

---

[1] See Genesis 1:26–7.

Our power to act does not exempt us from being acted upon and restrained, or compelled by a superior power; and the power of God is always superior to that of man.

It would be great folly and presumption in us to pretend to know all the ways in which the government of the supreme being is carried on, and his purposes accomplished by men, acting freely, and having different or opposite purposes in their view. For as the heavens are high above the earth, so are his thoughts above our thoughts, and his ways above our ways.[2]

That a man may have great influence upon the voluntary determinations of other men by means of education, example, and persuasion, is a fact which must be granted, whether we adopt the system of liberty or necessity. How far such determinations ought to be imputed to the person who applied those means, how far to the person influenced by them, we know not, but God knows, and will judge righteously.

But what I would here observe is that, if a man of superior talents may have so great influence over the actions of his fellow-creatures without taking away their liberty, it is surely reasonable to allow a much greater influence of the same kind to him who made man. Nor can it ever be proved that the wisdom and power of the Almighty are insufficient for governing free agents, so as to answer his purposes.

He who made man may have ways of governing his determinations, consistent with moral liberty, of which we have no conception. And he who gave this liberty freely may lay any restraint upon it that is necessary for answering his wise and benevolent purposes. The justice of his government requires that his creatures should be accountable only for what they have received, and not for what was never entrusted to them. And we are sure that the judge of all the earth will do what is right.[3]

Thus, I think, it appears that, upon the supposition of necessity, there can be no moral government of the universe. Its government must be perfectly mechanical, and everything

---

[2] See Isaiah 55:9.
[3] See Genesis 18:25.

done in it, whether good or ill, must be God's doing; and that, upon the supposition of liberty, there may be a perfect moral government of the universe, consistent with his accomplishing all his purposes in its creation and government.

The arguments to prove that man is endowed with moral liberty which have the greatest weight with me are three: *first*, because he has a natural conviction or belief, that, in many cases, he acts freely; *secondly*, because he is accountable; and, *thirdly*, because he is able to prosecute an end by a long series of means adapted to it.[4]

Chapter IX
Of Arguments for Necessity

Some of the arguments that have been offered for necessity were already considered in this essay.

It has been said that human liberty respects only the actions that are subsequent to volition; and that power over the determinations of the will is inconceivable and involves a contradiction. This argument was considered in the first chapter.

It has been said that liberty is inconsistent with the influence of motives, that it would make human actions capricious, and man ungovernable by God or man. These arguments were considered in the fourth and fifth chapters.

I am now to make some remarks upon other arguments that have been urged in this cause. They may, I think, be reduced to three classes. They are intended to prove either that liberty of determination is impossible, or that it would be hurtful, or that, in fact, man has no such liberty.

To prove that liberty of determination is impossible, it has been said that there must be a sufficient reason for everything. *For every existence, for every event, for every truth, there must be sufficient reason.*[5]

---

[4] Chapters VI, VII, and VIII address each of these arguments, respectively.
[5] For the arguments in this section, see *A Collection of Papers, Which passed between the late Learned Mr Leibnitz, and Dr Clarke, in the Years 1715 and 1716.*

The famous German philosopher Leibniz boasted much of having first applied this principle to philosophy, and of having, by that means, changed metaphysics from being a play of unmeaning words, to be a rational and demonstrative science. On this account it deserves to be considered.

A very obvious objection to this principle was, that two or more means may be equally fit for the same end; and that, in such a case, there may be a sufficient reason for taking one of the number, though there be no reason for preferring one to another, of means equally fit.

To obviate this objection, Leibniz maintained that the case supposed could not happen; or, if it did, that none of the means could be used, for want of a sufficient reason to prefer one to the rest. Therefore, he determined, with some of the schoolmen, that if an ass could be placed between two bundles of hay, or two fields of grass equally inviting, the poor beast would certainly stand still and starve; but the case, he says, could not happen without a miracle.

When it was objected to this principle that there could be no reason but the will of God why the material world was placed in one part of unlimited space rather than another, or created at one point of unlimited duration rather than another, or why the planets should move from west to east, rather than in a contrary direction; these objections Leibniz obviated by maintaining that there is no such thing as unoccupied space or duration; that space is nothing but the order of things coexisting, and duration is nothing but the order of things successive; that all motion is relative, so that, if there were only one body in the universe, it would be immoveable; that it is inconsistent with the perfection of the deity that there should be any part of space unoccupied by body; and, I suppose, he understood the same of every part of duration. So that, according to this system, the world, like its author, must be infinite, eternal, and immoveable; or, at least, as great in extent and duration as it is possible for it to be.

When it was objected to the principle of a sufficient reason that, of two particles of matter perfectly similar, there can be no reason but the will of God for placing *this* here and *that* there; this objection Leibniz obviated by maintaining that it is impossible that there can be two particles of matter, or any two things, perfectly similar. And this seems to have led him to another of his grand principles, which he calls *the identity of indiscernibles*.

When the principle of a sufficient reason had produced so many surprising discoveries in philosophy, it is no wonder that it should determine the long disputed question about human liberty. This it does in a moment. The determination of the will is an event for which there must be a sufficient reason, that is, something previous, which was necessarily followed by that determination, and could not be followed by any other determination; therefore it was necessary.

Thus we see that this principle of the necessity of a sufficient reason for everything is very fruitful of consequences; and by its fruits we may judge of it.[6] Those who will adopt it must adopt all the consequences that hang upon it. To fix them all beyond dispute, no more is necessary but to prove the truth of the principle on which they depend.

I know of no argument offered by Leibniz in proof of this principle, but the authority of Archimedes,[7] who, he says, makes use of it to prove that a balance loaded with equal weights on both ends will continue at rest.

I grant it to be good reasoning with regard to a balance, or with regard to any machine, that, when there is no external cause of its motion, it must remain at rest, because the machine has no power of moving itself. But to apply this reasoning to a man is to take for granted that the man is a machine, which is the very point in question.

Leibniz and his followers would have us to take this principle of the necessity of a sufficient reason for every existence, for every event, for every truth, as a first principle, without proof, without explanation; though it be evidently a vague proposition, capable of various meanings, as the word *reason* is. It must have different meanings when applied to things of so different nature as an event and a truth; and it may have different meanings when applied to the same thing. We cannot, therefore, form a distinct judgement of it in

---

[6] See Matthew 7:15–20 and Luke 6:43–5.
[7] Archimedes of Syracuse (c. 287–c. 212 BC).

the gross, but only by taking it to pieces and applying it to different things, in a precise and distinct meaning.

It can have no connection with the dispute about liberty, except when it is applied to the determinations of the will. Let us therefore suppose a voluntary action of a man; and that the question is put, whether was there a sufficient reason for this action or not?

The natural and obvious meaning of this question is, was motive to the action sufficient to justify it to be wise and good, or, at least, innocent? Surely, in this sense, there is not a sufficient reason for every human action, because there are many that are foolish, unreasonable, and unjustifiable.

If the meaning of the question be, was there a cause of the action? Undoubtedly there was: of every event there must be a cause that had power sufficient to produce it, and that exerted that power for the purpose. In the present case, either the man was the cause of the action, and then it was a free action, and is justly imputed to him; or it must have had another cause, and cannot justly be imputed to the man. In this sense, therefore, it is granted that there was a sufficient reason for the action; but the question about liberty is not in the least affected by this concession.

If, again, the meaning of the question be, was there something previous to the action which made it to be necessarily produced? Every man who believes that the action was free will answer to this question in the negative.

I know no other meaning that can be put upon the principle of a sufficient reason when applied to the determinations of the human will besides the three I have mentioned. In the first, it is evidently false; in the second, it is true, but does not affect the question about liberty; in the third, it is a mere assertion of necessity without proof.

Before we leave this boasted principle, we may see how it applies to events of another kind. When we say that a philosopher has assigned a sufficient reason for such a phenomenon, what is the meaning of this? The meaning surely is that he has accounted for it from the known laws of nature. The sufficient reason of a phenomenon of nature must therefore be some law or laws of nature, of which the phenomenon is a necessary consequence. But are we sure that, in this sense, there is a sufficient reason for every phenomenon of nature? I think we are not.

For, not to speak of miraculous events, in which the laws of nature are suspended or counteracted, we know not but that, in the ordinary course of God's providence, there may be particular acts of his administration that do not come under any general law of nature. Established laws of nature are necessary for enabling intelligent creatures to conduct their affairs with wisdom and prudence, and prosecute their ends by proper means; but still it may be fit that some particular events should not be fixed by general laws, but be directed by particular acts of the divine government, that so his reasonable creatures may have sufficient inducement to supplicate his aid, his protection, and direction, and to depend upon him for the success of their honest designs.

We see that in human governments, even those that are most legal, it is impossible that every act of the administration should be directed by established laws. Some things must be left to the direction of the executive power, and particularly acts of clemency and bounty to petitioning subjects. That there is nothing analogous to this in the divine government of the world, no man is able to prove.

We have no authority to pray that God would counteract or suspend the laws of nature in our behalf. Prayer therefore supposes that he may lend an ear to our prayers, without transgressing the laws of nature. Some have thought that the only use of prayer and devotion is to produce a proper temper and disposition in ourselves, and that it has no efficacy with the deity. But this is a hypothesis without proof. It contradicts our most natural sentiments, as well as the plain doctrine of Scripture, and tends to damp the fervour of every act of devotion.

It was indeed an article of the system of Leibniz that the deity, since the creation of the world, never did anything, excepting in the case of miracles; his work being made so perfect at first as never to need his interposition. But, in this, he was opposed by Sir Isaac Newton and others of the ablest philosophers, nor was he ever able to give any proof of this tenet.[8]

There is no evidence, therefore, that there is a sufficient reason for every natural event; if, by a sufficient reason, we understand some fixed law or laws of nature, of which that event is a necessary consequence. But what, shall we say, is the sufficient reason for a truth? For our belief of a truth, I think, the sufficient reason is our having good evidence; but what may be meant by a sufficient reason for its being a truth, I am not able to guess, unless the sufficient reason of a contingent truth be, that it *is* true; and, of a necessary truth, that it *must be* true. This makes a man little wiser.

From what has been said, I think, it appears that this principle of the necessity of a sufficient reason for everything is very indefinite in its signification. If it mean that of every event there must be a cause that had sufficient power to produce it, this is true, and has always been admitted as a first principle in philosophy and in common life. If it mean that every event must be necessarily consequent upon something (called a sufficient reason) that went before it; this is a direct assertion of universal fatality, and has many strange, not to say absurd, consequences: but, in this sense, it is neither self-evident, nor has any proof of it been offered. And, in general, in every sense in which it has evidence, it gives no new information; and, in every sense in which it would give new information, it wants evidence.

Another argument that has been used to prove liberty of action to be impossible is, that it implies 'an effect without a cause'.

To this it may be briefly answered that a free action is an effect produced by a being who had power and will to produce it; therefore it is not an effect without a cause.

To suppose any other cause necessary to the production of an effect than a being who had the power and the will to produce it is a contradiction; for it is to suppose that being to have power to produce the effect, and not to have power to produce it.

---

[8] See Isaac Newton, *Philosophiae Naturalis Principia Mathematica* [*The Mathematical Principles of Natural Philosophy*], General Scholium.

But as great stress is laid upon this argument by a late zealous advocate for necessity,[9] we shall consider the light in which he puts it.

He introduces this argument with an observation to which I entirely agree: it is, that to establish this doctrine of necessity, nothing is necessary but that, throughout all nature, the same consequences should invariably result from the same circumstances.

I know nothing more that can be desired to establish universal fatality throughout the universe. When it is proved that, through all nature, the same consequences invariably result from the same circumstances, the doctrine of liberty must be given up.

To prevent all ambiguity, I grant that, in reasoning, the same consequences, throughout all nature, will invariably follow from the same premises: because good reasoning must be good reasoning in all times and places. But this has nothing to do with the doctrine of necessity. The thing to be proved, therefore, in order to establish that doctrine, is, that, through all nature, the same events invariably result from the same circumstances.

Of this capital point, the proof offered by that author is, that an event not preceded by any circumstances that determined it to be what it was would be *an effect without a cause*. Why so? 'For', says he, 'a *cause* cannot be defined to be anything but *such previous circumstances as are constantly followed by a certain effect*; the constancy of the result making us conclude, that there must be a *sufficient reason,* in the nature of things, why it should be produced in those circumstances'.[10]

I acknowledge that, if this be the only definition that can be given of a cause, it will follow that an event not preceded by circumstances that determined it to be what it was, would be, not an *effect* without a cause, which is a contradiction in terms, but an *event* without a cause, which I hold to be impossible. The matter, therefore, is brought to this issue,

---

[9] Joseph Priestley (1733–1804).
[10] See Section II of Priestley's 'appendix' to the *Disquisitions Relating to Matter and Spirit, The Doctrine of Philosophical Necessity Illustrated.*

whether this be the only definition that can be given of a cause?

With regard to this point, we may observe, *first*, that this definition of a cause, bating the phraseology of putting a *cause* under the category *of circumstances*, which I take to be new, is the same, in other words, with that which Mr Hume gave, of which he ought to be acknowledged the inventor.[11] For I know of no author before Mr Hume who maintained that we have no other notion of a cause, but that it is something prior to the effect, which has been found by experience to be constantly followed by the effect. This is a main pillar of his system; and he has drawn very important consequences from this definition, which I am far from thinking this author will adopt.

Without repeating what I have before said of causes in the first of these Essays, and in the second and third chapters of this, I shall here mention some of the consequences that may be justly deduced from this definition of a cause, that we may judge of it by its fruits.

First, it follows from this definition of a cause that night is the cause of day, and day the cause of night. For no two things have more constantly followed each other since the beginning of the world.

Secondly, it follows from this definition of a cause that, for what we know, anything may be the cause of anything, since nothing is essential to a cause but its being constantly followed by the effect. If this be so, what is unintelligent may be the cause of what is intelligent; folly may be the cause of wisdom, and evil of good; all reasoning from the nature of the effect to the nature of the cause, and all reasoning from final causes, must be given up as fallacious.

Thirdly, from this definition of a cause, it follows that we have no reason to conclude that every event must have a cause. For innumerable events happen when it cannot be shown that there were certain previous circumstances that have constantly been followed by such an event. And though it were certain that every event we have had access to observe had a cause, it would not follow that every event

---

[11] See Hume, *Treatise*, I.iii.14, 'Of the idea of necessary connexion'.

must have a cause. For it is contrary to the rules of logic to conclude that, because a thing has always been, therefore it must be; to reason from what is contingent to what is necessary.

Fourthly, from this definition of a cause, it would follow that we have no reason to conclude that there was any cause of the creation of this world: for there were no previous circumstances that had been constantly followed by such an effect. And, for the same reason, it would follow from the definition that whatever was singular in its nature, or the first thing of its kind, could have no cause.

Several of these consequences were fondly embraced by Mr Hume, as necessarily following from his definition of a cause, and as favourable to his system of absolute scepticism. Those who adopt the definition of a cause, from which they follow, may choose whether they will adopt its consequences, or show that they do not follow from the definition.

A *second* observation with regard to this argument is that a definition of a cause may be given which is not burdened with such untoward consequences.

Why may not an efficient cause be defined to be a being that had power and will to produce the effect? The production of an effect requires active power, and active power, being a quality, must be in a being endowed with that power. Power without will produces no effect; but, where these are conjoined, the effect must be produced.

This, I think, is the proper meaning of the word *cause* when it is used in metaphysics; and particularly when we affirm that everything that begins to exist must have a cause; and when, by reasoning, we prove that there must be an eternal first cause of all things. Was the world produced by previous circumstances which are constantly followed by such an effect? Or, was it produced by a being that had power to produce it, and willed its production?

In natural philosophy, the word *cause* is often used in a very different sense. When an event is produced according to a known law of nature, the law of nature is called the cause of that event. But a law of nature is not the efficient cause of any event. It is only the rule, according to which the efficient cause acts. A law is a thing conceived in the mind of a rational being, not a thing that has a real existence; and, therefore, like a motive, it can neither act nor be acted upon, and consequently cannot be an efficient cause. If there be no being that acts according to the law, it produces no effect.

This author takes it for granted that every voluntary action of man was determined to be what it was by the laws of nature, in the same sense as mechanical motions are determined by the laws of motion; and that every choice, not thus determined, 'is just as impossible, as that a mechanical motion should depend upon no certain law or rule, or that any other effect should exist without a cause'.[12]

It ought here to be observed that there are two kinds of laws, both very properly called *laws of nature*, which ought not to be confounded. There are moral laws of nature, and physical laws of nature. The first are the rules which God has prescribed to his rational creatures for their conduct. They respect voluntary and free actions only; for no other actions can be subject to moral rules. These laws of nature ought to be always obeyed, but they are often transgressed by men. There is, therefore, no impossibility in the violation of the moral laws of nature, nor is such a violation an effect without a cause. The transgressor is the cause, and is justly accountable for it.

The physical laws of nature are the rules according to which the deity commonly acts in his natural government of the world; and, whatever is done according to them is not done by man, but by God, either immediately or by instruments under his direction. These laws of nature neither restrain the power of the author of nature, nor bring him under any obligation to do nothing beyond their sphere. He has sometimes acted contrary to them, in the case of miracles, and perhaps often acts without regard to them, in the ordinary course of his providence. Neither miraculous events, which are contrary to the physical laws of nature, nor such ordinary acts of the divine administration as are without their sphere, are impossible, nor are they *effects without a cause.* God is the cause of them, and to him only they are to be imputed.

---

[12] Priestley, *The Doctrine of Philosophical Necessity Illustrated*, II.

That the moral laws of nature are often transgressed by man is undeniable. If the physical laws of nature make his obedience to the moral laws to be impossible, then he is, in the literal sense, *born under one law, bound unto another*,[13] which contradicts every notion of a righteous government of the world.

But though this supposition were attended with no such shocking consequence, it is merely a supposition; and until it be proved that every choice or voluntary action of man is determined by the physical laws of nature, this argument for necessity is only the taking for granted the point to be proved.

Of the same kind is the argument for the impossibility of liberty, taken from a balance, which cannot move but as it is moved by the weights put into it. This argument, though urged by almost every writer in defence of necessity, is so pitiful, and has been so often answered, that it scarce deserves to be mentioned.

Every argument in a dispute which is not grounded on principles granted by both parties is that kind of sophism which logicians call *petitio principii*;[14] and such, in my apprehension, are all the arguments offered to prove that liberty of action is impossible.

It may farther be observed that every argument of this class, if it were really conclusive, must extend to the deity, as well as to all created beings; and necessary existence, which has always been considered as the prerogative of the supreme being, must belong equally to every creature and to every event, even the most trifling.

This I take to be the system of Spinoza,[15] and of those among the ancients who carried fatality to the highest pitch. I before referred the reader to Dr Clarke's argument, which professes to demonstrate that the first cause is a free agent.[16] Until that argument shall be shown to be fallacious, a thing

---

[13] From *The Tragedy of Mustapha*, by Baron Brooke Fulke Greville (1554–1628).
[14] i.e. 'begging the question'.
[15] Baruch Spinoza (1632–1677).
[16] Clarke, *Demonstration of the Being and Attributes of God*, IX.

which I have not seen attempted, such weak arguments as have been brought to prove the contrary ought to have little weight.

Chapter X
The Same Subject

With regard to the *second* class of arguments for necessity, which are intended to prove that liberty of action would be hurtful to man, I have only to observe that it is a fact too evident to be denied, whether we adopt the system of liberty or that of necessity, that men actually receive hurt from their own voluntary actions and from the voluntary actions of other men; nor can it be pretended that this fact is inconsistent with the doctrine of liberty, or that it is more unaccountable upon this system than upon that of necessity.

In order, therefore, to draw any solid argument against liberty from its hurtfulness, it ought to be proved that, if man were a free agent, he would do more hurt to himself, or to others, than he actually does.

To this purpose it has been said that liberty would make men's actions capricious; that it would destroy the influence of motives; that it would take away the effect of rewards and punishments; and that it would make man absolutely ungovernable. These arguments have been already considered in the fourth and fifth chapters of this essay; and, therefore, I shall now proceed to the *third* class of arguments for necessity, which are intended to prove that, in fact, men are not free agents.

The most formidable argument of this class and, I think, the only one that has not been considered in some of the preceding chapters is taken from the prescience of the deity.

God foresees every determination of the human mind. It must therefore be what he foresees it shall be; and therefore must be necessary.

This argument may be understood three different ways, each of which we shall consider, that we may see all its force.

The necessity of the event may be thought to be a just consequence, either barely from its being certainly future, or barely from its being foreseen, or from the impossibility of its being foreseen, if it was not necessary.

First, It may be thought that, as nothing can be known to be future which is not certainly future; so, if it be certainly future, it must be necessary.

This opinion has no less authority in its favour than that of Aristotle, who indeed held the doctrine of liberty, but believing, at the same time, that whatever is certainly future must be necessary, in order to defend the liberty of human actions, maintained that contingent events have no certain futurity; but I know of no modern advocate for liberty, who has put the defence of it upon that issue.[17]

It must be granted that as whatever was, certainly was, and whatever is, certainly is, so whatever shall be, certainly shall be. These are identical propositions, and cannot be doubted by those who conceive them distinctly.

But I know no rule of reasoning by which it can be inferred that, because an event certainly shall be, therefore its production must be necessary. The manner of its production, whether free or necessary, cannot be concluded from the time of its production, whether it be past, present, or future. That it shall be no more implies that it shall be necessarily than that it shall be freely produced; for neither present, past, nor future, have any more connection with necessity than they have with freedom.

I grant, therefore, that, from events being foreseen, it may be justly concluded that they are certainly future; but from their being certainly future, it does not follow that they are necessary.

Secondly, if it be meant by this argument that an event must be necessary merely because it is foreseen, neither is this a just consequence. For it has often been observed that prescience and knowledge of every kind, being an immanent act, has no effect upon the thing known. Its mode of existence, whether it be free or necessary, is not in the least affected by its being known to be future, any more than by its being known to be past or present. The deity foresees his own future free actions, but neither his foresight nor his purpose makes them necessary. The argument, therefore, taken in this view, as well as in the former, is inconclusive.

---

[17] See *De Interpretatione* [*On Interpretation*], IX.

A *third* way in which this argument may be understood is this: it is impossible that an event which is not necessary should be foreseen; therefore every event that is certainly foreseen must be necessary. Here the conclusion certainly follows from the antecedent proposition, and therefore the whole stress of the argument lies upon the proof of that proposition.

Let us consider, therefore, whether it can be proved that no free action can be certainly foreseen. If this can be proved, it will follow, either that all actions are necessary, or that all actions cannot be foreseen.

With regard to the general proposition that it is impossible that any free action can be certainly foreseen, I observe,

First, that every man who believes the deity to be a free agent must believe that this proposition not only is incapable of proof, but that it is certainly false: for the man himself foresees that the judge of all the earth will always do what is right[18] and that he will fulfil whatever he has promised; and, at the same time, believes that, in doing what is right and in fulfilling his promises, the deity acts with the most perfect freedom.

Secondly, I observe that every man who believes that it is an absurdity or contradiction that any free action should be certainly foreseen must believe, if he will be consistent, either that the deity is not a free agent, or that he does not foresee his own actions; nor can we foresee that he will do what is right and will fulfil his promises.

Thirdly, without considering the consequences which this general proposition carries in its bosom, which give it a very bad aspect, let us attend to the arguments offered to prove it.

Dr Priestley has laboured more in the proof of this proposition than any other author I am acquainted with, and maintains it to be not only a difficulty and a mystery, as it has been called, that a contingent event should be the object of knowledge, but that, in reality, there cannot be a greater absurdity or contradiction. Let us hear the proof of this.

'For', says he, 'as certainly as nothing can be known to exist, but what does exists so certainly can nothing be known

---

[18] See note 3.

to *arise from what does exist*, but what does arise from it or depend upon it. But, according to the definition of the terms, a contingent event does not depend upon any previous known circumstances, since some other event might have arisen in the same circumstances'.[19]

This argument, when stripped of incidental and explanatory clauses, and affected variations of expression, amounts to this: nothing can be known to arise from what does exist, but what does arise from it: but a contingent event does not arise from what does exist. The conclusion, which is left to be drawn by the reader, must, according to the rules of reasoning, be: therefore a contingent event cannot be known to arise from what does exist.

It is here very obvious that a thing may arise from what does exist {in} two ways, freely or necessarily. A contingent event arises from its cause, not necessarily but freely, and so, that another event might have arisen from the same cause, in the same circumstances.

The second proposition of the argument is that a contingent event does not depend upon any previous known circumstances, which I take to be only a variation of the term of *not arising from what does exist*. Therefore, in order to make the two propositions to correspond, we must understand by *arising from what does exist*, arising necessarily from what does exist. When this ambiguity is removed, the argument stands thus: nothing can be known to arise necessarily from what does exist, but what does necessarily arise from it: but a contingent event does not arise necessarily from what does exist; therefore a contingent event cannot be known to arise necessarily from what does exist.

I grant the whole but the conclusion of this argument is not what he undertook to prove, and therefore the argument is that kind of sophism which logicians call *ignoratio elenchi*.[20]

The thing to be proved is not that a contingent event cannot be known to arise necessarily from what exists; but that a contingent future event cannot be the object of knowledge.

---

[19] Priestley, *The Doctrine of Philosophical Necessity Illustrated*, III.
[20] i.e. 'irrelevant conclusion'.

To draw the argument to this conclusion, it must be put thus: nothing can be known to arise from what does exist, but what arises necessarily from it: but a contingent event does not arise necessarily from what does exist; therefore a contingent event cannot be known to arise from what does exist.

The conclusion here is what it ought to be; but the first proposition assumes the thing to be proved, and therefore the argument is what logicians call *petitio principii*.[21]

To the same purpose he says, 'That nothing can be known at present, except itself or its necessary cause exist at present'.[22]

This is affirmed, but I find no proof of it.

Again he says, 'That knowledge supposes an object, which, in this case, does not exist'.[23] It is true that knowledge supposes an object, and everything that is known is an object of knowledge, whether past, present, or future, whether contingent or necessary.

Upon the whole, the arguments I can find upon this point bear no proportion to the confidence of the assertion, that there cannot be a greater absurdity or contradiction than that a contingent event should be the object of knowledge.

To those who, without pretending to show a manifest absurdity or contradiction in the knowledge of future contingent events, are still of {the} opinion that it is impossible that the future free actions of man, a being of imperfect wisdom and virtue, should be certainly foreknown, I would humbly offer the following considerations.

1) I grant that there is no knowledge of this kind in man; and this is the cause that we find it so difficult to conceive it in any other being.

All our knowledge of future events is drawn either from their necessary connection with the present course of nature, or from their connection with the character of the agent that produces them. Our knowledge, even of those future events that necessarily result from the established laws of nature, is

---

[21] See note 14.
[22] Priestley, *The Doctrine of Philosophical Necessity Illustrated*, III.
[23] Ibid.

hypothetical. It supposes the continuance of those laws with which they are connected. And how long those laws may be continued, we have no certain knowledge. God only knows when the present course of nature shall be changed, and therefore he only has certain knowledge even of events of this kind.

The character of perfect wisdom and perfect rectitude in the deity gives us certain knowledge that he will always be true in all his declarations, faithful in all his promises, and just in all his dispensations. But when we reason from the character of men to their future actions, though, in many cases, we have such probability as we rest upon in our most important worldly concerns, yet we have no certainty, because men are imperfect in wisdom and in virtue. If we had even the most perfect knowledge of the character and situation of a man, this would not be sufficient to give certainty to our knowledge of his future actions; because, in some actions, both good and bad men deviate from their general character.

The prescience of the deity, therefore, must be different not only in degree, but in kind, from any knowledge we can attain of futurity.

2) Though we can have no conception how the future free actions of men may be known by the deity, this is not a sufficient reason to conclude that they cannot be known. Do we know, or can we conceive, how God knows the secrets of men's hearts? Can we conceive how God made this world without any pre-existent matter? All the ancient philosophers believed this to be impossible: and for what reason but this, that they could not conceive how it could be done. Can we give any better reason for believing that the actions of men cannot be certainly foreseen?

3) Can we conceive how we ourselves have certain knowledge by those faculties with which God has endowed us? If any man thinks that he understands distinctly how he is conscious of his own thoughts; how he perceives external objects by his senses; how he remembers past events, I am afraid that he is not yet so wise as to understand his own ignorance.

4) There seems to me to be a great analogy between the prescience of future contingents and the memory of past

contingents. We possess the last in some degree, and therefore find no difficulty in believing that it may be perfect in the deity. But the first we have in no degree, and therefore are apt to think it impossible.

In both, the object of knowledge is neither what presently exists, nor has any necessary connection with what presently exists. Every argument brought to prove the impossibility of prescience proves, with equal force, the impossibility of memory. If it be true that nothing can be known to arise from what does exist, but what necessarily arises from it, it must be equally true that nothing can be known to have gone before what does exist, but what must necessarily have gone before it. If it be true that nothing future can be known unless its necessary cause exist at present, it must be equally true that nothing past can be known unless something consequent, with which it is necessarily connected, exist at present. If the fatalist should say that past events are indeed necessarily connected with the present, he will not surely venture to say that it is by tracing this necessary connection that we remember the past.

Why then should we think prescience impossible in the Almighty, when he has given us a faculty which bears a strong analogy to it, and which is no less unaccountable to the human understanding than prescience is? It is more reasonable, as well as more agreeable to the sacred writings, to conclude with a pious father of the church,

> Therefore we are in no way compelled either to abolish free will when we keep the foreknowledge of God, or blasphemously to deny that God foreknows the future because we keep free will. Instead we embrace both truths; with faith and trust we assert both. The former is required for correct belief, the latter for right living.[24]

---

[24] Augustine, *City of God*, 5.10. Reid quotes the Latin.

Chapter XI
Of the Permission of Evil

Another use has been made of divine prescience by the advocates for necessity, which it is proper to consider before we leave this subject.

It has been said that all those consequences follow from the divine prescience which are thought most alarming in the scheme of necessity; and particularly God's being the proper cause of moral evil. For, to suppose God to foresee and permit what it was in his power to have prevented is the very same thing as to suppose him to will and directly to cause it. He distinctly foresees all the actions of a man's life and all the consequences of them: if, therefore, he did not think any particular man and his conduct proper for his plan of creation and providence, he certainly would not have introduced him into being at all.

In this reasoning we may observe that a supposition is made which seems to contradict itself.

That all the actions of a particular man should be distinctly foreseen, and, at the same time, that that man should never be brought into existence, seems to me to be a contradiction: and the same contradiction there is in supposing any action to be distinctly foreseen and yet prevented. For, if it be foreseen, it shall happen; and, if it be prevented, it shall not happen and therefore could not be foreseen.

The knowledge here supposed is neither prescience nor science, but something very different from both. It is a kind of knowledge which some metaphysical divines, in their controversies about the order of the divine decrees, a subject far beyond the limits of human understanding, attributed to the deity, and of which other divines denied the possibility, while they firmly maintained the divine prescience.

It was called *scientia media*,[25] to distinguish it from prescience; and by this *scientia media* was meant, not the knowing from eternity all things that shall exist, which is prescience, nor the knowing all the connections and relations

---

[25] i.e. 'middle knowledge'.

of things that exist or may be conceived, which is science, but a knowledge of things contingent that never did nor shall exist. For instance, the knowing every action that would be done by a man who is barely conceived, and shall never be brought into existence.

Against the possibility of the *scientia media* arguments may be urged which cannot be applied to prescience. Thus it may be said that nothing can be known but what is true. It is true that the future actions of a free agent shall exist, and therefore we see no impossibility in its being known that they shall exist: but with regard to the free actions of an agent that never did nor shall exist, there is nothing true, and therefore nothing can be known. To say that the being conceived would certainly act in such a way, if placed in such a situation, if it have any meaning, is to say that his acting in that way is the consequence of the conception; but this contradicts the supposition of its being a free action.

Things merely conceived have no relations or connections but such as are implied in the conception, or are consequent from it. Thus I conceive two circles in the same plane. If this be all I conceive, it is not true that these circles are equal or unequal, because neither of these relations is implied in the conception; yet if the two circles really existed, they must be either equal or unequal. Again, I conceive two circles in the same plane, the distance of whose centres is equal to the sum of their semidiameters. It is true of these circles that they will touch one another, because this follows from the conception; but it is not true that they will be equal or unequal, because neither of these relations is implied in the conception, nor is consequent from it.

In like manner, I can conceive a being who has power to do an indifferent action or not to do it. It is not true that he would do it, nor is it true that he would not do it, because neither is implied in my conception nor follows from it; and what is not true cannot be known.

Though I do not perceive any fallacy in this argument against a *scientia media*, I am sensible how apt we are to err in applying what belongs to our conceptions and our knowledge to the conceptions and knowledge of the supreme being; and, therefore, without pretending to determine for or against a *scientia media*, I only observe that, to suppose that the deity prevents what he foresees by his prescience is a contradiction, and that to know that a contingent event which he sees fit not to permit would certainly happen if permitted is not prescience, but the *scientia media*, whose existence or possibility we are under no necessity of admitting.

Waving all dispute about *scientia media*, we acknowledge that nothing can happen under the administration of the deity which he does not see fit to permit. The permission of natural and moral evil is a phenomenon which cannot be disputed. To account for this phenomenon under the government of a being of infinite goodness, justice, wisdom, and power, has, in all ages, been considered as difficult to human reason, whether we embrace the system of liberty or that of necessity. But, if the difficulty of accounting for this phenomenon upon the system of necessity be as great as it is upon the system of liberty, it can have no weight when used as an argument against liberty.

The defenders of necessity, to reconcile it to the principles of theism, find themselves obliged to give up all the moral attributes of God, excepting that of goodness, or a desire to produce happiness. This they hold to be the sole motive of his making and governing the universe. Justice, veracity, {and} faithfulness are only modifications of goodness, the means of promoting its purposes, and are exercised only so far as they serve that end. Virtue is acceptable to him and vice displeasing, only as the first tends to produce happiness and the last misery. He is the proper cause and agent of all moral evil as well as good; but it is for a good end, to produce the greater happiness to his creatures. He does evil that good may come, and this end sanctifies the worst actions that contribute to it. All the wickedness of men being the work of God, he must, when he surveys it, pronounce it, as well as all his other works, to be very good.[26]

This view of the divine nature, the only one consistent with the scheme of necessity, appears to me much more shocking than the permission of evil upon the scheme of

---

[26] See Genesis 1:31.

liberty. It is said that it requires only *strength of mind*[27] to embrace it: To me it seems to require much strength of countenance to profess it.

In this system, as in Cleanthes' tablature of the Epicurean system,[28] pleasure or happiness is placed upon the throne as the queen, to whom all the virtues bear the humble office of menial servants.

As the end of the deity, in all his actions, is not his own good, which can receive no addition, but the good of his creatures; and, as his creatures are capable of this disposition in some degree, is he not pleased with this image of himself in his creatures, and displeased with the contrary? Why then should he be the author of malice, envy, revenge, tyranny, and oppression in their hearts? Other vices that have no malevolence in them may please such a deity, but surely malevolence cannot please him.

If we form our notions of the moral attributes of the deity from what we see of his government of the world, from the dictates of reason and conscience, or from the doctrine of revelation, justice, veracity, faithfulness, the love of virtue, and dislike of vice appear to be no less essential attributes of his nature than goodness.

In man, who is made after the image of God,[29] goodness or benevolence is indeed an essential part of virtue, but it is not the whole.

I am at a loss what arguments can be brought to prove goodness to be essential to the deity which will not, with equal force, prove other moral attributes to be so; or what objections can be brought against the latter, which have not equal strength against the former, unless it be admitted to be an objection against other moral attributes, that they do not accord with the doctrine of necessity.

If other moral evils may be attributed to the deity as the means of promoting general good, why may not false declarations and false promises? And then what ground

---

[27] Priestley, *Doctrine of Philosophical Necessity Illustrated*, Preface.
[28] See Cicero, *De Finibus* [*On Ends*] II.xxi.
[29] See note 1.

have we left to believe the truth of what he reveals or to rely upon what he promises?

Supposing this strange view of the divine nature were to be adopted in favour of the doctrine of necessity, there is still a great difficulty to be resolved. Since it is supposed that the supreme being had no other end in making and governing the universe but to produce the greatest degree of happiness to his creatures in general, how comes it to pass that there is so much misery in a system made and governed by infinite wisdom and power for a contrary purpose?

The solution of this difficulty leads us necessarily to another hypothesis, that all the misery and vice that is in the world is a necessary ingredient in that system which produces the greatest sum of happiness upon the whole. This connection betwixt the greatest sum of happiness and all the misery that is in the universe must be fatal and necessary in the nature of things, so that even almighty power cannot break it: for benevolence can never lead to inflict misery without necessity.

This necessary connection between the greatest sum of happiness upon the whole and all the natural and moral evil that is, or has been, or shall be, being once established, it is impossible for mortal eyes to discern how far this evil may extend or on whom it may happen to fall; whether this fatal connection may be temporary or eternal, or what proportion of the happiness may be balanced by it.

A world made by perfect wisdom and almighty power, for no other end but to make it happy, presents the most pleasing prospect that can be imagined. We expect nothing but uninterrupted happiness to prevail forever. But, alas! When we consider that in this happiest system there must be necessarily all the misery and vice we see, and how much more we know not, how is the prospect darkened!

These two hypotheses, the one limiting the moral character of the deity, the other limiting his power, seem to me to be the necessary consequences of necessity when it is joined with theism; and they have accordingly been adopted by the ablest defenders of that doctrine.

If some defenders of liberty, by limiting too rashly the divine prescience, in order to defend that system, have raised high indignation in their opponents; have they not equal ground of indignation against those who, to defend necessity, limit the moral perfection of the deity and his almighty power?

Let us consider, on the other hand, what consequences may be fairly drawn from God's permitting the abuse of liberty in agents on whom he has bestowed it.

If it be asked, why does God permit so much sin in his creation? I confess I cannot answer the question, but must lay my hand upon my mouth. He giveth no account of his conduct to the children of men. It is our part to obey his commands, and not to say unto him, why dost thou thus?[30]

Hypotheses might be framed; but, while we have ground to be satisfied that he does nothing but what is right, it is more becoming us to acknowledge that the ends and reasons of his universal government are beyond our knowledge, and perhaps beyond the comprehension of human understanding. We cannot penetrate so far into the counsel of the Almighty as to know all the reasons why it became him, of whom are all things, and to whom are all things,[31] to create, not only machines, which are solely moved by his hand, but servants and children, who, by obeying his commands, and imitating his moral perfections, might rise to a high degree of glory and happiness in his favour, or, by perverse disobedience, might incur guilt and just punishment. In this he appears to us awful in his justice, as well as amiable in his goodness.

But, as he disdains not to appeal to men for the equity of his proceedings towards them when his character is impeached, we may, with humble reverence, plead for God, and vindicate that moral excellence which is the glory of his nature, and of which the image is the glory and the perfection of man.

Let us observe, first of all, that *to permit* has two meanings. It signifies not to forbid; and it signifies not to hinder by superior power. In the first of these senses, God never permits sin. His law forbids every moral evil. By his laws and by his government, he gives every encouragement to

---

[30] See Job, especially chapters 38–42.
[31] Westminster Confession, II.2.

good conduct, and every discouragement to bad. But he does not always, by his superior power, hinder it from being committed. This is the ground of the accusation; and this, it is said, is the very same thing as directly to will and to cause it.

As this is asserted without proof, and is far from being self-evident, it might be sufficient to deny it until it be proved. But, without resting barely on the defensive, we may observe that the only moral attributes that can be supposed inconsistent with the permission of sin are either goodness or justice.

The defenders of necessity, with whom we have to do in this point, as they maintain that goodness is the only essential moral attribute of the deity and the motive of all his actions, must, if they will be consistent, maintain that to will and directly to cause sin, much more not to hinder it, is consistent with perfect goodness, nay, that goodness is a sufficient motive to justify the willing and directly causing it.

With regard to them, therefore, it is surely unnecessary to attempt to reconcile the permission of sin with the goodness of God, since an inconsistency between that attribute and the causing of sin would overturn their whole system.

If the causing of moral evil and being the real author of it be consistent with perfect goodness, what pretence can there be to say that not to hinder it is inconsistent with perfect goodness?

What is incumbent upon them, therefore, to prove, is that the permission of sin is inconsistent with justice; and, upon this point, we are ready to join issue with them.

But what pretence can there be to say that the permission of sin is perfectly consistent with goodness in the deity, but inconsistent with justice?

Is it not as easy to conceive that he should permit sin, though virtue be his delight, as that he inflicts misery when his sole delight is to bestow happiness? Should it appear incredible that the permission of sin may tend to promote virtue, to them who believe that the infliction of misery is necessary to promote happiness?

The justice, as well as the goodness of God's moral government of mankind, appears in this: that his laws are not arbitrary nor grievous, as it is only by the obedience of them that our nature can be perfected and qualified for future happiness; that he is ready to aid our weakness, to help our infirmities, and not to suffer us to be tempted above what we are able to bear; that he is not strict to mark iniquity or to execute judgement speedily against an evil work, but is long-suffering and waits to be gracious; that he is ready to receive the humble penitent to his favour; that he is no respecter of persons, but in every nation he that fears God and works righteousness is accepted of him;[32] that of every man he will require an account, proportioned to the talents he hath received;[33] that he delights in mercy, but hath no pleasure in the death of the wicked;[34] and therefore in punishing will never go beyond the demerit of the criminal, nor beyond what the rules of his universal government require.

There were, in ancient ages, some who said, 'the way of the Lord is not equal'; to whom the prophet, in the name of God, makes this reply, which, in all ages, is sufficient to repel this accusation.

> Hear now, O house of Israel, is not my way equal, are not your ways unequal? When a righteous man turneth away from his righteousness, and committeth iniquity, for his iniquity which he hath done shall he die. Again, when a wicked man turneth away from his wickedness that he hath committed, and doth that which is lawful and right, he shall save his soul alive. O house of Israel, are not my ways equal, are not your ways unequal? Repent, and turn from all your transgressions, so iniquity shall not be your ruin. Cast away from you all your transgressions whereby you have transgressed, and make you a new heart and a new spirit, for why will ye die, O house of Israel? For I have no pleasure in the death of him that dieth, saith the Lord God.[35]

Another argument for necessity has been lately offered, which we shall very briefly consider.

---

[32] See Acts 10:34.
[33] See Matthew 25:14–30.
[34] See Ezekiel 33:11.
[35] Ezekiel 18:25–32a.

It has been maintained that the power of thinking is the result of a certain modification of matter and that a certain configuration of brain makes a soul; and, if man be wholly a material being, it is said, that it will not be denied that he must be a mechanical being; that the doctrine of necessity is a direct inference from that of materialism and its undoubted consequence.

As this argument can have no weight with those who do not see reason to embrace this system of materialism; so, even with those who do, it seems to me to be a mere sophism.

Philosophers have been wont to conceive matter to be an inert passive being and to have certain properties inconsistent with the power of thinking or of acting. But a philosopher arises who proves, we shall suppose, that we were quite mistaken in our notion of matter; that it has not the properties we supposed, and, in fact, has no properties but those of attraction and repulsion; but still he thinks that, being matter, it will not be denied that it is a mechanical being, and that the doctrine of necessity is a direct inference from that of materialism.[36]

Herein, however, he deceives himself. If matter be what we conceived it to be, it is equally incapable of thinking and of acting freely. But if the properties from which we drew this conclusion have no reality, as he thinks he has proved; if it have the powers of attraction and repulsion and require only a certain configuration to make it think rationally, it will be impossible to show any good reason why the same configuration may not make it act rationally and freely. If its reproach of solidity, inertness, and sluggishness be wiped off; and if it be raised in our esteem to a nearer approach to the nature of what we call spiritual and immaterial beings, why should it still be nothing but a mechanical being? Is its solidity, inertness, and sluggishness to be first removed to make it capable of thinking and then restored in order to make it incapable of acting?

---

[36] According to Haakonssen and Harris, Reid here refers to Roger Boscovich (1711–1787), whose theories were endorsed by Priestley in his *Disquisitions Relating to Matter and Spirit*. See *Active Powers* 267n.

Those, therefore, who reason justly from this system of materialism will easily perceive that the doctrine of necessity is so far from being a direct inference that it can receive no support from it.

To conclude this essay: extremes of all kinds ought to be avoided; yet men are prone to run into them; and, to shun one extreme, we often run into the contrary.

Of all extremes of opinion, none are more dangerous than those that exalt the powers of man too high, on the one hand, or sink them too low, on the other.

By raising them too high, we feed pride and vainglory, we lose the sense of our dependence upon God, and engage in attempts beyond our abilities. By depressing them too low, we cut the sinews of action and of obligation and are tempted to think that, as we can do nothing, we have nothing to do, but to be carried passively along by the stream of necessity.

Some good men, apprehending that, to kill pride and vainglory, our active powers cannot be too much depressed, have been led, by zeal for religion, to deprive us of all active power.

Other good men, by a like zeal, have been led to depreciate the human understanding, and to put out the light of nature and reason, in order to exalt that of revelation.

Those weapons which were taken up in support of religion are now employed to overturn it; and what was, by some, accounted the bulwark of orthodoxy, is become the stronghold of atheism and infidelity.

Atheists join hands with theologians in depriving man of all active power, that they may destroy all moral obligation and all sense of right and wrong. They join hands with theologians in depreciating the human understanding, that they may lead us into absolute scepticism.

God, in mercy to the human race, has made us of such a frame that no speculative opinion whatsoever can root out the sense of guilt and demerit when we do wrong, nor the peace and joy of a good conscience when we do what is right. No speculative opinion can root out a regard to the testimony of our senses, of our memory, and of our rational faculties. But we have reason to be jealous of opinions which run counter to those natural sentiments of the human mind and tend to shake, though they never can eradicate, them.

There is little reason to fear that the conduct of men, with regard to the concerns of the present life, will ever be much affected either by the doctrine of necessity or by scepticism. It were to be wished that men's conduct, with regard to the concerns of another life, were in as little danger from those opinions.

In the present state, we see some who zealously maintain the doctrine of necessity, others who as zealously maintain that of liberty. One would be apt to think that a practical belief of these contrary systems should produce very different conduct in them that hold them; yet we see no such difference in the affairs of common life.

The fatalist deliberates, and resolves, and plights his faith. He lays down a plan of conduct and prosecutes it with vigour and industry. He exhorts and commands, and holds those to be answerable for their conduct to whom he has committed any charge. He blames those that are false or unfaithful to him as other men do. He perceives dignity and worth in some characters and actions, and in others demerit and turpitude. He resents injuries, and is grateful for good offices.

If any man should plead the doctrine of necessity to exculpate murder, theft, or robbery, or even wilful negligence in the discharge of his duty, his judge, though a fatalist, if he had common sense, would laugh at such a plea and would not allow it even to alleviate the crime.

In all such cases, he sees that it would be absurd not to act and to judge as those ought to do who believe themselves and other men to be free agents, just as the sceptic, to avoid absurdity, must, when he goes into the world, act and judge like other men who are not sceptics.

If the fatalist be as little influenced by the opinion of necessity in his moral and religious concerns, and in his expectations concerning another world, as he is in the common affairs of life, his speculative opinion will probably do him little hurt. But, if he trust so far to the doctrine of necessity as to indulge sloth and inactivity in his duty, and hope to exculpate himself to his maker by that doctrine, let him consider whether he sustains this excuse from his servants and dependants when they are negligent or unfaithful in what is committed to their charge.

Bishop Butler, in his *Analogy*, has an excellent chapter upon *the opinion of necessity considered as influencing practice*, which I think highly deserving the consideration of those who are inclined to that opinion.[37]

---

[37] Reid is referring to the *Analogy of Religion*, by Bishop Butler (1692–1752), specifically Part I, Chapter iv, 'Of a State of Probation, as Implying Trial, Difficulties, and Danger'.

Appendix II
Lecture Notes

Eloquence of the Pulpit[1]

The pulpit {is} a very noble field of eloquence, as the speaker has the noblest and most sublime subjects to handle: the nature, the attributes, and the administration of the supreme being; the various dispensations of his grace and goodness towards the children of men; a future judgement and state of rewards and punishment; the end we ought to propose to ourselves in the conduct of life; {and} the wisdom and intrinsic excellence of virtue, and the folly and baseness of vice. These are grand and interesting subjects which the preacher has frequent occasion to display. And they require to be handled in a manner becoming their dignity and importance. His province leads him to touch every spring of the human heart and to draw forth every noble and generous sentiment, as well as to present the most beautiful and grand objects to the imagination. He has an opportunity of instructing the ignorant on things of the highest moment, of convincing the infidel and those who are in dangerous error by sound argument, of comforting the dejected, of rousing and awakening the thoughtless and secure, of determining the resolutions of those who waver between vice and virtue, of fortifying the weak, {and} of open{ing} the eyes of the most wicked to see the folly, the pravity, and the danger of the course they are taking. From all which it is evident that there

---

[1] The placing of several sections of this lecture is uncertain. Reid makes several cryptic notes to himself to insert material written in the margin or on various pages into the body of the lecture. For an alternative ordering see *Logic, Rhetoric, and Fine Arts*, 240–250.

is no species of human eloquence, from the lowest to the most sublime and vehement, which the preacher has not frequent occasion to exercise.

Yet, it may be observed that, notwithstanding the great number of pulpit orators in all Christian countries, yet fewer have attained to the highest pitch in that kind than almost any other kind of eloquence. For, I think it cannot be said that Chrysostom in the more early ages of Christianity, or that Fleshier, Bourdalou, or the Bishop of Clermont among the Roman Catholics, or Saurin, or Tillotson, or Secker, or Blair among the Protestants, have been celebrated for their eloquence as much as Demosthenes and Cicero; not to mention many others who have displayed an uncommon power of persuasion either as senators or barristers.[2] Several reasons may be assigned for this phenomenon, that very few if any pulpit orators have ever acquired that power of persuasion in the pulpit which many have attained at the bar or in the senate house. I shall mention some of those reasons that serve to account for this, as it may serve to give some light to the nature of the eloquence of the pulpit.

1) A higher degree of purity and sanctity of manners is required in the preacher than in any other public speaker. And where this is not conspicuous in his character, it will weaken much the force of his eloquence. Every speaker is heard with more attention and regard if we believe him to be a wise and a good man. But of all speakers, the least indulgence is shown to him whose very profession and business it is to be an authorized censor of manners and to point out every deviation from the line of our duty. Men never fail to compare the path of duty which he points out and recommends with his own practice. And if any discrepancy is observed, this must greatly weaken the force of his exhortations and reproofs.

---

[2] John Chrysostom (c. 349–407), Bishop Valentin-Esprit Fléchier (1632–1704), Lousi Bourdaloue (1632–1704), Bishop Jean-Baptiste Massillon (1663–1742), Jacques Saurin (1677–1730), John Tillotson (1630–1694), Thomas Secker (1693–1768), Hugh Blair (1718–1800), Demosthenes (384–322 BC), and Marcus Tullius Cicero (106–43 BC).

When it appears that a man's arguments do not convince himself, they can have little weight to convince others. He is like a commander that exhorts his men to stand against the enemy while he himself runs away. There are many occasions of public speaking in civil and political matters in which it matters little to the hearers what is the private character of the speaker. And if it is not remarkably odious, they can show a great indulgence and consider more what is said than who says it. But little or no indulgence will be given to him who takes upon him to correct others for vices from which he himself is not free. There is, therefore, required in the pulpit orator, in order to {assure} his success, an uncommon degree of purity of morals and sanctity of life, an unfeigned concern for the honour of God and the salvation of men's souls, {and} a severity against vice joined with pity and compassion towards the vicious. For as an apostle who was himself a very successful preacher tells us, 'the servant of the Lord must not strive, but be gentle to all men, apt to teach, patient, in meekness instructing those that oppose themselves'.[3]

It may be observed that the preachers of Christianity have been always most successful when they were most exposed to persecution and suffering for the sake of religion. They have then an opportunity of and of showing in the most convincing manner that is possible for men to prefer the concerns of another world to all the interests of this.

2) We may observe that the hearers to whom the preacher addresses himself are more diversified in character than those of other orators. A Christian congregation, especially in a populous city, is of all audiences the most promiscuous. And, therefore, it requires the greatest judgement and art to suit what is said and the manner of saying it to the audience. What would be both agreeable and useful to the one part of the audience may be above the capacity of others and quite useless to them. What may suit the manner of thinking and the innocent prejudices of one part may be disgusting to another part. It requires great attention and judgement in the speaker in such an assembly that, while he avoids either in

---

[3] St. Paul the Apostle (c.4–c. 64 AD), 2 Timothy 2:24–25a.

style or in sentiment soaring above the capacity of the lower class, he may not on the other hand sink below the regard of the higher. To attain simplicity without flatness, delicacy without refinement, {and} perspicuity without recurring to low idioms and similitudes will require his utmost care. The barrister in this respect has a peculiar advantage when he addresses one judge or a few judges, who are men of the same rank, of similar education, and not differing greatly in their studies and attainments. When he addresses the jury he has a greater variety of auditors. A speaker in the House of Peers has not so various an auditory as one who harangues in the House of Commons. It has often happened, as we had occasion to observe before, that the eloquence which carried all before it in the lower house has fallen greatly in its force when carried up to the higher.[4] Even in the lower house, the audience have all the education of gentlemen, and is not nearly so promiscuous as the popular assemblies of Athens and Rome. Yet even of these women, minors, and servants make no part. We may, therefore, justly reckon the audience which the preacher addresses the most promiscuous of any, and by that means he is deprived of some advantages which other speakers have from a greater uniformity of character in the persons to be wrought upon.

3) If we compare the subjects that are handled in the pulpit and at the bar or in the senate, we shall find that in this respect the preacher has indeed some advantages over other speakers, but these are balanced and perhaps more than balanced by other disadvantages. The perfections and providence of the supreme being, the relation we stand in to him and to our fellow creatures, and the duties consequent thereupon are without doubt the most sublime and the most important of all subjects of discourse. And in this the preacher may be conceived to have a great advantage of other speakers. The barrister must often be employed in explaining ambiguous statutes {or} in reconciling contradictory laws or precedents. Critical discussions and nice distinctions are a subject not very favourable to a display of

---

[4] Reid is referring to a previous lecture on rhetoric. See *Logic, Rhetoric, and Fine Arts*, 225.

rhetorical powers. Nor is the discussing {of} the testimony of witnesses in matters of fact much more favourable. In criminal cases, however, where there is accusation and defence, there is ample field for the descriptive, the pathetic, and the vehement, as well as the argumentative.[5]

In deliberations of the senate, the advantage or hurt to the state of measures that are under deliberation are the principal topics to be used, and these undoubtedly give great scope to every species of eloquence. But, after all, the preacher has objects to present that are still more important and affecting. The most important concerns of our present life vanish when compared with those of the life to come.

This seeming advantage which the pulpital orator has from the great weight and importance of his subject is perhaps counterbalanced or outweighed by its being more spiritual and intellectual, and less an object of the senses. The virtues and vices are things of an abstract nature, which do not make so strong an impression on men's imagination as objects of sense. The attention is more easily roused to individual things than to abstract notions, to things present than to things that may be at a great distance, {and} to objects of sense than to the objects of faith. On this account, preachers that have talents affect most when they descend to particular and real characters, as in funeral orations, and when virtues are illustrated by the examples of them exhibited in the life of our saviour and of good men whose history is recorded in the sacred writings. In the Church of Rome, the lives of canonized saints and the history of holy relics, which are frequently exhibited in their discourses, have a powerful tendency to enflame the devotion of the credulous multitude.

---

[5] Reid is referring to the five-fold division of the kinds of serious eloquence, divided according to their end, described in his previous lectures. They are 1) didactic, 'which is addressed to the understanding in order to inform, instruct, or explain'; 2) argumentative, 'which is intended to convince or create belief'; 3) descriptive, 'which is addressed to the fancy, imagination or taste and is intended to please'; 4) pathetic, 'which is addressed to the passions'; and 5) vehement, which 'is addressed to the will to persuade to action'. Ibid, 229.

4) I would observe in the last place that the pure doctrine of Jesus Christ is most opposite to the principles, the passions, and the habits by which the greater part of men are governed, so that the pulpit orator has greater obstacles to oppose his success than any other. By the wise destination of the Almighty, man is placed in such a station in this world as that his cares and his labours must be, for the greatest part, employed about things pertaining to the present life. The necessities of his nature and the care of his animal life occupy much of his time and thoughts, and the habit of attending to objects of a temporal kind indisposes him for the contemplation of those of a spiritual nature, though {the latter are} in themselves much more important. The things of another world to which the preacher would call our attention are hid, as it were, behind a veil. They are the objects of faith, and not of sense, attended indeed with sufficient evidence to convince the candid and ingenuous who have a hearty concern to know the will of God and to do it, but not with that irresistible conviction which sense or memory affords. Were we to discern the things of a future world with the same irresistible evidence as we see those which occupy our thoughts and cares here, we should be rendered altogether unfit for the occupations of our present state. Earthly concerns would not have the power of engaging our attention for a single moment. All human objects would be annihilated in our eye, and a total stagnation in the affairs of this world would be the consequence all the studies and pursuits; the arts and labours which now employ the activity of man would be neglected and abandoned. Man would no longer be a fit inhabitant of this world, nor be qualified for those exertions which are allotted to him in his present state of being. His views being raised above the measure of humanity, he would regard the pursuits of men with scorn, as dreams and puerile amusements. That veil which hides the future world from our eyes is wisely adapted to the state of humanity, and is fit and proper to beings in that stage of existence which we occupy.

Our present state is intended by our maker as a state of trial and improvement in which, by proper discipline, we may be trained to be fit for a higher state. Difficulty and temptation are proper for such a state. The virtues of fortitude, temperance, and self-denial, of moderation in prosperity, patience in adversity, submission to the will of God, charity, and a forgiving disposition towards men are not to be acquired without labour and difficulty amid the various temptations wherewith we are surrounded. One part of our trial is that we are surrounded with objects that are apt to take possession of our hearts and engross all our attention. This strong attachment to the objects of sense, the preacher has to oppose his efforts; and, therefore, it need not appear wonderful that he often speaks with less effect on his hearers than those who move them by those very passions which govern their ordinary conduct in life.

And indeed, it deserves our notice that this noble and ample field for every strain of eloquence is peculiar to the Christian religion, as that is the only institution we know in which there is an order of men appointed for this very purpose of instructing, admonishing, and persuading their fellow men in all matters pertaining to their moral and religious conduct in life, and preserving in their minds a lively sense of those great arguments and motives which both reason and revelation suggest to engage us to the practice of our duty. And it must be acknowledged, by every candid person, that this institution is truly worthy of God as one of the best means of carrying on the improvement of mankind in knowledge and virtue.

Every institution, through the weakness and imperfection of men, may be abused: so may this. But it ought to be honoured on account of its manifest tendency to promote the good of mankind, as well as on account of its divine authority. And those who dedicate their lives to this office ought surely to weigh well the importance of it and to exert their utmost endeavours to qualify themselves duly for it. It is my business only to speak of that kind of eloquence or power of speech which is fitted to this office.

As we distinguished eloquence into grave and facetious,[6] it is obvious that the grave kind is that which is suited to the pulpit. When men are met together for religious worship and with a view to be instructed and admonished in things

---

[6] Ibid.

pertaining to their salvation, strains of wit, of humour, or of ridicule can hardly be suitable. Yet I do not deny that there may be occasions wherein the folly of vice may be reproached so as to be an object of ridicule, and in like manner where errors are to be refuted that are truly absurd and contrary to the first principles of human belief. That absurdity may be laid open even in the pulpit. Wit and humour can hardly at any time be made consistent with the gravity and solemnity of pulpit discourses. Ridicule sometimes may, but requires delicate management a great restraint. {See, for example,} South, Sanderson,[7] Tillotson.

It is not necessary, I apprehend, that every discourse from the pulpit should be pathetic or vehement. There may be very useful preachers whose talents are not adapted to the higher strains of eloquence, and such should not attempt what is above their force. The didactic style in sermons, if accompanied with a proper degree of seriousness and fervour, may be very useful to well disposed hearers. In subjects where the main intention of the speaker is to enlighten the understanding, it is the most proper style. Even the didactic style, as we had occasion before to observe, may be more simple or more elevated according to the dignity of the subject.[8] Indeed, if the talents of a preacher to move the passions were ever so great, I apprehend he ought to make it a chief object of his preaching to enlighten the understanding of his hearers. That fervour of piety which is not grounded upon a sound understanding of the principles of religion is commonly of short duration and has but a small influence upon the conduct of life when that fervour cools, and even while it lasts it borders more upon enthusiasm than upon rational piety. A certain tone of voice and the use of favourite phrases are apt to catch the multitude, who measure their edification by sermons by the emotions they feel at the time, and not by what they learn, or the purposes and resolutions they form with regard to their future conduct.

---

[7] Robert South (1634–1716) and Robert Sanderson (1587–1663) were both celebrated Anglican preachers.

[8] See note 5.

As in every subject where the didactic style is used, so particularly in instruction from the pulpit, perspicuity ought carefully to be studied. There is no instruction where the understanding of the hearer is not carried along. And the preacher having, of all audiences, the most promiscuous, ought to adapt his style to the capacity of the greater part, which in all congregations are the unlearned and unimproved. There may {be} a want of perspicuity even when scriptural phrases are used, if they are not explained or so used as to make their meaning obvious. There are many words and phrases in use among the learned and among the persons in the higher spheres of life which are not understood by the vulgar, which ought to be avoided in popular discourses, in order to {provide} perspicuity. There are even theological terms of this kind which ought to be kept within the schools of theology and ought not to be carried to the pulpit.

On the other hand, I apprehend, a preacher ought never to affect vulgarity either in his words, or phrases, or pronunciation. Some may have attempted by such vulgarities to gain popular applause, at the same time that they give disgust to hearers of more understanding. But the applause got by this means, if any is got, will be short lived; for no man will long maintain the reputation of good preacher who is unacceptable to the more intelligent part of his audience.

As to the matter of the preacher's instructions, that is the whole doctrine of the gospel and the rules of Christian life. The doctrines of the Christian religion have all a tendency to promote piety and virtue in life, and they are more or less important in proportion to that tendency. Many of them have been variously explained, and many subtle disputes raised about {them} in the schools of theologians. Where the points that are controverted have no tendency to make men better men and better Christians, they may safely be left to the schools and ought never to enter the pulpit. But it is necessary that the great doctrines of Christianity should be set in the clearest light and their practical tendency pointed out that the hearers may be well instructed in them, and that they may not consider them only as matters of barren speculation.

Errors that are pernicious to morals or piety, where the hearers may be in danger to be drawn into them, ought without doubt to be solidly and judiciously refuted, whether they tend to nourish superstition or enthusiasm, whether their tendency be to relax Christian morals or to impose burdens upon men's consciences which the author of our religion has not imposed.

To execute these parts of his office properly, so as to give his attentive hearers sober, just, and rational sentiments of the scheme of the Christian religion and to establish them firmly in the belief of it, though it requires abilities and application, yet is perhaps the easiest part of the preacher's business.

To inculcate the precepts of religion, so as to give men a right apprehension of them without swerving either to the right hand or to the left, either the extreme of too much rigour and precision on the one hand, or into the more dangerous extreme, laxness and indulgence to vicious inclinations and practices on the other, requires both soundness of judgement and purity of heart, and much knowledge of the artifices by which men are wont to impose upon themselves, either in order to extenuate their faults or to put an undue value upon their good qualities.

Besides instructing his hearers and enlightening their understanding, it is the business of the preacher to please, that his instructions may be received with better effect. But here it is of the greatest importance that he seek to please only in order to profit his hearers, and not in order to gain a vain applause either with those of rank or with the vulgar. The vanity of hunting after applause is a weakness that cleaves fast to human nature, and every speaker ought to guard against it, but the preacher more than any other. It is a greater fault in him who ought to have ends in view of so much superior a nature. And it will not be so easily overlooked. It is a vice which cannot be long concealed. It will show itself in one way or another. No veil of hypocrisy is able to conceal it from a discerning eye. And in proportion as it appears, it will bring a man into contempt and defeat its own end. The only lawful way, therefore, and, we may say, the only effectual way in which a preacher should study to please is not by following the vices and follies of the great or the prejudices of the vulgar, but by sanctity of manners in his life and that dignity in his public performances which fits them for the end he ought to have in view, of enlightening the understandings, of mending the hearts, and {of} reforming the lives of his hearers. If this appears to be his end in his performances, and it will be difficult if at all possible to make it appear to be unless it really is so, this is of all the most effectual way to please. It will make many imperfections to be overlooked in his pronunciation and action, many lesser defects in matter and in style. Although, he ought not be inattentive even to these lesser defects and imperfections, but to use his best skill and diligence to get the better of them by all means in his power that his performances may be the more acceptable, and by that means the more useful.

The third branch of the preacher's business according to the division I have mentioned[9] is to move and to persuade. In this he has access to display whatever talent he may possess, all his abilities, natural and acquired, in the descriptive, the pathetic, and the vehement.

The descriptive kind of eloquence, of which I before gave an account, may be intended merely to please the fancy by presenting to the imagination agreeable pictures adorned with the ornaments of tropes and figures and allusions. Or, secondly, it may be intended to make a deeper impression upon the mind of what is described, so as to give that force and vivacity to things distant which they naturally have when at hand, that force to things intellectual and objects of faith which we feel in the objects of sense. As to the first of these ends of descriptive eloquence, it can only be allowed to take place in trivial subjects. In grave and important subjects, no ornaments of speech ought to be admitted but what spring naturally from the subject and either throw light upon it or give it a deeper impression upon the mind. Even a judicious historian, whose eloquence is chiefly of the descriptive kind, descends below the dignity of history when he addresses himself merely to the fancy of his readers and seeks to please by similes, antitheses, or other ornaments of

---

[9] At the end of this manuscript Reid briefly records 'The Business of the Preacher, 1. to instruct... 2. to please... 3. to move...'

speech which have no relation to the end he professes to have in view. This is still more applicable to the preacher, who exposes his vanity if he seeks, even in description, such ornaments of speech as have no tendency to throw light upon the subject or to make it enter with more force into the mind of the audience. His descriptions, therefore, ought to be chaste, without lace and trappings, but such as may {be} fitted to make an impression upon the mind corresponding to the dignity and importance of the subject, and such as directs the attention solely to the subject and not to the speaker.

When description is properly executed, it facilitates belief. For, although belief is not merely, as Mr Hume conceives, a lively idea of the thing believed,[10] yet it must be allowed that in things that are not objects of sense, a description which produces a lively conception of the thing contributes much to make the belief of it more easy and more steady.

In the pathetic and vehement {kinds of eloquence}, the pulpit orator makes his address chiefly to the consciences of men, and to their hopes and fears and their other principles of action only as far as they are connected with conscience. There are, therefore, many strains of eloquence that may be used at the bar or in popular assemblies which are unfit for the pulpit. Other orators may enflame the resentment of their audience for injuries done to themselves or their indignation for injuries done to others, almost to fury and malice. But the spirit of a pulpit orator ought to be far different, and when he attempts to enflame party rage, under the guise of religious zeal, he departs from his character and knows not what manner of spirit he is of.[11] His business is rather to allay such angry passions. He must not strive but be gentle to all men, and meek even to those that oppose him.[12] His zeal must be employed against the vices and corruptions of men, but not against their persons.

There is no kind of persuasion that has a greater force of argument to support it, yet there is none that is commonly

---

[10] See Hume, *Treatise*, I.i.1.
[11] See Luke 9:55.
[12] See note 3.

attended with less success than that which is employed to persuade men to amend their moral conduct, to correct their vices, to subdue their passions, and to act the part which their own minds dictate to them they ought to act. This is the chief part of the business of the preacher and, of all, the most difficult. The difficulty, as was just now observed, arises not from the want of solid arguments, but from the strength of evil habits and of animal passions, and the weakness of the governing principles of reason and conscience.

What I said before of the best and most effectual way of pleasing is equally applicable to the end of persuading: that nothing renders sermons so persuasive as known sanctity of life and manners in the preacher, and seriousness and fervour in delivering them. What comes from the heart of the speaker has power to reach the hearts of the hearers. And, without this, all the ornaments of rhetoric will be of little avail. The most important thing of all, therefore, is that the preacher appear, both from the general tenor of his life and from the manner of his preaching, to have a real and a deep conviction on his own mind of the things of which he would convince his hearers.

Of the Immortality of the Soul

January 20, 1776

The last question concerning the soul in general that I intend to consider is that which regards its duration, whether it perishes with the body or survives the funeral of the body and continues to live, to think, and {to} act in some future state.[13]

The wisest, the bravest, and the most virtuous men in all ages and in all nations which were but a little emerged from barbarity—nay, even most of the more barbarous nations— have been persuaded that there is a future life, wherein the good will be happy and wherein the murderer, the adulterer, the unjust, {and} the oppressor, who by their person, or interest, or cunning escaped the just punishment of their crimes in this world, shall be obliged to appear before a

---

[13] In previous lectures, Reid addressed the questions of the soul's immateriality and place.

higher and an impartial tribunal, by which they shall receive the just reward for their evil deeds.

This tribunal has been considered as the last refuge of oppressed innocence, where it may expect to be vindicated from open violence or secret calumny and detraction, as the hope of every good man and the terror of the most powerful villain. These sentiments of a future state have been extremely general. Nor are we able to trace the origin of them. The improvements made in philosophy in different ages have furnished arguments for this opinion, but it has been generally entertained by men before they could reason upon the subject. Socrates,[14] the wisest of all the Greek philosophers, supported himself by the hope of a future state under an unjust accusation of his enemies and an unjust sentence of the Athenians. He drank with perfect composure and serenity the cup of poison, after he had entertained his friends for many hours on this very subject of the immortality of the soul.[15] Confucius,[16] the great philosopher of the Chinese, who lived near about the same time with Socrates and seems very much to have resembled him in his opinions and in his character, appears to have been persuaded of the same doctrine of the future existence of men. The priests of Egypt, the Brahmins of India, the druids of Gaul, {and} the bards of our rude ancestors agreed in this opinion with the philosophers of Greece and Rome, while they hardly agreed in any thing else.

It may therefore be enquired, what is the origin of this notion of a future state so general among mankind? It appears to be so general and so ancient that it could not take its rise from any refined notions or subtle reasoning concerning the soul. These are of a much later date, and, although they may give a great confirmation to this opinion, they do not seem to {have} given birth to it. It seems to me to arise very naturally from the consciences of men and from some general observation of the administration of things in this world. For:

---

[14] Socrates (c. 470–399 BC).
[15] Plato (c. 428–c. 347 BC), *Phaedo*.
[16] Confucius (551–479 BC).

1) Men's consciences dictates to them that atrocious crimes ought to be punished, that oppressed innocence ought to be vindicated and defended, and that heroic virtue ought to be rewarded. These are opinions which are interwoven into our constitution and which cannot be rooted out while men have that faculty which we call conscience. And what we are persuaded ought to be, we are very prone to believe will actually be one time or another. Nothing appears to us more becoming the supreme being than a universal retribution according to the merit or demerit of persons.

2) When we observe the administration of things in the world, we cannot but take notice of a kind of justice or retribution that generally prevails, although not always. Wisdom and industry are generally rewarded with success. Justice, generosity, and humanity are rewarded, not only by the great pleasure and satisfaction, {and} the security and tranquillity of mind that attends the exercise of those virtues, but by the love, the esteem, and the confidence of mankind. On the contrary, every vice commonly brings its own punishment along with it, or is followed by it sooner or later. Indolence and prodigality bring on poverty. Lying and deceit are punished by the want of trust and the contempt of mankind. Secret villainies are often strangely and unexpectedly brought to light. Injurious conduct draws after it the hatred {and} resentment {of} the injured, and is often retaliated by their posterity. Intemperance and dissolute pleasures have their natural punishments, which are well known to those that pursue them. And crimes that are hurtful to society have their just punishment often from the civil magistrate. Thus a light observation of the source of things may satisfy us that there is a regard to justice manifested in the general constitution of nature and in the administration of the world. And as it cannot be denied that there are instances, both of successful villainies which are not punished as they deserve in this world and of virtuous actions for which men suffer or are not rewarded, we are led to think that justice completes that work in another state (which we evidently see begun here) of a universal retribution according to the merit and demerit of persons.

These sentiments are very obvious and require no deep or subtle reasoning. We may trace them among all nations that are but a little removed from barbarity. And, as they naturally lead to the belief of a future state, I am apt to think that it is by them that men who had not the benefit of revelation have been so generally led to this belief. Nor do I know any other reasonable account that can be given why this opinion began so early and spread so wide.

But it may be asked whether this reasoning which has led men so generally to believe a future state of existence is really conclusive. I answer that, to me, it appears to have very considerable force. For must we not allow that virtue ought to be rewarded and vice punished? Must we not allow that we are accountable for our conduct and should receive accordingly? This is the voice of every man's conscience. And the voice of conscience is the voice of God. That natural and unavoidable expectation which every man has of recompense for what he has done well or ill is a kind of revelation from heaven. It is an anticipation, given us by the author of our nature, of what he intends to do. But, although virtue is very often rewarded and vice punished in the present state, there is the greatest probability that this is not always the case. Have there not been useful schemes for the good of mankind, continued with the best intention, which have perished with their authors and were never brought to light? Have there not been many wise and good men, great benefactors to mankind and an honour to humanity, who have perished in a noble struggle in the cause of their country or in the cause of truth and virtue? Their fall was glorious, and the generous mind would wish for their fate even if there was no future state. But shall they have no reward? Will death put them upon a level with the tyrant that wallowed in human blood and spread dissolution through provinces and kingdoms to gratify his ambition and lust of power? Is there no ear to hear the groans of those whom his sword has made widows and fatherless? Surely, reason could not approve of such an administration of the world as this. We behoved to lay our hand upon our mouth,[17] but we could not possibly think that these ought to go thus. But, when we suppose a future state of retribution,

---

[17] Job 40:4.

the black and gloomy scene clears up. The future is made consistent with the present, and a just and righteous administration shines forth in the whole plan of the universe.

The sum of this argument is that virtue ought to be rewarded and vice punished by a just and equal retribution. And it is reasonable to expect this under the divine administration. What we see of the divine administration here gives us still more reason to expect an equal retribution, although it can only be in a future state. There are many other arguments that corroborate this argument from the dictates of our conscience and our observation of the general administration of things. But before we take notice of them, it may {be} proper to consider what arguments have been used to prove that the soul does not continue to exist after death, but perishes with the body.

There have not been wanting some persons in ancient and modern times who have exercised their wit and genius to prove that mankind have no reason to expect any continuance of their existence after the present life, and endeavour to solace themselves and their readers with the comfortable and high-spirited prospect of perpetual annihilation.

The whole Epicurean sect adopted this opinion, and these arguments in support of it are at large displayed by Lucretius.[18] The arguments of Pomponatius are much to the same purpose.[19] The sum of them amounts to this, that the soul begins to exist with the body, it grows up with it, and its faculties ripen in the same manner as those of the body. Its operations are exercised only by means of the bodily organs, it gradually decays and dotes, as the body droops and stiffens with old age. It seems, therefore, to depend entirely upon the structure of the body, and when that structure is destroyed, the soul must perish in the wreck, as the liquor is spilt and dissipated when the vessel that contained it is broke.

In answer to these arguments, I would observe that there would be some strength in them if the soul be supposed to be

---

[18] See *De Rerum Natura* [*On the Nature of Things*], especially Book III.
[19] Pietro Pomponazzi (1462–1525).

no distinct substance from the body, but only some modification of matter. It might be supposed with some probability that death destroys that modification upon which thinking depends. But nothing can be more absurd than to conceive mind to be a modification of body. Take a piece of matter, put into the form of a sphere, a cube, a prism, a pyramid, etc. It is nothing nearer to a thinking being in one of these forms that another. 'For in these elements there is nothing to possess the power of memory, thought, reflection, nothing capable of retaining the past, or foreseeing the future and grasping the present.'[20] Nay, we have endeavoured to show that the mind must be a substance that is not divisible that does not consist of parts.[21] Consequently, the destroying {of, or} any modification in, the body cannot destroy the soul, which is a substance distinct from the body. These different substances are indeed, in our present state, so connected that many of the operations of the mind are performed by means of the organs of the body. And the good or bad constitution of the body affects the mind. But we have no evidence that this connection with such a body must last forever. It is more surprising that such a connection should ever have existed than that it should at last be dissolved. If a limb of the body is cut off, the soul is left entire, though it is no more connected with that limb. This Epicurean argument therefore does not conclude; we grant the premises, but deny the conclusion. We grant that the soul is presently so connected with the body as to be greatly affected by the good or bad state of it. But it follows not from this that it may not continue to exist when that connexion is totally broke. We may with better reason conclude, on the contrary, that as the operations of the mind are limited and confined by its connexion with the body, those operations will be more free and unconfined when that connexion is dissolved.

Indeed, we may observe, and it deserves our notice, that neither the principles of Epicurus nor those of any other of the atheistic sects can afford any solid argument against the

---

[20] Cicero, *Tusculan Disputations*, I.xxvii.66. Reid quotes the Latin.
[21] Reid is referring to his first lecture on the soul. See 'About These Texts', above pages 14–19.

duration of the soul after death. For if body and soul were both produced by a fortuitous dance of atoms, it does not follow that the one should be destroyed when the other loses its vital form. The same chance that produced it may as well continue it after death. If the soul did consist of some subtle matter, this subtle matter may be separated from the body at death and continue to exist after it. If blind necessity produced this world without any governing mind, the same necessity may change it into another wherein we may continue to exist. There is, therefore, no argument of any force against the duration of the soul upon any hypothesis whatsoever. Let us proceed to mention some other arguments that serve to corroborate what we have already advanced for its duration after death.

1. We have strong ground to believe that no substance that ever God made is annihilated. In all the operations of nature that fall under our notice, of generation, growth, decay, corruption, {and} putrefaction in animals and vegetables, of fermentation, solution, precipitation, evaporation, calcination, and concretion in other substances, there does not appear to be any new matter created or any single atom annihilated which before existed. In all these operations, there is nothing but various compositions and decompositions of the matter which already existed without any addition of new or annihilation of the old. When we reduce matter to its least parts, these have always been and continue to be the same under all their various arrangements and successive forms. There does not appear in nature any destruction of any simple substances, but only a resolution of those that are compounded into their parts. The mind is a simple substance which cannot be destroyed by resolving it into its compounding parts. If it is destroyed, it must be annihilated, but this is an operation of which the whole course of nature and all that has been discovered in natural philosophy and chemistry does not afford a single instance, and therefore we can have no reason to suppose it in the case of the soul. This argument is elegantly expressed by the Roman orator in the words:

> But if nothing is mixed in souls, nothing compounded, nothing joined together, nothing connected, nothing two-

fold; certainly it cannot be separated, nor divided, nor rent, nor pulled apart: nor, therefore, can it die. For death, just as a departure, is both a separation and breaking up of those parts which before death were held together by some union. (And indeed if no body perishes, although it is diminished by the division itself, and assumes diverse forms, less by far will its spiritual substance be destroyed, which has no parts into which it is able to dissolve: especially when nothing disappears into nothing, least of all a thing more exceptional than any body.)[22]

2. The powers and capacities of the human soul strongly indicate its being intended for a longer duration than the present life. I shall mention only its powers of improving continually in knowledge and in virtue. The noblest minds pursue these noble objects and thirst after them with ardour. But very often, while they are but setting out in the glorious course, death cuts it short. Shall we think that he who feeds the ravens and hears the cry of the young lions; he who hath provided means for the gratification of every bodily appetite of the human species as far as is proper;[23] shall we think, I say, that this bountiful father of the universe hath given desires and appetites to men of a far nobler kind which he intends should never be satisfied? Even when men live out their days to the common period of human life, the time is not sufficient for making that progress in knowledge and virtue of which the soul is capable. How much of human life is consumed in the weakness of infancy, the folly of childhood, the giddiness of youth, and languor of sickness or old age? How much in sleep, how much in the necessary care of the body and relaxation of the mind? And in the far greater part of mankind, whose natural capacities are not inferior to the rest, is not almost all that remains employed in some

---

[22] According to Derek R. Brookes, this quotation is from *De mente humana* [*The Human Mind*], VI.vi, by Jean-Baptist du Hamel (1624–1706). See *Intellectual Powers*, 624n. The first half of the quotation is a slightly adapted quotation from Cicero's *Tusculan Disputations*, I.xxix. Reid placed du Hamel's gloss in parentheses. Translation by Rocki Wentzel.

[23] See Psalm 104:21 and 147:9.

laborious calling which gives but little exercise to the noblest powers of the mind? How many savage nations {are there} in whom their capacity for knowledge and virtue lies dead through life for want of the means of culture? So that, if there was no future life, we could not but conceive that the souls of most men were made in vain, having no part assigned them in life wherein the noblest powers of their minds can have access to exert themselves and to acquire that enlargement and improvement of which they are capable.

3. It is agreeable to all that we see of the course of nature that man and other animals should pass through various successive states, as different as the present life can be supposed to be from a future. Nay, we see many instances wherein animals pass from one of these states to another by a change not very unlike that which we call death. Consider a bird in the egg. It has a close and seemingly inseparable connection with the egg, and if the egg is broke, the bird perishes, all the air and the food that sustains it is contained in the egg, and if we were to trust to analogical reasoning drawn from the former state of the being, we should be apt to conclude that when this food and air contained in the egg are exhausted, the bird must then die. It seems, accordingly, to be in great distress. It has a convulsive struggle and agony not unlike the agony of death, but by this struggle the shell is burst, and it is so brought into a new world with powers far more enlarged and objects more extensive than those it was acquainted with in the prison of the egg. What a difference is there between the state of the bird confined to the dark prison of the egg and its after-state, when it wings the air or tastes the sweets of a delightful grove, and makes an addition to them by its cheerful melody.

I might trace the many successive states of a caterpillar which first is enclosed in an egg and bursts out from it in the form of a caterpillar, much in the same manner as the bird does. In this new form, it has locomotive powers, it sees and gathers its food, it spins and has many curious arts by means of its spinning of conveying itself from one leaf to another and escaping the birds that would prey upon it. But it is still enclosed in a horny coat of mail which seems to be an essential part of its body and cannot be broke without destroying it. As it grows up, it is straitened in this coat of mail and has no longer room for that enlargement of its size which nature intends. What should we expect of a child shut up in a coat of mail that will not permit it to grow to the size of a man? It might be expected that it should turn diseased and deformed, and sicken and die. The caterpillar sickens in like manner and gives over eating. It retires to some convenient place and falls into an agony which seems to be its last, but in this agony, the coat of mail bursts and is thrown off and discovers a new one under it, which allows the animal to grow to a greater size. The last agony of the caterpillar is that by which it is transformed into an aurelia,[24] which seems to be an animal of a quite different form from the caterpillar, having neither feet, nor head, nor any power of transporting itself from one place to another, nor does it take any food in this state. The aurelia grows in the bowels of the caterpillar, and the butterfly, which is the last state of the insect that we perceive, grows in the bowels of the aurelia. The death of the caterpillar was only the birth of the aurelia, and the death of the aurelia is the birth of the butterfly. Nor is this passage from one state to another by a kind of death or convulsive agony to be observed in the inferior animals only. This general law of nature extends to man also. If we consider the state of a child in the womb, it seems as different from its state after birth as we can conceive our present state different from a future state. In this state, it is enclosed in a dark prison, without the use of any of those powers which afterward appear in it, excepting, perhaps, those of drawing nourishment and feeling pain. It grows from the mother as a branch from a tree, her blood fills its veins and arteries and supplies its nourishment, and there is one course of circulation of the vital fluid through the mother and the infant. One would think it impossible that it could live any longer than it is separated from the parent that gave it nourishment in its former state. This separation is not without agonizing throes on the part of the child as well as of the mother. And although, if we were only acquainted with that state of children when they are in the womb, it would be very natural to think that they must perish as soon as excluded,

---

[24] An archaic term for 'chrysalis'.

yet we know that this is only the birth of the child into a new world, where its powers are vastly enlarged and where it acquires a kind of new existence. Thus we see that it is a general law of nature that man and other animals pass from one state of existence to another extremely different, which is, as it were, an entrance into a new world. And, that this passage from one state of existence into another is often made by an event not very unlike to that which we call death. And, that death should be a passage into a new state of existence is much more agreeable to the analogy of nature than that it should put a final period to our existence. Nor is this way of thinking concerning death new. The Indian Brahmins, as Strabo tells us, taught that the present life is the infancy of man and that death is our being born into another world where those shall be happy who lived according to the precepts of virtue.[25]

I cannot put an end to this subject without observing that, of all questions in philosophy, this concerning the future existence of the soul is the most important, and the determination of it has the greatest influence upon the conduct of life. For, if there be a hereafter, then the present life is education for eternity. And the part of a wise man is to conduct it with that view. This gives an elevation to the mind and is the only source of true magnanimity. The soul that is animated by this hope rises superior to the love of pleasure, superior to the fears of death, superior to the applause or the censure of weak and silly men; supported by its own integrity. And, by the hope {of} approbation of the supreme judge, it steers its course to eternity without being sunk by adversity or unduly elated by prosperity, secure of arriving in a safe port at last if it hold the proper course, whatever storms it may meet with in the way.

I shall only farther add that, though this question concerning a future state of existence is of the highest importance to mankind, yet it must be acknowledged that the arguments that philosophy suggests upon this head are not of such strength but that they may leave some doubt in minds of wise and thinking men.

---

[25] Strabo (c. 64 BC–24 AD). See *Geography*, XV.i.59.

The arguments I have advanced are, I think, aboundantly sufficient to prove that we have no reason to conclude that the soul shall perish with the body; but that there may be a future state of existence, for anything we know to the contrary. Nay, I will be bold to say that those arguments make it much more probable that there shall be a future state of existence than that there shall not. The first is more agreeable to all that we see of the divine administration than the last. The probability, therefore, is on that side of the question. But, as there are very different degrees of probability which fall below that degree of evidence which we call certainty, so I think it must be acknowledged that all the evidence we have of a future state from reason or philosophy amounts to probability only and not to certainty. Allowing, then, as I think we ought to allow, that it is highly probable from reason that the souls of men shall continue to exist after death, it cannot be said to be certain from reason. Far less can we know from reason what the nature or duration of this future state shall be, whether we shall pass through a succession of different states hereafter or not, and whether we shall exist forever or at last have a final period put to our existence. These things must depend upon the will and pleasure of the Almighty. Nor can we without arrogance pretend to know these things without a revelation from heaven. Such a revelation, God has been pleased to give us. And surely it must be acknowledged, by every sober and candid mind, that to aid our feeble reason in this most important point by a revelation from heaven—to give us full assurance of a future and immortal state of existence, and of such a state as gives an immense additional force to every argument which reason suggests in favour of virtuous and wise conduct, and deprives vice and folly of every subterfuge—such a revelation, I say, must be acknowledged, by every candid and sober mind, highly beneficial to mankind, and therefore it must appear suitable to the goodness of the indulgent parent of mankind to bestow it.

It is, therefore, agreeable to reason, and it is moreover made certain by revelation, that we shall live forever; that of all the things which we desire and pursue, of all the things we are apt to value ourselves upon in this life, nothing will go along with us or be of any use to us hereafter but our good works and our good habits; that of all the evils we dread or feel here, nothing can hurt us hereafter but our guilt and bad conduct. What elevation of mind the belief of this doctrine must give to the good man? What strength to virtue and to every noble purpose? What consolation under all the calamities that can befall him? What a plain and sure rule it affords us for estimating things according to their real value and importance? And what influence it ought to have upon the whole of our conduct? {All this} is so obvious that I shall only recommend {it} to your own serious reflection.

Of the Duty We Owe to the Supreme Being

March 7, 1766

As all that duty we owe to God must be grounded upon just sentiments of him, our first duty must be to endeavour, by the best use of our reason, to attain just notions of him, his perfections, and universal government. But having already in the lectures on natural theology endeavoured to point out what reason teaches us concerning his nature, his attributes, and his government, we shall not resume what was then delivered, but suppose it as the proper ground {of} all that piety and devout affection which is due to him.

2.[26] Supposing then that we have just sentiments of the supreme being, it is our {second} duty to maintain upon our mind a constant and lively impression of our dependence upon {him}, as we are his creatures. It is the saying of a heathen poet, adopted by one of the sacred writers, that we are his offspring.[27] We are so in a much stricter sense than we are the offspring of our natural parents. He is the universal mind and soul that pervades all nature, that upholds its whole frame, and directs all its movements. From his infinite intelligence all created intelligence is derived.

In what sense God may be said to be the soul of the world: all the life and light that is found in finite beings are

---

[26] Haakonssen suggests that this '2' is in contrast to the first duty, 'to attain just notions of him, his perfections, and universal government' mentioned above. *Practical Ethics*, 181.

[27] See Acts 17:28.

emanations from him, the father of lights,[28] the foundation of life. The curious texture of our bodies, the more curious and wonderful structure of our minds, with all their several intelligent and active powers, are his workmanship. Our noblest powers, our rational and moral powers, which are the glory of the human nature, are a faint image of the deity, and by them it is that we are capable of resembling him in some degree, as well as of knowing him. The inanimate and brute creation are his property and his servants, for he is Lord of all. But the human kind, by their rational and moral natures, are so far exalted as to be dignified with the title of his children, his offspring. And as he has given to man some resemblance of his intellectual and moral perfections in the constitution of the human nature, he has likewise given him some image of his dominion in this world.[29] The extent of human power is so very considerable when it is properly exerted, especially in the higher stations of life, that such persons are justly represented as God's vicegerents on Earth.

Now it is evidently most just and reasonable that our minds should be constantly impressed with a lively sense and conviction that we derive our being and all the privileges and prerogatives of it from our father in heaven; that every blessing we taste is his gift, that every degree of power we are possessed of is derived from him, that all the tender charities of relations, friends, benefactors, {and} country are rays of his benignity and goodness; that all human excellence, even the most exalted and most heroic virtues which every heart admires and every tongue celebrates are only faint images and copies of that perfection of moral excellence which is in the supreme being. It is just and reasonable that we should see the supreme beauty in all the beauties of nature, the supreme wisdom in the admirable contrivance of all his works, the supreme goodness in everything that is agreeable to us or to our fellow creatures.

The duty to the supreme being consists in the devout and loyal affection of the heart towards him, corresponding to his nature and the relations we stand in to him: love, esteem,

---

[28] See James 1:17.
[29] See Genesis 1:28.

veneration, gratitude, submission, obedience, and external religion.[30] It is just and reasonable that we have a constant and lively conviction of his presence with us and of his perfect knowledge of all our actions and even of our most secret thoughts, so that no secret wickedness can escape his eye nor any good intention fail of his gracious notice and approbation. Men see not our intentions, they only guess at them by their outward signs, and these signs are sometimes ambiguous, and often misinterpreted from prejudice, envy, or malignity. These considerations ought to moderate our desire of praise and applauses of men, especially of the foolish and ignorant rabble, and make their censure more tolerable when we are conscious that it is unjust. It is no small comfort to a good man in such circumstances that he has a witness in his own breast that cannot be bribed. But it is still a much greater comfort that he has a higher witness whose judgement is {as} infallible as his knowledge is perfect, and whose approbation is of more avail than of all the world besides. He can discern integrity of heart where it is the prevailing principle, under every disadvantage that may cloud or disfigure it in the eyes of the world. He only can make the proper allowances for the frailty of our nature, for our involuntary errors, and for the strength of temptations, for he knows our frame and remembers our frailty, and pities us as a father pities his children.[31] It is, therefore, most reasonable that our desire of the approbation of our supreme judge and the supreme judge of men and angels should, in a great measure, swallow up our desire of the approbation of our fellow men. This {is} the true, the proper, and natural direction of that thirst of honour which God himself hath planted in the human breast: that as the gravitation of the planets bends chiefly towards the sun, the centre of the system, and in a much inferior degree towards one another; so this desire of honour should lean chiefly toward that

---

[30] The placing of this sentence is uncertain. It appears as a marginal note labelled '2' on the previous page. I have placed it here because Reid writes a '2' in the margin at this point. See *Practical Ethics*, 17, for an alternative placement.

[31] See Psalm 103:13–14.

honour that is from God, the fountain of true honour and the sole infallible judge of worth, and more weakly towards the honour that is from men.

3. It is just and reasonable that we consider the supreme being not only as the witness and the judge of our whole conduct, but as our compassionate father and faithful guardian, whose goodness sympathizes with us even in the afflictions and trials which his wisdom sees necessary for our discipline and culture, who does not afflict willingly, but only for the best purposes, and as a father may sometimes chastise, and sometimes prescribe severe tasks to his dear children. Reason and revelation concur in representing the deity as the refuge of the distressed and those who have none to help them. We are led by a kind of instinct to implore his mercy when all help of man fails. Nor will he who gave us the instinct be deaf to its voice. Reason and revelation concur in representing him to us as a faithful guardian, ready to afford divine aid to every soul that makes any virtuous effort and pants after true glory and honour. The wisdom of God for ends which perhaps it is impossible now fully to comprehend has placed us in such a state that the path of virtue is not always smooth and easy. It is sometimes beset with briars and thorns, sometimes steep and difficult. Reason can discover some causes of this, and there may be others which our reason cannot discover.

¶ Our appetites and passions are of quicker growth than reason and conscience, and ripen more early. They are strengthened by habits of indulgence before the governing powers can exercise their authority. And although there is no natural appetite, affection, or passion which is not useful and necessary as a subordinate part of the human constitutions, yet, however useful they may be as servants, they are hurtful as masters and give often a violent impulse to courses which are contrary both to our real happiness and our duty. If we add to this the influence of bad example and bad education, it is easy to see that a steady course of virtue requires a continued effort. It is a conflict between the flesh and the spirit,[32] between the inferior principles of our nature and

---

[32] See Galatians 5:13–26.

those which ought to bear sway. In this conflict, a man who has good purposes in the main finds many reasons to be diffident of himself. He can recollect many instances wherein his purposes have failed him and have been baffled by a strong temptation. As between winter or summer there is a season wherein these two seem to struggle against each other, and sometimes one seems to gain the ascendant sometimes the other, it happens so in the struggle in the human mind between virtue and vice, especially while good habits have not been long confirmed or bad ones retain a considerable degree of their power. In this dubious conflict, as in every other circumstance of distress or danger, a mind impressed with just sentiments of the supreme being naturally looks up to him for divine aid to strengthen his weakness, to fortify his good purposes, {and} to guard him in the course of his providence from such temptations as might be too strong for him. Nor will the hearer of prayer be deaf to these requests. Virtue is his care. Its votaries are under his protection and guardianship. He will cherish the divine principle as his own offspring till it grows up to maturity.

Lastly, it is just and reasonable to consider what befalls us, whether in itself agreeable or disagreeable, as a part of the divine administration, as what seems meet to the supreme governor to do or permit as part of that culture and discipline which he sees meet for us. In distress and affliction, to which all men are equally liable from the accidents of life, the firm persuasion that nothing befalls us but by the appointment or permission of our father in heaven is the truest source of consolation to a pious mind. He pretends not to a stoical insensibility to pain and grief. But he is persuaded that the evils that befall him are a part of that discipline which a wise and compassionate father sees necessary for his good. He takes them, therefore, as he does a harsh but salutary medicine. The cup which my father hath given me shall I not drink?[33] To bear our afflictions in this way, as it is an essential part of true piety, so it is the most sovereign cordial to the afflicted. Resignation to God is the

---

[33] John 18:11.

softest pillow upon which man can lay his head in distress.[34] That perfect indifference with regard to pain, sickness, poverty, {or} loss of friends which the Stoics pretended to, grounded on the persuasion that there are no evils, I say, this indifference, were it really attainable by human nature, would be so far from adding to the worth of the virtue of patience under these evils and perfect resignation to the will of God that it would diminish it, or rather totally annihilate {it}. For where lies the merit of bearing patiently what is no evil or the loss of what is no {good}?

An indifference with regard to what happens to us, whether health or sickness, poverty or riches, the favour of great men or their neglect, a public employment or a private station, was much inculcated by the Stoics. They taught men to employ their whole concern not about what should happen to them but about what they should do and how they should behave themselves in that station and in those circumstances in which they were placed whatever they were. This was surely a very noble lesson and does great honour to that ancient system of morals. Yet Zeno[35] and the more ancient Stoics seem to have built this elevated system upon too weak a foundation, when they left out of their system the consideration of the providence of the deity and maintained that health, riches, {and} honour were not at all goods, nor the contrary, evils; that the former were not objects of desire but of election, the latter were not objects of aversion but of rejection; that virtue was the only good and therefore the only object that ought to be desired, and vice the only evil that ought {to be} shunned. The solidity and firmness of the foundation does not answer to the grandeur and sublimity of the superstructure. And a man must already be possessed of a very high love and admiration of virtue who can enter into the reasonings of the ancient Stoical school and feel the force of them so strongly as to influence his conduct. They have too much the appearance of rant and enthusiasm rather than of sober reason. But when

---

[34] See Bolingbroke, *Fragments or Minutes of Essays*, L.
[35] Zeno of Citium (c. 335–c. 263 BC). See Diogenes Laertius, *Lives of Eminent Philosophers*, VII.102–4.

we consider a good man as under the paternal care of the supreme being, so that nothing can befall him but by the order and direction of infinite wisdom and goodness, his conduct may be justified to the soberest reason, whereof he leaves the care of his happiness to him that made him, being perfectly assured that he can never suffer in that respect while he is careful to do his duty and to act properly.

But though Zeno and some of the more ancient Stoics left the consideration of the providence of God out of their system, yet we find even some of the heathen philosophers urging this as an argument to moderate our concern about our external goods or evils that happen to us. Plato, in his *{Second} Alcibiades*, represents Socrates as urging this doctrine in a most beautiful manner and with great strength of reason. The later Stoics — Epictetus, Arrian, and M.A. Antoninus[36] — frequently use the same argument, none of them in a more beautiful and striking manner than Juvenal in his tenth satire.

> So is there nothing for people to pray for? If you want my advice, you'll let the gods themselves estimate what will suit us and benefit our circumstances: you see, the gods will bestow gifts that are the most appropriate rather than nice. They care more about people than people do themselves. While we are led by our blind emotional impulses and by empty desire to seek marriage and children from a wife, it is the gods who know who our boys will be and what kind of wife she'll be… You should ask for a sound mind in a sound body. Ask for a heart that is courageous, with no fear of death, that reckons long life among the least of Nature's gifts, that can put up with long anguish, that is unfamiliar with anger, that longs for nothing, that prefers the troubles and gruelling labours of Hercules to the sex and feasts and downy cushions of Sardanapallus.[37]

These oracles of right reason correspond exactly with the oracles of divine wisdom in the Christian religion. 'Not my

---

[36] Epictetus (c. 50–c. 135), Lucius Flavius Arrianus (c. 86–c. 160) and Marcus Aurelius (121–180).

[37] Juvenal (c. 55–127), Satire 10, 345–7 & 356–62. Reid quotes the Latin.

will but thine be done', says our divine teacher.[38] 'Take no thought what ye shall eat or what ye shall drink or wherewithall ye shall be clothed. Your heavenly Father knoweth that ye have need of these things. But seek ye first the Kingdom of God and his righteousness and all these things shall be added unto you.'[39] The passage I have quoted from Juvenal looks as if it had been intended for a paraphrase upon these precepts of our divine teacher.

I must not omit as a part of the duty we owe to the supreme being, obedience to his commands.

Every act of virtue becomes an act of piety towards God when it is done from a regard to his authority, a desire to imitate his perfection and obtain his approbation.

The vices contrary to piety come under the denomination of impiety, the neglect or contempt of those duties of true piety. Dishonourable sentiments of the supreme being lead to those corruptions of true piety: superstition; a persecuting spirit; enthusiasm; fanaticism; irreverence to the deity in common swearing; contempt of public worship; attributing to chance, fortune, and luck the events that befall us; discontent with our condition; {and} undue anxiety about events. Every vice is in some sense impiety.

Reflexions: 1) Piety an essential part of virtue and one of the strongest inducements to every other part of it. A source of joy. 2) Too little considered by heathen philosophers on this view. 3) The Christian system more rational in this respect.

March 8, 1768

There are some persons who pretend to high notions of virtue and honour, who seem to entertain a very mean opinion of piety and devotion as something that may be fit for the entertainment of monks and old women, but is rather an unnecessary encumbrance to a man in active life; and that one may be a man of virtue and honour without minding religion at all.

---

[38] Luke 22:42.
[39] See Matthew 6:32-33.

Nothing in human character is more surprising or unaccountable than the manner in which some men impose upon themselves by empty forms of virtue and honour, others by no less empty forms of religion. No man can bear the thought of his being perfectly worthless. This would make a man detestable to himself and to account his existence a curse. Therefore a man, to preserve a character with himself as well as with the rest of mankind, will cultivate some good quality which may cover all his faults with himself and, perhaps, with others. His good qualities, however, must be dignified with the sacred names of virtue, honour, or religion.

But I cannot help thinking that such virtue as disdains any aid of religion stands upon a very slippery foundation, and will hardly be able to endure any severe trial. For how can we conceive a man to believe himself under an obligation to reverence his parents and at the same time to owe no reverence or filial affection to his maker and father in heaven, whose offspring he is in a stronger sense than of his earthly parents? Is a man bound to be grateful to his benefactors and under no obligation of gratitude to his greatest and best benefactor? A man who vainly imagines that he has no need of the aid the protection and guardianship of the Almighty must be extremely arrogant and ignorant of himself. And he who has a just sense of his own weakness and frailty, but thinks it useless and unprofitable to implore divine aid and direction, must have very wrong notions of the deity and be deaf to the voice of his own conscience.

The exercises of a rational piety and devotion have a manifest and powerful tendency in their very nature to strengthen every virtuous principle, to confirm every good purpose, to fortify the mind against every temptation, to raise it in adversity, to temper the giddiness of prosperity, and to enlarge our hearts in sentiments of humanity and kind affection towards the whole creation of God.

Besides the exercises of piety towards God, as they have the most salutary effects for cherishing and strengthening every virtuous disposition, so they have afforded to the worthiest and best men in every age the most rational and most elevated joy and consolation, especially in circumstances of the greatest distress, when men stand most in need of consolation. The testimony of Christians, Jews, and heathens who have experienced this leaves no room to doubt the fact. For these reasons I conceive that those who profess to be friends to virtue while they hold in contempt piety towards God must either be hypocrites or very grossly deluded. {See, for example this quotation from} Shaftesbury's *Inquiry*, end of the first book.

> Hence we may determine justly the relation which virtue has to piety; the first being not complete but in the later: since where the later is wanting, there can neither be the same benignity, firmness, nor constancy; the same good composure of the affections or uniformity of mind. And thus the perfection and height of virtue must be owing to the belief of a God.[40]

The same noble author elsewhere observes 'that the notion of a real divinity is not dry and barren, but such consequences are necessarily drawn from it as must set us in action and find employment for our strongest affections. All the duties of religion evidently flow hence and no exception remains against any of those great maxims which revelation has established'.[41] These are the sentiments of my Lord Shaftesbury, whose freedom of thinking in matters that concern religion will not be questioned. Let me add to this the opinion of a free-thinking heathen. The person I mean is the great Roman orator and philosopher Tully[42] in his second book {of} *de Legibus* [*of Laws*]. The passage I am to recite is the preface to his code of laws, the passage is rather long for a quotation, but on account of its sublimity and eloquence, as well as justness of sentiment, it deserves to be got by heart.

Cicero *de Legibus* [*of Laws*] 2.7:

> So in the very beginning we must persuade our citizens that the gods are the lords and rulers of all things, and that what is done, is done by their will and authority; that they are likewise great benefactors of man, observing the character of

---

[40] Shaftesbury, *An Inquiry Concerning Virtue or Merit*, I.iii.
[41] Shaftesbury, *Characteristics of Men, Manners, Opinions, Times*, Vol. II, 'The Moralists', II.iii.
[42] i.e. Cicero.

every individual, what he does, of what wrong he is guilty, and with what intentions and with what piety he fulfils his religious duties; and that they take note of the pious and the impious. For surely minds which are imbued with such ideas will not fail to form true and useful opinions. Indeed, what is more true than that no one ought to be so foolishly proud as to think that, though reason and intellect exist in himself, they do not exist in the heavens and the universe, or that those things which can hardly be understood by the highest reasoning powers of the human intellect are guided by no reason at all? In truth, the man that is not driven to gratitude by the orderly courses of the stars, the regular alteration of the day and night, the gentle progress of the seasons, and the produce of the earth brought forth for our sustenance — how can such a one be accounted a man at all? And since all things that possess reason stand above those things which are without reason, and since it would be sacrilege to say that anything stands above universal nature, we must admit that reason is inherent in nature. Who will deny that such beliefs are useful when he remembers how often oaths are used to confirm agreements, how important to our well-being is the sanctity of treaties, how many persons are deterred from crime by the fear of divine punishment, and how sacred an association of citizens becomes when the immortal gods are made members of it, either as judges or witnesses?[43]

To this I shall add an authority which I respect as much as any human authority whatsoever. Sir I{saac} Newton, in the queries subjoined to his *Opticks*, Q{uestion} 31, at the end observes that this is the first principle of the moral law given to all nations.

'God is to be acknowledged as the one highest Lord, and his worship is not to be transferred to others', to which he subjoins this remark of his own, 'Indeed, without this principle virtue would be nothing but a mere name.'[44]

---

[43] Reid quotes the Latin.
[44] Reid quotes the Latin. Translation by Rocki Wentzel. As Haakonssen points out, this quotation only appears in Samuel Clarke's second Latin edition of Newton's *Opticks*. See *Practical Ethics*, 186-7.

Appendix III

Personal Papers

Reid's Prayer for his Wife

March 30, 1746

O God, I desire humbly to supplicate thy divine majesty in behalf of my distressed wife, who is by thy hand brought very low and in imminent danger of death, if thou, who alone doest wonders, do not in mercy interpose thy almighty arm and bring her back from the gate of death. I deserve justly, O Lord, that thou shouldst deprive me of the greatest comfort of my life, because I have not been so thankful to thee as I ought for giving me such a kind and affectionate wife. I have forgot thy goodness in bringing us happily together by an unforeseen and undesigned train of events and blessing us with so much love and harmony of affection and so many of the comforts and conveniences of life. I have not been so careful as I ought to have been to stir her up to piety and Christian virtues. I have not taken that pains with my children and servants and relatives as I ought. Alas! I have been too negligent of my pastoral duty and my private devotions, too much given to the pleasures and satisfactions of this world, and too little influenced by the promises and the hope of a future state. I have employed my studies, reading, and conversation rather to please myself than to edify myself and others. I have sinned greatly in neglecting many opportunities of making private applications to my flock and family in the affairs of their souls, and in using too slight preparation for my public exercises. I have thrown away too much of my time in sloth and sleep, and have not done so much for the relief of the poor and destitute as I might have done. The means that providence has afforded me of correcting my evil inclinations I have abused to pamper and feed them in various instances. For these and many other sins which have escaped my memory, thou mightst justly inflict so great a chastisement on me, as to make my children motherless and deprive me of my dear wife. O Lord, accept of my humble and penitent confession of these my offences, which I desire to acknowledge with shame and sorrow, and am resolved by thy grace to amend. If thou art pleased to hearken to the voice of my supplications and grant my request on behalf of my dear wife in restoring her to health, I do promise and covenant through grace to turn from these backslidings, to express my thankfulness by a vigorous discharge of my duty as a Christian, a minister, and master of a family, and by an alms of ten pounds sterling to the poor in meat and money. Lord, pardon if there is anything in this presumptuous or unbecoming a humble penitent sinner; and, Lord, accept of what is sincerely designed as a new bond upon my soul to my duty, through Jesus Christ, my Lord and Saviour.

Prayer from Inaugural Lecture at Glasgow University

Do thou O God, who givest wisdom to them that ask it of thee, enlighten our understanding and purify our hearts. May we partake deeply more of thy divine image, by the uprightness and integrity of our hearts, the innocence of our lives, by a fervent charity towards all men, and by the love of truth and of virtue. May we abhor everything that is evil and unbecoming the dignity of our nature. May we study and practice those things that are pure and just and lovely and of good report, the things that are virtuous and praiseworthy. Purge our minds from all prejudices and errors that may be hurtful to us, and lead us into the knowledge of those truths which tend to enlarge and elevate the mind, and which both enable and dispose us to be more useful to our fellow men. From a deep conviction of the importance of our present behaviour to our future happiness, from a conviction that as we now sow we shall afterwards reap, may we shake off sloth and indolence, and apply ourselves with vigour to the work which thy providence calls us to be employed in. Teach us a due contempt of the pleasures of sense and of the pomp and luxury and vain amusements of this life, and give us a just relish of those intellectual and moral enjoyments which are suited to the dignity of our natures and which lead to true felicity and glory. May thy countenance shine upon this university. May the instructors of the youth be exemplary of everything that is praiseworthy. May they be furnished every talent necessary for discharging the duty of their several professions with honour to themselves and advantage to those who hear them. May the youth be kept in the paths of innocence and preserved from the allurements of vice and from the contagion of evil company. Inspire them with the love of truth, with the desire of improvement, with reverence to thee their creator, and due respect to all to whom they stand related.

Lord bless this city. May the magistrates be always endowed with that wisdom and public spirit which becomes their station. May they be zealous for promoting the good of the place, justice, industry, virtue, and true religion, and for discouraging vice, profaneness, idleness, and fraud of every kind. May they be wise to discern the proper means of answering those good purposes. Lord help the ministers of thy gospel, and may they by their doctrine, by their conversation, and by their example, be the happy instruments of gaining many souls to the love of God and goodness.

May we, O God, incline our ears to wisdom and apply our heats to understanding. May we by thy grace be continually improving in the knowledge of those things which are truly useful in the conduct of life, and in those habits of virtue and true goodness without which we can neither enjoy true felicity, nor be acceptable to thee, nor useful to our fellow men. Give us such a sense of the dignity of that rational and immortal nature which thou hast given us as may engage us to live and to act suitably to it. May we look down with contempt upon those pleasures and enjoyments which we have in common with the brutes that perish, and place our happiness in the imitation of thy moral perfections.

Public Prayer for an Unidentified Occasion

Gracious and merciful God, we implore thy favour and the light of thy countenance as our chief good. Thou alone who made us canst make us happy. Do thou, O God, who has given us understanding above the brutes that perish, enlighten and elevate our minds, give us just views of the noblest objects. Teach us to act suitably to the dignity of our natures and to aspire after that immortal glory and felicity which thou hast set before us.

Having this prize in our eye, may we run the race set before us, and act the part which thy providence assigns us upon the stage of life, so as we shall be approved of our great judge at last. May we every day be improving in useful knowledge, in good habits, and in the capacity and disposition to be useful to our fellow creatures and the obedient subjects of thy kingdom. Make us to understand our errors, our prejudices, and all our faults and imperfections, that we may not think of ourselves above what we ought to think.

Letter to Unidentified Roman Catholic Correspondent

Dear Sir,[1]

I have been in your debt as a correspondent since Christmas. You then rejoiced in the return of that anniversary and in the great events which had happened in our neighbouring kingdom both civil and ecclesiastical.[2] In all this I think you did what might become a good Praefactorian, and I give you the right hand of fellowship. Among the other wonders of the day, let the pure wine of Rome and Geneva mix,[3] leaving the dregs behind!

---

[1] Reid's correspondent is not directly identified, but Paul Wood suggests that it may have been the Scottish Roman Catholic Bishop George Hay (1729–1811) or the Catholic priest and philosopher Joseph Berington (1740–1827). See *Correspondence*, 314.

[2] Reid is referring to the French Revolution.

[3] Here, 'Rome' indicates the Roman Catholic Church and 'Geneva' the Reformed protestant churches, of which the Church of Scotland is one.

I give you joy with all my heart upon the relief granted to protesting Roman Catholics; and I doubt not but we both rejoice in the new constitution of Poland and in the wise and magnanimous conduct of the French Assembly in the elopement and return of the king.[4]

I have been very long persuaded that a nation, to be free, needs only to know the rights of man. I have lived to see this knowledge spread far beyond my most sanguine hopes and produce glorious effects. God grant it may spread more and more, and that those who taste the sweets of liberty may not turn giddy, but make a wise and sober use of it.

Some few here think, or affect to think, that to be a friend to the revolution of France is to be an enemy to the constitution of Britain, or at least to its present administration. I know the contrary to be true in myself, and verily believe that most of my acquaintances who rejoice in that revolution agree with me in this.

In this belief, upon the solicitation of some friends in the college and others, I permitted my name to be used for a meeting of Friends to the French Revolution on the 14th of July, upon the condition and promise of my fellow stewards that no unfavourable reflection, direct or oblique, either on the constitution or present administration of Great Britain was to be heard. I meant nothing more than to own myself not ashamed to be thought a friend to the French Revolution, and thought no mortal needed to take offence at this. But I have within this four and twenty hours received an anonymous letter in a feigned hand professing friendship and great surprize *'that my name should appear at the bottom of an advertisement calling together a set of political madmen and blackguards; and acquainting me that the time is fast approaching when I and some of my brethren will repent the steps we have taken'*.[5]

---

[4] Reid refers to three recent events. 1) The passing of The Catholic Relief Act of 1791, 2) the establishment of a constitutional monarchy in Poland, and 3) the so-far peaceful treatment of the Louis XVI and his family by the French National Assembly.

[5] Reid attended the meeting and read his paper 'Some Thoughts on the Utopian System'. See *Society and Politics*, 134–54.

Whether do you think it more odd: that an old deaf dotard should be announced as a steward of such a meeting, or that it should give any man such offence?

Bibliography

Ahnert, Thomas. 2014. *The Moral Culture of the Scottish Enlightenment, 1690–1805*. The Lewis Walpole Series in Eighteenth-Century Culture and History. New Haven, CT, and London: Yale University Press.

Anaxagoras of Clazomenae. 2007. *Anaxagoras of Clazomenae: Fragments and Testimonia, A Text and Translation with Notes and Essays*. Edited by Patricia Curd. Phoenix Presocratics. Toronto: University of Toronto Press.

Anonymous. 1766. 'Reid's Essays'. Aberdeen. Special Collections, Aberdeen University Library. MS 2131/8/VII.

Anonymous. 1768. 'Dr Reid's Lectures'. Edinburgh. New College Library. MS Box 32.3.

Aquinas, Thomas. 1948. *Summa Theologica*. Translated by Fathers of the English Dominican Province. 5 vols. Notre Dame, IN: Ave Maria Press.

Aristotle. 1984a. *De Interpretatione* [*On Interpretation*]. In *The Complete Works of Aristotle*, edited by Jonathan Barnes, translated by J.L. Ackril. Vol. 1. Bollingen, LXXI. Princeton, NJ: Princeton University Press.

Aristotle. 1984b. *History of Animals*. In *The Complete Works of Aristotle*, edited by Jonathan Barnes, translated by d'A.W. Thompson. Vol. 1. Bollingen, LXXI. Princeton, NJ: Princeton University Press.

Aristotle. 1984c. *Metaphysics*. In *The Complete Works of Aristotle*, edited by Jonathan Barnes, translated by W.D. Ross. Vol. 2. Bollingen, LXXI. Princeton, NJ: Princeton University Press.

Aristotle. 1984d. *Nicomachean Ethics*. In *The Complete Works of Aristotle*, edited by Jonathan Barnes, translated by W.D. Ross and J.O. Urmson. Vol. 2. Bollingen, LXXI. Princeton, NJ: Princeton University Press.

Augustine of Hippo. 1963. *City of God*. Edited by Jeffrey Henderson. Translated by H. William M. Green. Vol. II. VII vols. Loeb Classical Library 412. Cambridge, MA, and London: Harvard University Press.

Baird, George. 1780. 'Notes from the Lectures of Thomas Reid'. Glasgow. Mitchell Library. Ref. No. 104929–104936. V5 pp. 17–

179 and V6 pp. 1–28. ©CSG CIC Glasgow Museums and Libraries Collection: The Mitchell Library, Special Collections.

Bayes, Thomas. 1731. *Divine Benevolence, or an Attempt to Prove That the Principal End of the Divine Providence and Government Is the Happiness of His Creatures.* London: John Noon. https://archive.org/details/DivineBenevolenceOrAnAttemptToProveThatThe.

Bolingbroke, Henry St. John, Lord Viscount. 1754. 'Fragments or Minutes of Essays'. In *The Philosophical Works of the Right Honorable Henry St. John, Lord Viscount Bolingbroke.* Vol. 4. London: David Mallet. https://archive.org/details/philosophicalwor04boli.

Borelli, Giovanni Alfonso. 1685. *De Motu Animalium [On the Movement of Animals].* 2 vols. Batavis: Lugduni.

Buffon, Georges-Leclerc, comte de. 1749–1804. *Historie Naturelle [Natural History].* 36 vols. Paris: Imprimerie Royale.

Butler, Joseph. [1736] 1927. *The Analogy of Religion, Natural and Revealed.* Edited by Ernest Rhys. Everyman's Library 90. New York: J.M. Dent & Sons. https://archive.org/details/analogyreligion00butliala.

Calvin, John. 1960. *Institutes of the Chrstian Religion.* Edited by John T. McNeil. Translated by Ford Lewis Battles. 2 vols. Library of Christian Classics, XX. Philadelphia, PA: The Westminster Press.

Cicero, Marcus Tullius. 1928. *De Legibus [On the Laws].* In *De Re Publica. De Legibus.*, edited by Jeffrey Henderson, translated by Clinton Walker Keyes, Revised. Loeb Classical Library 213. Cambridge, MA, and London: Harvard University Press.

Cicero, Marcus Tullius. 1931. *De Finibus [On Ends].* Edited by Jeffrey Henderson. Translated by H. Rackham. Second. Loeb Classical Library 40. Cambridge, MA, and London: Harvard University Press.

Cicero, Marcus Tullius. 1945. *Tusculan Disputations.* Edited by Jeffrey Henderson. Translated by H. King, J.E. Revised. Loeb Classical Library 141. Cambridge, MA, and London: Harvard University Press.

Cicero, Marcus Tullius. 1951. *De Natura Deorum [On the Nature of the Gods].* In *De Natura Deorum. Academica.*, edited by Jeffrey Henderson, translated by H. Rackham, Revised. Loeb Classical Library 268. Cambridge, MA, and London: Harvard University Press.

Clark, Kelly James, and Justin L. Barrett. 1–37. 'Reidian Religious Epistemology and the Cognitive Science of Religion'. *Journal of the American Academy of Religion* 79 (3): 639–75.

Clarke, Samuel. [1705] 1998. *Demonstration of the Being and Attributes of God and Other Writings.* Edited by Ezio Vailati. Cambridge Texts in the History of Philosophy. Cambridge: Cambridge University Press.

Cleghorn, Robert. 1796. *Sketch of the Character of the Late Thomas Reid, DD. Professor of Moral Philosophy in the University of Glasgow; with Observations on the Danger of Political Innovation, From a Discourse Delivered in 28th Nov. 1794, by Dr. Reid, before the Literary Society in Glasgow College*. Glasgow: J. McNayr & Co.

Cudworth, Ralph. 1678. *The True Intellectual System of the Universe*. Vol. 1. 3 vols. London: Richard Royston. https://archive.org/details/bub_gb_HKbl4NOjBr8C.

Descartes, René. [1641] 1993. *Meditations on First Philosophy*. Translated by Donald A. Cress. Third. Indianapolis, IN, and Cambridge: Hackett.

Evans, G. Stephen. 2010. *Natural Signs and Knowledge of God*. Oxford: Oxford University Press.

Fénelon, François. 1712. *Demonstration de L'existence de Dieu* [*A Demonstration of the Existence God*]. Translated by Anonymous. London: W. Taylor and J. Baker. https://books.google.com/books?id=cNUDAAAAQAAJ.

Fraser, Alexander Campbell. 1898. *Thomas Reid*. Famous Scots. Edinburgh and London: Oliphant Anderson. https://archive.org/details/thomasreid00frasuoft.

Graham, Archibald. 1769. 'Notes of Thomas Reid's Lectures on Pneumatology'. Glasgow. Special Collections, Glasgow University Library. MS Gen 760.

Greville, Fulke, Baron Broke. 1604. *The Tragedy of Mustapha*. London: Nathaniel Butter. https://archive.org/details/tragedyofmustaph00grev.

Halley, Edmund. 1705. *A Synopsis of the Astronomy of Comets*. London: John Senex. https://archive.org/details/synopsisofastron00hall.

Harris, John. 1725. *Lexicon Technicum* [*Technical Lexicon*], *Or, an Universal Dictionary of Arts and Sciences*. 4th ed. London: Dan Browne et al. https://books.google.com/books?id=0GdEAAAAcAAJ.

Harvey, William. 1628. *Exercitatio Anatomica de Motu Cordis et Sanguinis in Animalibus* [*Anatomical Exercise on the Motion of the Heart and Blood in Living Beings*]. Frankfurt: William Fitzer.

Hume, David. [1739] 1978. *A Treatise of Human Nature*. Edited by L.A. Selby-Bigge and P.H. Nidditch. 2nd ed. Oxford: Clarendon Press.

Hume, David. [1748, 1751] 1997. *Enquiries Concerning Human Understanding and Concerning the Principles of Morals*. Edited by L.A. Selby-Bigge and P.H. Nidditch. Third. Oxford: Clarendon Press.

Hume, David. [1779, 1757] 2008. *Principal Writings on Religion Including Dialogues Concerning Natural Religion and The Natural*

History of Religion. Edited by J.C.A Gaskin. Oxford World's Classics. Oxford: Oxford University Press.

Hutcheson, Francis. 1744. *Synopsis Metaphysicae, Ontologiam et Pneumatologiam Complectens* [*Synopsis of Metaphysics, Including Ontology and Pneumatology*]. 3rd ed. Glasgow: Robert and Andrew Foulis.

Jack, Robert. 1775. 'Dr Reid's Lectures'. Glasgow. Special Collections, Glasgow University Library. MS Gen 117.

Juvenal. 2004. 'Satire 10'. In *Juvenal and Persius*, edited by Jeffrey Henderson, translated by Susanna Morton Braund. Loeb Classical Library 91. Cambridge, MA, and London: Harvard University Press.

Kepler, Johannes. [1609] 2015. *Astronomia Nova* [*New Astronomy*]. Translated by William H. Donahue. Revised. Santa Fe, NM: Green Lion Press.

Kolbe, Peter. 1719. *Caput Bonae Spei Hodiernum* [*Today's Cape of Good Hope*]. Nurnberg: Peter Conrad Monath. https://archive.org/details/bub_gb_MbxYAAAAcAAJ.

Kroeker, Esther. 2015. 'Thomas Reid Today'. *Journal of Scottish Philosophy* 13 (2): 95–114.

Laertius, Diogenes. 1931. *Lives of Eminent Philosophers, Books 6–10*. Edited by Jeffrey Henderson. Translated by R.D. Hicks. Revised. Vol. 2. 2 vols. Loeb Classical Library 185. Cambridge, MA, and London: Harvard University Press.

Leibniz, Gottfried, and Samuel Clarke. 1718. *A Collection of Papers, Which Passed Between the Late Mr. Leibnitz, and Dr. Clarke, In the Years 1715 and 1716, Relating to the Principles of Natural Philosophy and Religion*. London: James Knapton. http://www.newtonproject.sussex.ac.uk/catalogue/viewcat.php?id=THEM00224.

Lucretius. 1992. *De Rerum Natura* [*On the Nature of Things*]. Edited by Jeffrey Henderson. Translated by W.H.D. Rouse and Martin Ferguson Smith. Revised. Loeb Classical Library 181. Cambridge, MA, and London: Harvard University Press.

MacPherson, John, ed. 1958. *The Westminster Confession of Faith*. Second. Edinburgh: T&T Clark. https://archive.org/details/westminsterconf00unknuoft.

Milton, John. 2008. *Paradise Lost*. Edited by Stephen Orgel and Jonathan Goldberg. Oxford World's Classics. Oxford: Oxford University Press.

Newton, Isaac. 1719. *Optices* [*Opticks*]. Edited by Samuel Clarke. 2nd ed. London.

Newton, Isaac. 1729. *Philosophiae Naturalis Principia Mathematica* [*The Mathematical Principles of Natural Philosophy*]. Translated by Andrew Motte. 2 vols. London: Benjamin Motte. https://archive.org/details/opticesivederef00clargoog.

Paley, William. [1802] 2008. *Natural Theology*. Edited by Matthew D. Eddy and David Knight. Oxford World's Classics. Oxford: Oxford University Press.

Plantinga, Alvin. 2000. *Warranted Christian Belief*. Oxford: Oxford University Press.

Plato. 1997. *Second Alcibiades*. In *Plato: Complete Works*, edited by John M. Cooper and D.S. Hutchinson, translated by Anthony Kenny. Indianapolis, IN, and Cambridge: Hackett.

Plato. 1997. *Euthyphro*. In *Plato: Complete Works*, edited by John M. Cooper and D.S. Hutchinson, translated by G.M.A Grube. Indianapolis, IN, and Cambridge: Hackett.

Priestley, Joseph. 1775. *An Examination of Dr. Reid's Inquiry into the Human Mind on the Principles of Common Sense, Dr. Beattie's Essay on the Nature and Immutability of Truth, and Dr. Oswald's Appeal to Common Sense in Behalf of Religion*. Second. London: J. Johnson. https://archive.org/details/examinationofdrr00prieuoft.

Priestley, Joseph. 1777. *Disquisitions Relating to Matter and Spirit*. London: J. Johnson. https://archive.org/details/disquisitionsrel00prie.

Priestley, Joseph. 1782. *The Doctrine of Philosophical Necessity Illustrated, Being an Appendix to the Disquisitions Relating to Matter and Spirit*. Second. Birmingham: Pearson and Rollason. https://archive.org/details/disquisitionsre00priegoog.

Racine, Jean. [1691] 2009. 'Athalié [Athaliah]'. In *Britannicus, Phaedra, and Athaliah*, translated by C.H. Sisson. Oxford World's Classics. Oxford: Oxford University Press.

Ramsay of Ochtertyre, John. 1888. *Scotland and Scotsmen in the Eighteenth Century*. Edited by Alexander Allardyce. 2 vols. Edinburgh and London: William Blackwood and Sons.

Reid, Thomas. 1788. *Essays on the Active Powers of Man*. Edinburgh and London: John Bell and G.G.J. & J. Robinson. https://books.google.com/books?id=5ksOAAAAQAAJ.

Reid, Thomas. 1995. *Thomas Reid on Animate Creation*. Edited by Paul B. Wood. The Edinburgh Edition of Thomas Reid. Edinburgh: Edinburgh University Press.

Reid, Thomas. [1764] 2000. *An Inquiry into the Human Mind on the Principles of Common Sense*. Edited by Derek R. Brookes. The Edinburgh Edition of Thomas Reid. Edinburgh: Edinburgh University Press.

Reid, Thomas. [1785] 2002a. *Essays on the Intellectual Powers of Man*. Edited by Derek R. Brookes and Knud Haakonssen. The Edinburgh Edition of Thomas Reid. Edinburgh: Edinburgh University Press.

Reid, Thomas. 2002b. *The Correspondence of Thomas Reid*. Edited by Paul B. Wood. The Edinburgh Edition of Thomas Reid. Edinburgh: Edinburgh University Press.

Reid, Thomas. 2004. *Thomas Reid on Logic, Rhetoric and Fine Arts*. Edited by Alexander Broadie. The Edinburgh Edition of Thomas Reid. Edinburgh: Edinburgh University Press.

Reid, Thomas. 2007. *Thomas Reid on Practical Ethics*. Edited by Knud Haakonssen. The Edinburgh Edition of Thomas Reid. Edinburgh: Edinburgh University Press.

Reid, Thomas. [1788] 2010. *Essays on the Active Powers of Man*. Edited by Knud Haakonssen and James A. Harris. The Edinburgh Edition of Thomas Reid. Edinburgh: Edinburgh University Press.

Reid, Thomas. 2015. *Thomas Reid on Politics and Society*. Edited by Knud Haakonssen and Paul B. Wood. The Edinburgh Edition of Thomas Reid. Edinburgh: Edinburgh University Press.

Shaftesbury, Anthony Ashley Cooper, Earl of. [1711] 2016. *Characteristicks of Men, Manners, Opinions, Times*. Edited by Douglas den Uyl. 3 vols. Indianapolis, IN: Liberty Fund. http://oll.libertyfund.org/titles/1851.

Sher, Richard. 2016. *Church and University in the Scottish Enlightenment: The Moderate Literati of Edinburgh*. 2nd ed. Edinburgh Classic Editions. Edinburgh: Edinburgh University Press.

Strabo. 1930. *Geography, Books 15–16*. Translated by Horace Leonard Jones. Vol. 7. 8 vols. Loeb Classical Library 241. Cambridge, MA, and London: Harvard University Press.

Suarez, Francisco. 2002. *On Creation, Conservation, and Concurrence: Metaphysical Disputations 20–22*. Translated by A.J. Freddoso. South Bend, IN: St. Augustine Press.

Tillotson, John. 1743. 'Sermon CXXXVII, The Wisdom of God in the Creation of the World'. In *Sermons on Several Subjects and Occasions*. Vol. 8. Works of the Most Reverend John Tillotson, Late Archbishop of Canterbury. London: R. Ware et al. https://archive.org/details/worksofmostrever08till.

Tuggy, Dale. 2004. 'Reid's Philosophy of Religion'. In *The Cambridge Companion to Thomas Reid*, edited by Terence Cuneo and René van Woudenberg. Cambridge Companions to Philosophy. Cambridge: Cambridge University Press.

Whiston, William. 1738. *A New Theory of the Earth*. Fifth. London: John Whiston. https://books.google.com/books?id=vZI5AAAAcAAJ.

Wolterstorff, Nicholas. 1996. *John Locke and the Ethics of Belief*. Cambridge Studies in Religion and Critical Thought. Cambridge: Cambridge University Press.

Wood, Paul B. 1984. 'Thomas Reid, Natural Philosopher: A Study of Science and Philosophy in the Scottish Enlightenment'. Ph.D. Dissertation, Leeds University. University of Aberdeen, Special Collections. MS 3412.

Xenophon of Athens. 1914. *Cyropaedia, Books I–IV*. Edited by Jeffrey Henderson. Translated by Walter Miller. Volume 1. 2 vols. Loeb Classical Library 51. Cambridge, MA, and London: Harvard University Press.

Xenophon of Athens. 2013. *Oeconomicus* [*Economics*]. In *Memorabilia. Oeconomicus. Symposium. Apology.*, edited by Jeffrey Henderson, translated by E.C. Marchant, Revised. Loeb Classical Library 168. Cambridge, MA, and London: Harvard University Press.

Aberdeen University (AUL) Library Manuscripts —
Courtesy of the Special Collections Centre,
The Sir Duncan Rice Library, University of Aberdeen

MS 2814
1/45
1/80

MS 2131
2/I/7
3/III/8
4/II/9
4/II/19
6/I/26
6//I/27
7/VII/16
8/I/6
8/IV/2

Index of Names

Adam, 48
Ahnert, Thomas, 3n, 12
Alcibiades, 209
Alexander the Great, 57
Alphonzo, 76
Anaxagoras of
 Clazomenae, 31–2
Aquinas, Thomas, 21, 24, 85n
Archimedes of Syracuse, 151
Ariadne, 119
Aristotle, 32n, 40, 53n, 57, 106n, 161
Arrianus, Lucius Flavius, 209
Athalié, 138n
Augustine, 9, 16, 166n

Baird, George, 2, 12–7, 20, 30n, 43n, 53n, 54n, 60n, 65n, 66n, 77n, 89n, 103n, 107n, 114n, 125n
Banks, Joseph, 53n
Barrett, Justin, 22
Bayes, Thomas, 114n
Bayle, Pierre, 36, 38n
Berington, Joseph, 217n
Blair, Hugh, 180
Bolingbroke, Henry St. John, Viscount, 111, 206n
Borelli, Giovanni Alfonso, 63

Boscovich, Roger, 175n
Bourdaloue, Louis, 180
Bouvet, Joachim, 113n
Broadie, Alexander, 16n, 17
Brookes, Derek, 17, 198n
Brown, Michael, 19
Buffon, Georges-Louis Leclerc, Comte de, 52n, 78
Butler, Joseph, 178

Caesar, Julius, 57
Calvin, John, 3, 9, 12n, 16, 21–2
Charles I of England, 61
Chrysostom, John, 180
Cicero, Marcus Tullius, 31n, 74, 77, 140, 170n, 180, 196n, 198n, 212
Clark, Kelly James, 22
Clarke, Samuel, 4, 92n, 97, 125n, 126n, 149n, 159n, 213n
Cleanthes, 170
Cleghorn, Robert, 12n
Confucius, 192
Cook, James, 53n
Cousin, Victor, 1
Craig, Cairns, 19
Cudworth, Ralph, 123n
Cuvier, Georges, 52n
Cyrus the Great, 107

Democritus, 40

Demosthenes, 180
Descartes, René, 77, 78, 92
d'Holbach, Paul Henri Thiry, Baron, 80
Diagoras of Melos, 31
Du Hamel, Jean-Baptist, 198n

Edmond, J., 18
Epictetus, 209
Epicurus, 32, 35, 40, 66, 77–9, 100, 108, 111, 170, 195–6
Evans, Christmas, 4
Evans, G. Stephen, 22
Ezekiel, 174n

Fénelon, François, 78
Fischer, Archie, 19
Fléchier, Valentine-Esprit, 180
Foster, James, 1–20
Fu Xi, 41
Fraser, Alexander Campbell, 4n, 5, 10n, 18

Gait, Michelle, 19
Galen of Pergamum, 66, 77
Galileo, 66n
Graham, Archibald, 14n, 20
Graham, Gordon, 14, 19
Grandi, Giovanni, 18
Greville, Baron Brook Fulke, 159n
Grew, Nehemiah, 55

Haakonssen, Knud, 17, 30n, 36n, 38n, 175n, 203n, 213n
Halley, Edmond, 48n
Hanna, Adam, 19
Harris, James, 175n
Harris, John, 49n
Harvey, William, 61
Hay, George, 217n

Hippocrates of Kos, 53, 67
Hobbes, Thomas, 111
Homer, 100, 120
Horrocks, Jeremiah, 47, 48n
Hume, David, 1, 5, 21, 26, 38n, 39, 78, 83, 108, 110–1, 112n, 135, 156–7, 190
Hutcheson, Francis, 30, 74

Isaiah, 148n

Jack, Robert, 15n, 20, 43n
St. James the Apostle, 29n, 104n, 204n
Jesus Christ, 9, 99, 183–4, 210, 215
Job, 172n, 194n
St. John the Evangelist, 99n, 207n
Juvenal, 209n

Kant, Immanuel, 1
Kepler, Johannes, 45, 47
Kolbe, Peter, 59
Kroeker, Esther, 1n

Laertius, Diogenes, 32n, 40n, 45n, 100n, 123n, 208n
Leibniz, Gottfried Wilhelm, 92, 113–5, 125–6, 149n, 150–1, 153
Locke, John, 28
Louis XVI of France, 218n
Lucifer, 111
Lucretius, 32, 40, 42n, 51n, 195
St. Luke the Evangelist, 151n, 190n, 210n

Malpighi, Marcello, 55
Mandeville, Bernard, 38n
Marcus Aurelius, 209
Massillon, Jean-Baptist, 180
St. Matthew the Evangelist, 151n, 174n, 210n

Maupertuis, Pierre Louis, 78
McCosh, James, 18
Milton, John, 111
Molina, Luis de, 97n
More, Henry, 77–8
More, Thomas, 11
Moses, 120
Motte, Andrew, 89n
St. Mungo, 11
Mustapha, 159n

Newton, Isaac, 46, 82n, 88, 89, 121n, 153, 154n, 213
Noah, 41n

Paley, William, 47n
St. Paul the Apostle, 137n, 181n
Pelagius, 9
Pierce, Charles Sanders, 1
Pomponazzi, Pietro, 195
Pope, Alexander, 89
Plantinga, Alvin, 21, 22n
Plato, 32n, 107, 123, 192n, 209
Priestley, 10, 155n, 158n, 162, 163n, 164n, 170n, 175n
Protagoras of Abdera, 31
Pythagoras, 45, 123

Racine, Jean, 138n
Ramsay, John, 4n
Reid, Elizabeth, 4–5, 11, 18, 214–5
Reid, George, 4
Reid, Lewis, 3
Reid, Margaret, 3
Reid, Martha, 5
Reid, Thomas, 1–18, 20–7, 30n, 33n, 38n, 39n, 43n, 47n, 48n, 52n, 53n, 66n, 78n, 89n, 102n, 121n, 123n, 129n, 166n, 175n, 178n, 179n, 182n, 183n, 189n, 191n, 196n, 198n, 205n, 209n, 213n, 214, 217n, 218n

Sanderson, Robert, 186
Saurin, Jacques, 180
Secker, Thomas, 180
Shaftesbury, Anthony Ashley Cooper, 3rd Earl of, 139, 212
Sher, Richard, 3n
Smith, Adam, 6
Smith, Jan, 19
Socinus, Faustis, 10
Socrates, 32n, 69, 192, 209
South, Robert, 186
Spinoza, Baruch, 159
Stahl, Lisa, 19
Stewart, John, 4
Strabo, 201
Suarez, Francisco, 124n

Theodorus of Cyrene, 31
Theseus, 119n
Tillotson, John, 4, 48, 79, 180, 186
Tuggy, Dale, 15n

Vanni, Lucilio, 31

Watts, Isaac, 125
Wentzel, Rocki, 19, 198n, 213n
Whiston, William, 41n
Wolterstorff, Nicholas 2, 15n, 20–8
Wood, Paul, 10n, 19, 43n, 53n, 217n

Xenophon of Athens, 68, 69n

Zeno of Citium, 208–9